The World Book Student Information Finder

The World Book

STUDENT INFORMATION FINDER

Math
and Science

Published by
World Book, Inc.
a Scott Fetzer company
Chicago

The World Book Student Information Finder

Copyright © 1988
World Book, Inc.
Merchandise Mart Plaza
Chicago, IL 60654

Portions of the text and certain illustrations previously published under the title
The World Book Student Handbook
Copyright © 1978, 1981 by
World Book-Childcraft International, Inc.

Printed in the United States of America

ISBN 0-7166-3208-X (set)
ISBN 0-7166-3209-8 (Math and Science volume)
Library of Congress Catalog Card No. 88-50713

a/hh

Staff

Publisher
William H. Nault

Editorial

Editor in Chief
Robert O. Zeleny

Executive Editor
Dominic J. Miccolis

Associate Editor
Maureen M. Mostyn

Staff Editor
Karen Zack Ingebretsen

Permissions Editor
Janet T. Peterson

Freelance Editor
Kathy Klein

Indexer
Joyce Goldenstern

Writers
James I. Clark
William D. Leschensky
Mary Alice Molloy
Betty Van Wyk
Joseph A. Zullo

Cartographic Services
George Stoll, head

Research and Library Services
Mary Norton, director

Art

Art Director
Roberta Dimmer

Assistant Art Director
Joe Gound

Photography Director
John S. Marshall

Photographs Editor
Geralyn Swietek

Designer
Stuart Paterson

Production Artists
Kelly Shea
Ann Tomasic

Product Production

Executive Director
Peter Mollman

Manufacturing
Henry Koval, director
Sandra Van den Broucke,
  manager

Pre-Press Services
Jerry Stack, director

Production Control
Barbara Podczerwinski
Janice Rossing

Using the *World Book Student Information Finder*

During your years in school, you are asked to read and learn a tremendous amount of information. Sometimes it may seem to you—no matter how much you like school in general or any subject in particular—that you are almost overwhelmed by the many facts that you need to know.

The World Book Student Information Finder has been designed to help you review essential facts in nine key content areas: mathematics; physical sciences; earth sciences; life sciences; language, writing, and spelling; geography; world history and American history; biography; and United States Presidents and Canada's Prime Ministers. Reviewing the facts in a given area can help you maintain or regain your sense of perspective.

This key concept of *review* was foremost in the minds of the editors of THE WORLD BOOK ENCYCLOPEDIA when they planned and prepared this two-volume set. *The World Book Student Information Finder* is organized by units. Each unit presents the highlights of a content area in a clear, concise fashion. Naturally, two volumes cannot cover all the information you need to know, but a strong attempt was made to include the crucial highlights of your studies.

Helping you review your schoolwork is but one major purpose of the *Student Information Finder*. Another is to provide you with useful reference material. For example, you can look up the preferred method for using footnotes in a research paper.

You should familiarize yourself with the table of contents in the front of each volume before attempting to use the set. To make the best possible use of each volume, you should also consult the indexes frequently. Cross-references within the volumes will help you find related material.

The *Student Information Finder* is intended as a companion to your textbooks, your encyclopedia, other reference works, and books of other kinds. No book can take the place of all those others, but these volumes—properly used—can aid you in an important way.

This volume contains information on math and science. Unit 1 contains review information on a topic that is troublesome to many students—mathematics. Clear, concise information is presented on selected math topics; this includes the subjects of arithmetic, algebra, geometry, and trigonometry.

Also, new math is presented, for students and parents alike.

For the student intent on reviewing topics in the physical sciences, Unit 2 will be of interest. Diagrams are used along with text material to present selected information on astronomy, chemistry, and physics.

The earth sciences are presented for review in Unit 3. Again, diagrams are freely used to present some important facts about the earth, the atmosphere, weather, and climate.

A third science unit, Unit 4, deals with the life sciences. This unit uses diagrams and text to present a selection of key information from cell biology, botany, zoology, and human physiology.

Volume 2 of this set contains information on the language arts and social studies.

The editors hope that this brief summary has given you ideas on how *The World Book Student Information Finder* can help you. Use of this book can give you not only a fund of important facts, but also many hours of interesting and pleasurable reading.

Contents

1

Basic Information about Mathematics

What is your most difficult school subject to understand? If you are like most students, you will probably answer "math." More students have trouble with math than with any other subject. This is because math is a cumulative subject. Previously learned math skills are the foundation on which new skills are built. If you fail to understand some math skill today, this will keep you from understanding a new math skill tomorrow.

This unit will help you to "firm-up" your foundation of math skills. It will help you to review skills you should already understand. And it will help you to understand additional math skills as you are taught them.

Physicists, computer programmers, and many other professionals use mathematics in their work.

1

Reviewing Arithmetic

You may want to begin by reviewing four basic arithmetic operations—addition, subtraction, multiplication, and division—and their uses.

Whole numbers

Addition of whole numbers can be done horizontally or vertically. For example:

$$4 + 19 + 36 = 59$$

$$\begin{array}{r} 2579 \\ 346 \\ +83 \\ \hline 3008 \end{array}$$

When columns are used, the "ones" digits must be aligned, as must the "tens" digits, the "hundreds" digits, and so on. The individual numbers are called *addends* and the answer is called the *sum*.

Addition is defined for only two numbers at a time. So, to add 5 and 7 and 9 you could

1 add 5 and 7 first
$(5 + 7) + 9$
$12 + 9$
21

2 add 7 and 9 first
$5 + (7 + 9)$
$5 + 16$
21

3 add 5 and 9 first
$(5 + 9) + 7$
$14 + 7$
21

If two whole numbers are added, the sum is always a whole number.

Subtraction of whole numbers is also defined only for pairs of whole numbers. Subtraction can be done horizontally or vertically. For example:

$$16 - 7 = 9 \qquad \begin{array}{r} 16 \\ -7 \\ \hline 9 \end{array}$$

The number from which an amount is subtracted is called the *minuend,* the number being subtracted is called the *subtrahend,* and the answer is called the *difference.*

Sometimes when subtracting it is necessary to "borrow." Thus to perform the calculation

$$\begin{array}{r} 482 \\ -153 \\ \hline 329 \end{array}$$

you must borrow 10 from the 8 "tens" in the minuend and add the 10 to 2. Then you can subtract 3 from 12. When you borrowed in the example above, you really were thinking of 482 as

$$400 + 80 + 2 \text{ or } 4(100) + 8(10) + 2$$

and then as

$$4(100) + 7(10) + 12$$

to make the subtraction possible. The following example shows a mechanical way to do this.

Example: Subtract 297 from 534.

Solution: The minuend is 534 and the subtrahend is 297. Rewrite the problem as shown below.

$$\begin{array}{r} 534 \\ -297 \\ \hline \end{array} \quad \begin{array}{l} \text{minuend} \\ \text{subtrahend} \end{array}$$

To subtract, it is necessary to borrow twice. To show the borrowing, you cross out the number from which you borrowed in each case.

$$\begin{array}{r} 42 \\ \cancel{5}\cancel{3}4 \\ -297 \\ \hline 237 \end{array}$$

The difference is 237.

Subtraction of whole numbers is possible only when the minuend *is greater than* the subtrahend.

Multiplication of whole numbers can be thought of as "shorthand" addition. For instance,

$$2 + 2 + 2 + 2 + 2 = 5(2) = 10.$$

Numbers can be multiplied horizontally or vertically. For example:

$$7 \cdot 3 = 21$$

$$\begin{array}{r} 7 \\ \times 3 \\ \hline 21 \end{array}$$

The numbers being multiplied are called *factors* and the answer is called the *product*. If one of the factors has more than one digit, the multiplication is usually done vertically. In problems of this sort, the factor with the greatest number of digits is written first.

Example: Multiply 57 and 6.

Solution: Rewrite the problem as shown below.

$$\begin{array}{r} 57 \\ \times 6 \\ \hline \end{array}$$

To find the product:

$$\begin{array}{r} 4 \\ 57 \\ \times 6 \\ \hline 2 \end{array}$$

1. Multiply 6 and 7. The result is 42. Write down the 2 below the line under the 6 and "carry" the 4.

$$\begin{array}{r} 57 \\ \times 6 \\ \hline 342 \end{array}$$

2. Multiply 6 and 5. The result is 30. Add 4 and record 34 to the left of 2.

The product is 342.

When one of two factors in a multiplication problem has one digit, the product can usually be found mentally. However, the procedure becomes more involved as the number of digits increases. For example:

$$\begin{array}{r} 38 \\ \times 42 \\ \hline 76 \\ 152 \\ \hline 1596 \end{array}$$

76   first partial product
152   second partial product
1596 product

In problems of this kind, each partial product is obtained by multiplying a factor with more than one digit and a single digit factor. Each time, the right-most digit of the partial product is recorded in the *same* column as the single-digit multiplier.

Zeros in multiplication may appear troublesome.

Example: Multiply 327 and 400.

Solution: The factors are 327 and 400. The computation is simplified if you rewrite the problem as

$$
\begin{array}{cccc}
327 & \text{rather than} & 400 & \text{or} & 327 \\
\underline{\times 400} & & \underline{327} & & \underline{400} \\
130800 & & &
\end{array}
$$

The product is 130,800.

Example: Find the product of 547 and 309.

Solution: The factors are 547 and 309. To simplify the computation, rewrite the problem as

$$
\begin{array}{ccc}
547 & \text{instead of} & 309 \\
\underline{\times 309} & & \underline{\times 547} \\
4923 & & 2163 \\
(000) & & 1236 \\
\underline{1641} & & \underline{1545} \\
169023 & & 169023
\end{array}
$$

The product is 169,023.

Division is another operation used for pairs of whole numbers. Division may be done horizontally or vertically. For example:

$$
20 \div 4 = 5 \qquad 4\overline{)20}^{\,5}
$$

The number being divided is called the *dividend,* the number by which the dividend is divided is called the *divisor,* and the answer is called the *quotient.*

Sometimes when dividing with whole numbers, the quotient is not a whole number. In such cases, there is a remainder.

$$
\begin{array}{rl}
& \overset{\displaystyle 4}{} \quad \text{quotient} \\
\text{divisor} \quad 7\overline{)31} & \text{dividend} \\
\underline{28} & \\
3 & \text{remainder}
\end{array}
$$

If the divisor has a single digit and the dividend has several digits, we use a procedure called *long division* to find the quotient.

Example: Divide 1,579 by 6.

Solution: The dividend is 1,579 and the divisor is 6. You can rewrite the problem as $6\overline{)1579}$. You begin by selecting a *trial divisor.* In this case, the trial divisor is some whole number x such that 6 times x is less than or equal to 15. There are three numbers you could use: 0, 1, and 2. If you use 0, you have made no progress at all. If you use 1,

$$
\begin{array}{l}
\overset{\displaystyle 1}{6\overline{)1579}} \\
\underline{6}\qquad 6 \times 1 = 6 \quad \text{product} \\
9 \qquad 15 - 6 = 9 \quad \text{difference}
\end{array}
$$

the difference is greater than the divisor. This will not work. Instead, use 2 as the first digit of the quotient.

$$\begin{array}{r} 2 \\ 6\overline{)1579} \\ 12 \\ \hline 3 \end{array}$$

$6 \times 12 = 12$ product

$15 - 12 = 3$ difference

Next, you "bring down" the third digit (the "tens" digit) of the dividend. You then consider 37 as the new dividend and repeat the "trial divisor—product—difference" procedure.

Think: $6 \times 6 = 36$ and 36 is less than 37.

Write: 6 as the next digit of the quotient.

$$\begin{array}{r} 26 \\ 6\overline{)1579} \\ 12 \\ \hline 37 \\ 36 \\ \hline 1 \end{array}$$

$6 \times 6 = 36$ product

$37 - 36 = 1$ difference

Finally, you bring down the last digit (the "ones" digit) of the dividend, consider 19 as the new dividend, and again repeat the procedure.

Think: $6 \times 3 = 18$ and 18 is less than 19.

Write: 3 as the next digit of the quotient.

$$\begin{array}{r} 263 \\ 6\overline{)1579} \\ 12 \\ \hline 37 \\ 36 \\ \hline 19 \\ 18 \\ \hline 1 \end{array}$$

$6 \times 3 = 18$ product

$19 - 18 = 1$ difference

Since there are no other digits in the dividend, the final difference is the remainder. The quotient is 263 and the remainder is 1.

As your skill increases, you will be able to find such quotients without showing products or differences. However, if the divisor has more than one digit and the dividend has several digits, it is always advisable to write the steps.

Fractions

A fraction is an expression that represents the quotient of two numbers. For example, the fraction $\frac{5}{7}$ is the equivalent of the quotient of $5 \div 7$. In fractions, the dividend is called the *numerator* and the divisor is called the *denominator*. If the numerator is less than the denominator; the fraction is said to be a *proper* fraction. If the numerator is greater than the denominator, the fraction is said to be an *improper* fraction.

proper fraction

improper fraction

$\dfrac{2}{3}$ numerator denominator

$\dfrac{5}{4}$ numerator denominator

The sum of a whole number and a fraction is called a *mixed* number; *e.g.*, $3 + \frac{2}{5}$ or $3\frac{2}{5}$. Mixed numbers are usually written without the plus sign, but it is important to remember that every mixed number can be replaced with a sum. Mixed numbers can be changed to improper fractions as shown below.

mixed number   improper fraction

$$3\frac{2}{5} = \frac{5 \cdot 3 + 2}{5} = \frac{15 + 2}{5} = \frac{17}{5}$$

Notice that the "new" numerator is obtained by adding the original numerator to the product of the denominator and the whole number. But the "new" demoninator remains the same as the original denominator. To compute with fractions, it is important to be able to change from mixed numbers to improper fractions quickly.

Simplifying fractions

If the numerator and denominator of a proper fraction have no common factors (other than 1) the fraction is said to be in "lowest" terms or in "simplest" form. The following fractions are in lowest terms:

$$\frac{2}{3} \quad \frac{4}{5} \quad \frac{9}{11}$$

In mathematics, if two numbers have no common factors other than 1, you describe the numbers as *relatively prime*. In each of the fractions above, the numerator and denominator are relatively prime.

If the numerator and denominator of a proper fraction have common factors, they are not in lowest terms. The following fractions are not in lowest terms:

$$\frac{6}{8} \quad \frac{16}{20} \quad \frac{24}{36}$$

To rewrite a fraction in lowest terms:
1. find a common factor;
2. divide both the numerator and denominator by the common factor; and
3. continue in this way until the numerator and denominator are relatively prime.

Example: Rewrite (a) $\frac{6}{8}$ and (b) $\frac{18}{30}$ in simplest form.

Solution:
(a) Since $6 = 3 \cdot 2$ and $8 = 4 \cdot 2$, 2 is a common factor of 6 and 8. To simplify $\frac{6}{8}$, you divide both 6 and 8 by 2.

$$\frac{6 \div 2}{8 \div 2} = \frac{3}{4}$$

Notice that 3 and 4 are relatively prime.
Therefore, $\frac{6}{8}$ in simplest form is $\frac{3}{4}$.

(b) Since $18 = 9 \cdot 2$ and $30 = 15 \cdot 2$, 2 is a common factor of 18 and 30. To simplify $\frac{18}{30}$, you divide both 18 and 30 by 2.

$$\frac{18 \div 2}{30 \div 2} = \frac{9}{15}$$

Since $9 = 3 \cdot 3$ and $15 = 5 \cdot 3$, 3 is a common factor of 9 and 15. To simplify $\frac{9}{15}$, you divide both 9 and 15 by 3.

$$\frac{9 \div 3}{15 \div 3} = \frac{3}{5}$$

The numbers 3 and 5 are relatively prime.
Therefore, $\frac{18}{30}$ in simplest form is $\frac{3}{5}$.

You could have rewritten $\frac{18}{30}$ in simplest form in one step if you had divided by the *greatest* common factor. In this case, the greatest common factor is 6.

$$\frac{18 \div 6}{30 \div 6} = \frac{3}{5}$$

Two fractions are equal if they have the same simplest form. For example,

$$\frac{6}{10} = \frac{21}{35} \text{ because } \frac{6}{10} = \frac{6 \div 2}{10 \div 2} = \frac{3}{5}$$

$$\frac{21}{35} = \frac{21 \div 7}{35 \div 7} = \frac{3}{5}$$

You can also tell if two fractions are equal by "cross multiplying":

$$10 \cdot 21 = 210 \qquad \frac{6}{10} \diagdown \frac{21}{35}$$

$$6 \cdot 35 = 210$$

If two fractions are not equal, one is greater than (symbol $>$) the other. If both fractions have the same denominator, the one with the greater numerator is the greater fraction. Hence,

$$\frac{5}{16} > \frac{3}{16}$$

If both fractions have the same numerator, the one with the lesser denominator is the greater fraction. Hence,

$$\frac{7}{4} > \frac{7}{8}$$

If neither the denominators nor the numerators are equal, it is necessary to make the denominators equal to compare the fractions. This can be done by multiplying.

Example: Determine which fraction is greater, $\frac{7}{17}$ or $\frac{11}{34}$.

Solution: You can make the denominator of $\frac{7}{17}$ equal to the denominator of $\frac{11}{34}$ if you multiply both the numerator and the denominator of $\frac{7}{17}$ by 2.

$$\frac{7}{17} = \frac{7 \cdot 2}{17 \cdot 2} = \frac{14}{34}$$

Now, $\frac{14}{34} > \frac{11}{34}$ because both denominators are 34 and $14 > 11$.

When using multiplication (or division) to rewrite a fraction, always multiply (or divide) *both* the numerator and the denominator by the *same* number.

Multiplying fractions and mixed numbers

To multiply two (or more) fractions:
1. multiply the numerators to obtain the numerator of the product;
2. multiply the denominators to obtain the denominator of the product; and
3. rewrite the answer in simplest form.

Example: Multiply $\frac{4}{9}$ and $\frac{7}{8}$.

Solution: Rewrite the problem using symbols and multiply.

$$\frac{4}{9} \cdot \frac{7}{8} = \frac{4 \cdot 7}{9 \cdot 8} = \frac{28}{72}$$

Write $\frac{28}{72}$ in simplest form.

$$\frac{28 \div 4}{72 \div 4} = \frac{7}{18}$$

Sometimes when multiplying, it is possible to simplify before you obtain the product. To show that you are dividing the numerator and denominator by a number, the numerals are usually "crossed out." This procedure, called *cancellation,* is illustrated below.

$$\frac{4}{9} \cdot \frac{7}{8} = \frac{\overset{1}{\cancel{4}} \cdot 7}{9 \cdot \underset{2}{\cancel{8}}} = \frac{7}{18}$$

The numbers 4 and 8 were both divided by 4.
To multiply when mixed numbers are included:
1. rewrite the mixed numbers as improper fractions; and
2. use the procedure for multiplying fractions to find the product.

Example: Multiply $2\frac{1}{4}$ and $4\frac{5}{6}$.

Solution: Rewrite the problem using symbols.

$$\left(2\frac{1}{4}\right) \cdot \left(4\frac{5}{6}\right)$$

Replace each mixed number with its corresponding improper fraction and multiply.

$$\frac{9}{4} \cdot \frac{29}{6} = \frac{\overset{3}{\cancel{9}}}{4} \cdot \frac{29}{\underset{2}{\cancel{6}}} = \frac{87}{8}$$

Generally, when the product is an improper fraction, you rewrite the product as a mixed number. To do that, you simply divide the numerator by the denominator and write the remainder as a fraction. In simplest form, the product is $10\frac{7}{8}$.

Dividing fractions and mixed numbers

Division of fractions is defined in terms of multiplication. To divide two fractions:
1. find the reciprocal of the divisor;
2. multiply the dividend and the reciprocal of the divisor; and
3. write the answer in simplest form.

The reciprocal of a fraction can be found by interchanging the numerator and the denominator of the fraction.

fraction	reciprocal
$\dfrac{2}{5}$	$\dfrac{5}{2}$

Example: Divide $\frac{5}{27}$ by $\frac{2}{3}$.

Solution: The dividend is $\frac{5}{27}$ and the divisor is $\frac{2}{3}$. Rewrite the problem using symbols.

$$\frac{5}{27} \div \frac{2}{3}$$

The reciprocal of $\frac{2}{3}$ is $\frac{3}{2}$. Rewrite the problem as a product and multiply.

$$\frac{5}{27} \cdot \frac{3}{2} = \frac{5 \cdot \overset{1}{\cancel{3}}}{\underset{9}{\cancel{27}} \cdot 2} = \frac{5}{18}$$

Since 5 and 18 are relatively prime, the quotient in simplest form is $\frac{5}{18}$.

To divide when mixed numbers are included:
1. rewrite the mixed numbers as improper fractions; and
2. multiply the dividend by the reciprocal of the divisor to find the quotient.

Example: Divide $7\frac{1}{2}$ by $3\frac{1}{3}$.

Solution: The dividend is $7\frac{1}{2}$ and the divisor is $3\frac{1}{3}$. Rewrite the problem using symbols.

$$\left(7\frac{1}{2}\right) \div \left(3\frac{1}{3}\right)$$

Replace the mixed numbers with improper fractions.

$$\frac{15}{2} \div \frac{10}{3}$$

The reciprocal of $\frac{10}{3}$ is $\frac{3}{10}$. Rewrite the problem as a product and multiply.

$$\frac{15}{2} \cdot \frac{3}{10} = \frac{\overset{3}{\cancel{15}} \cdot 3}{2 \cdot \underset{2}{\cancel{10}}} = \frac{9}{4}$$

In simplest form, the quotient is $2\frac{1}{4}$.

Adding fractions and mixed numbers

If two fractions have the same denominator:
1. add the numerators to obtain the numerator of the sum;
2. write the common denominator as the denominator of the sum; and
3. rewrite the answer in simplest form.

Example: Add $\frac{5}{16}$ and $\frac{3}{16}$.

Solution: The denominators are the same. Rewrite the problem using symbols and add the numerators.

$$\frac{5}{16} + \frac{3}{16} = \frac{5 + 3}{16} = \frac{8}{16}$$

In simplest form, the sum of $\frac{5}{16}$ and $\frac{3}{16}$ is $\frac{1}{2}$.

If two fractions have different denominators:
1. multiply to make the denominators the same; and
2. apply the rule for adding fractions with the same denominator.

Example: Add $\frac{3}{5}$ and $\frac{4}{7}$.

Solution: The denominators are different. Rewrite the problem using symbols.

$$\frac{3}{5} + \frac{4}{7}$$

Since 5 and 7 have no common factors (except 1), you can find a common denominator by multiplying the two denominators. The common denominator is 35. Multiply to make both denominators equal to 35 and add.

$$\frac{3 \cdot 7}{5 \cdot 7} + \frac{4 \cdot 5}{7 \cdot 5} = \frac{21}{35} + \frac{20}{35} = \frac{21 + 20}{35} = \frac{41}{35}$$

In simplest form, the sum is $1\frac{6}{35}$.

When the denominators of two addends are not relatively prime, it is not advisable to choose the product of the two denominators as a common denominator. Instead, we look for the *least common denominator*.

Example: Add $\frac{5}{6}$ and $\frac{8}{15}$.

Solution: First, find the *greatest* common factor of 6 and 15.

$6 = 2 \cdot 3$ prime factors $15 = 3 \cdot 5$ prime factors

The number 3 is in both lists; hence, 3 is the greatest common factor. The least common multiple of 6 and 15 can be found by dividing their product by their greatest common factor.

$$\frac{6 \cdot 15}{3} = 30$$

Since 30 is the least common multiple of 6 and 15, 30 is the least common denominator. Rewrite the problem using symbols.

$$\frac{5}{6} + \frac{8}{15}$$

Multiply to make both denominators equal to 30 and add.

$$\frac{5 \cdot 5}{6 \cdot 5} + \frac{8 \cdot 2}{15 \cdot 2} = \frac{25}{30} + \frac{16}{30} = \frac{25 + 16}{30} = \frac{41}{30}$$

In simplest form, the sum is $1\frac{11}{30}$.

To add when mixed numbers are included:
1. rewrite the mixed numbers as improper fractions; and
2. add the resulting improper fractions.

Example: Add $2\frac{1}{2}$ and $3\frac{2}{3}$.

Solution: Rewrite the problem using symbols.

$$2\frac{1}{2} + 3\frac{2}{3}$$

Replace the mixed numbers with improper fractions.

$$\frac{5}{2} + \frac{11}{3}$$

Since 2 and 3 are relatively prime, the least common denominator is their product, 6. Multiply to make both denominators equal to 6 and add.

$$\frac{5 \cdot 3}{2 \cdot 3} + \frac{11 \cdot 2}{3 \cdot 2} = \frac{15}{6} + \frac{22}{6} = \frac{15 + 22}{6} = \frac{37}{6}$$

In simplest form, the sum is $6\frac{1}{6}$.

Subtracting fractions and mixed numbers

If two fractions have the same denominator:
1. subtract the numerator of the subtrahend from the numerator of the minuend to obtain the numerator of the difference;
2. write the common denominator as the denominator of the difference; and
3. rewrite the answer in simplest form.

Example: Subtract $\frac{3}{10}$ from $\frac{11}{10}$.

Solution: The minuend is $\frac{11}{10}$ and the subtrahend is $\frac{3}{10}$. Rewrite the problem using symbols and subtract.

$$\frac{11}{10} - \frac{3}{10} = \frac{11 - 3}{10} = \frac{8}{10}$$

In simplest form, the difference is $\frac{4}{5}$.

If two fractions have different denominators:
1. multiply to make the denominators the same; and
2. apply the rule for subtracting fractions with the same denominator.

Example: Subtract $\frac{3}{8}$ from $\frac{2}{3}$.

Solution: The minuend is $\frac{2}{3}$ and the subtrahend is $\frac{3}{8}$. Rewrite the problem using symbols.

$$\frac{2}{3} - \frac{3}{8}$$

Since 3 and 8 are relatively prime, the least common denominator is their product, 24. Multiply to make both denominators equal to 24 and subtract.

$$\frac{2 \cdot 8}{3 \cdot 8} - \frac{3 \cdot 3}{8 \cdot 3} = \frac{16 - 9}{24} = \frac{7}{24}$$

Since 7 and 24 are relatively prime, $\frac{7}{24}$ is in simplest form.

To subtract when mixed numbers are included:
1. rewrite the mixed numbers as improper fractions; and
2. subtract the resulting improper fractions.

Example: Subtract $2\frac{3}{5}$ from $7\frac{1}{2}$.

Solution: The minuend is $7\frac{1}{2}$ and the subtrahend is $2\frac{3}{5}$. Rewrite the problem using symbols.

$$7\frac{1}{2} - 2\frac{3}{5}$$

Replace the mixed numbers with improper fractions.

$$\frac{15}{2} - \frac{13}{5}$$

Since 2 and 5 are relatively prime, the least common denominator is 10. Multiply to make the denominators equal to 10 and subtract.

$$\frac{15 \cdot 5}{2 \cdot 5} - \frac{13 \cdot 2}{5 \cdot 2} = \frac{75}{10} - \frac{26}{10} = \frac{49}{10}$$

In simplest form, the difference is $4\frac{9}{10}$.

Decimals

Our number system is a "positional" number system. This means that the position a numeral occupies indicates the "unit" it represents.

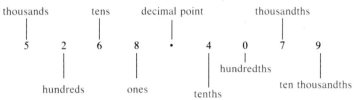

The decimal point always separates the whole-number part from the fractional part in a decimal number. The part of the decimal to the right of the decimal is sometimes called a *decimal fraction*.

The decimal 5,268.407 can be represented as

$$5(1,000) + 2(100) + 6(10) + 8(1) + 4\left(\frac{1}{10}\right) + 0\left(\frac{1}{100}\right) + 7\left(\frac{1}{1000}\right).$$
$$\text{unit} \qquad \text{unit} \qquad \text{unit} \quad \text{unit} \qquad\quad \text{unit} \qquad \text{unit} \qquad \text{unit}$$

As you move from left to right, each unit is $\frac{1}{10}$ of the preceding unit. None can be omitted; a zero is used to indicate that there are no $\frac{1}{100}$ units in the decimal above.

Adding decimals

To add decimals:
1. write the problem vertically, aligning the decimal points;
2. place a decimal point for the sum directly below those in the problem; and
3. add as you would for whole numbers.

This procedure assures that only units of the same kind will be added.

Example: Add 28.47, 7.062, and 135.9.

Solution: Rewrite the problem vertically, aligning the decimal points. Then place the decimal point for the sum and add.

$$\begin{array}{r} 28.47 \\ 7.062 \\ + 135.9 \\ \hline 171.432 \end{array}$$

Subtracting decimals

To subtract decimals:
1. write the problem vertically, aligning the decimal points;
2. place a decimal point for the difference directly below those in the problem; and
3. subtract as you would for whole numbers.

Because subtraction often involves borrowing, zeros are usually filled in so that there is a unit in the minuend for each unit in the subtrahend.

Example: Subtract 4.037 from 12.46.

Solution: The minuend is 12.46 and the subtrahend is 4.037. Rewrite the problem vertically, aligning the decimal points.

```
  12.46
 -4.037
```

Since no digit appears in the thousandths place of the minuend, you fill in a zero for this unit, place the decimal point for the difference, and subtract.

```
      5
  12.460
  -4.037
   8.423
```

Multiplying decimals

To multiply decimals:

1. write the problem vertically, aligning the right-hand digits of the two factors;
2. multiply as you would for whole numbers;
3. count the digits in the decimal-fraction part of each factor and place a decimal point that many digits from the right-hand digit of the product.

Example: Multiply 2.147 and 36.5.

Solution: Rewrite the problem vertically, aligning the right-hand digits of the factors. Since 2.147 has more digits than 36.5, write it first. Multiply.

```
                                    2.147
                                  × 36.5
Note: no decimal points            10735
appear in the partial product.     12882
                                    6441
                                  783655
```

There are *three* digits in the decimal fraction of the factor 2.147. There is *one* digit in the decimal fraction of the factor 36.5. Altogether there are *four* digits in the decimal fraction of the factors. Thus, you place the decimal point in the product between the 8 and the 3; that is, four digits from the right-hand digit of the product. The product is 78.3655.

Dividing decimals

To divide decimals:

1. write the problem in long-division form;
2. locate the decimal point for the quotient; and
3. divide as you would for whole numbers.

If the divisor is a whole number (no decimal fraction), the decimal point in the quotient will be directly above the decimal point in the dividend.

Example: Divide 45.36 by 21.

Solution: The dividend is 45.36 and the divisor is 21. Rewrite the problem in long-division form, place the decimal point, and divide.

```
        2.16
   21)45.36
      42
      ──
      33
      21
      ──
      126
      126
      ───
        0
```

If the divisor possesses a decimal fraction, you eliminate the fraction by multiplying dividend and divisor by a power of ten (*i.e.*, 10, 100, 1,000, etc.). This is usually done mechanically by drawing arrows or using carats. For instance:

```
          ┌────────  new location of decimal point
          ·
  3.7)21.462     Multiply both the divisor
                 and dividend by 10.
```

```
        ┌──────  new location of decimal point
        ·
  16.237)5.71963   Multiply both the divisor
                   and dividend by 1,000.
```

Example: Divide 5.6758 by .037.

Solution: The dividend is 5.6758 and the divisor is .037. Rewrite the problem as .037)5.6758.
The divisor has a decimal fraction. To eliminate the decimal fraction, you must multiply by 1,000.

```
      153.4
  .037)5.6758       Locate the decimal point
      3 7           for the quotient and divide.
      ───
      1 97
      1 85
      ────
       125
       111
       ───
       148
       148
       ───
         0
```

When dividing decimals, remainders are usually not left as the final difference in the division process. Instead, zeros are added to the right of the dividend and the division process is continued as long as you wish—most often, however, to a certain specified number of digits (*e.g.*, to the nearest hundredth). This procedure requires rules for rounding numbers.

For instance, if the quotient is to be rounded to the nearest hundredth, the division process is continued until the thousandths digit has been determined; then:

1. If the thousandths digit is 5, 6, 7, 8, or 9, the hundredths digit is increased by 1.
2. If the thousandths digit is 0, 1, 2, 3, or 4, the hundredths digit is kept unchanged.

A similar procedure is followed to round a quotient to the nearest tenth or to the nearest thousandth.

Changing fractions and mixed numbers to decimals

To change a fraction to a decimal, simply divide the numerator by the denominator. The resulting decimal will be either a repeating decimal or a terminal decimal.

Example: Change $\frac{5}{6}$ to a decimal fraction.

Solution: Use long division to find the quotient. The decimal point in the dividend is understood to be after the 5.

$$
\begin{array}{r}
.83 \\
6\overline{)5.000} \\
4\,8 \\
\hline
20 \\
18 \\
\hline
2
\end{array}
$$

Add zeros to the dividend.

If you continue the division process, each additional digit in the quotient will be 3. You can give the answer in either of the following two forms.

$.8\overline{3}$ or $.83\frac{1}{3}$

The bar over the 3 indicates that it repeats. The decimal is called a *repeating decimal*.

Example: Change $\frac{5}{8}$ to a decimal fraction.

Solution: Use long division to find the quotient.

$$
\begin{array}{r}
.625 \\
8\overline{)5.000} \\
4\,8 \\
\hline
20 \\
16 \\
\hline
40 \\
40 \\
\hline
0
\end{array}
$$

When the remainder is 0, the resulting decimal is called a *terminal decimal*.

To change a mixed number to a decimal:
1. rewrite the mixed number as an improper fraction; and
2. divide the numerator of the improper fraction by the denominator.

Example: Change $4\frac{2}{3}$ to a decimal.

Solution: Rewrite $4\frac{2}{3}$ as an improper fraction.

$$4\frac{2}{3} = \frac{14}{3}$$

Then use long division to divide 14 by 3.

$$
\begin{array}{r}
4.6 \\
3\overline{)14.0} \\
\underline{12} \\
2\,0 \\
\underline{1\,8} \\
2
\end{array}
$$

If the division process is continued, 6 will repeat in the quotient. So, the answer is $4.\overline{6}$ or $4.66\frac{2}{3}$.

Changing decimals to fractions and mixed numbers

To change a decimal fraction to a proper fraction:
1. multiply the digits of the decimal fraction by the smallest unit named; and
2. write the product in simplest form.

Example: Change .125 to a proper fraction.

Solution: The smallest unit named in .125 is $\frac{1}{1000}$ (thousandths). So you multiply 125 and $\frac{1}{1000}$ and simplify.

$$125\left(\frac{1}{1000}\right) = \frac{125}{1000} = \frac{1}{8}$$

Example: Change $.33\frac{1}{3}$ to a proper fraction.

Solution: The smallest unit named in $.33\frac{1}{3}$ is $\frac{1}{100}$ (hundredths). So you multiply $33\frac{1}{3}$ and $\frac{1}{100}$. Then simplify.

$$33\frac{1}{3}\left(\frac{1}{100}\right) = \frac{100}{3} \cdot \frac{1}{100} = \frac{1}{3}$$

To change a decimal to a mixed number:
1. express the decimal as the sum of a whole number and a decimal fraction;
2. change the decimal fraction to a proper fraction in simplest form; and
3. rewrite the sum as a mixed number.

Example: Change 5.75 to a mixed number.

Solution: Express 5.75 as a sum.

$$5.75 = 5 + .75$$

Change .75 to a proper fraction in simplest form.

$$75\left(\frac{1}{100}\right) = \frac{75}{100} = \frac{3}{4}$$

So $5 + .75$ becomes $5 + \frac{3}{4}$. This sum is $5\frac{3}{4}$.

Ratio and proportion

A ratio is a comparison of two quantities of the same kind by division. A ratio can be written by using a *fraction bar* or a *colon*. For example, the ratio of 3 to 4 can be written as $\frac{3}{4}$ or $3:4$. Both forms are useful.

In the ratio above, 3 is the first term of the ratio and 4 is the second term. If you were to use a fraction to express the ratio of 12 to 16, you would use a fraction in simplest form; namely, $\frac{3}{4}$.

Example: Mary's softball team won 16 games out of 24 games played. What is the ratio of games won to games played?

Solution: $\dfrac{\text{games won}}{\text{games played}} = \dfrac{16}{24} = \dfrac{2}{3}$

A proportion is an equation whose members are ratios. For example, $\frac{3}{4} = \frac{15}{20}$ and $3:4 = 15:20$ are both proportions. The numerators and denominators of the ratios are called *terms* of the proportion. The terms of a proportion are numbered. In the generalized proportion $\dfrac{a}{b} = \dfrac{c}{d}$ or $a:b = c:d$, a is the first term, b is the second term, c is the third term, and d is the fourth term. The first term and the fourth term of a proportion are called the *extremes* and the second and third terms are called the *means*.

In a proportion, the product of the means is always equal to the product of the extremes; that is, in general, $a \cdot d = b \cdot c$. By using this property of proportions, it is possible to solve a proportion for any one of the terms, given the other three. The letter x is generally used to represent the unknown term of a proportion.

Example: Solve for x: $\frac{3}{5} = \frac{x}{20}$.

Solution: The extremes are 3 and 20. The means are 5 and x. To solve the proportion, multiply the means and extremes, set the products equal, and solve for x.

$$5 \cdot x = 3 \cdot 20 \qquad \text{Divide both sides by 5.}$$
$$5x = 60 \qquad\qquad x = 12$$

Example: In a certain school, the ratio of the number of boys to the number of girls is 4 to 3. If there are 600 girls in the school, how many boys are in the school?

Solution: Let x represent the number of boys in the school. Write a proportion.

$$\frac{\text{number of boys}}{\text{number of girls}} = \frac{x}{600} = \frac{4}{3}$$

The extremes are x and 3. The means are 600 and 4.

$$3 \cdot x = 4 \cdot 600$$
$$3x = 2,400$$
$$x = 800$$

There are 800 boys in the school.

Per cent

A per cent is a ratio whose second term is 100. Because the second term is always the same, per cent offers a convenient way to compare two quantities. The symbol %, read "per cent," is used to indicate a per cent. For example:

$$5\% = \frac{5}{100} \qquad \frac{43}{100} = 43\%$$
$$17\% = \frac{17}{100} \qquad \frac{121}{100} = 121\%$$

When solving problems, it is useful to change decimals and fractions to per cents and to change per cents to decimals and fractions.

To change a decimal to a per cent:
1. express the decimal as a fraction whose denominator is 100; and
2. rewrite the fraction as a per cent.

Example: Change .37 to a per cent.

Solution: Change .37 to $\frac{37}{100}$. Rewrite $\frac{37}{100}$ as a per cent. The answer is 37%.

After becoming familiar with this kind of problem, many people omit the fraction step and simply move the decimal point two places to the right and add a % symbol when changing a decimal to a per cent. Hence:

$$.17 = 17\% \qquad .027 = 2.7\%$$
$$.01 = 1\% \qquad 4.67 = 467\%$$

To change a fraction to a per cent:
1. rewrite the fraction so the denominator is 100; and
2. rewrite the resulting fraction as a per cent.

Example: Change $\frac{5}{8}$ to a per cent.

Solution: Make x the first term of the per cent ratio and write a proportion.

$$\frac{5}{8} = \frac{x}{100}$$

Solve the proportion for x.

$$8 \cdot x = 5 \cdot 100$$
$$8x = 500$$
$$x = 62\frac{1}{2}$$

The per cent is $\dfrac{62\frac{1}{2}}{100}$ or $62\frac{1}{2}\%$.

You can also change a fraction to a per cent by using long division to change the fraction to a decimal and then change the resulting decimal to a per cent.

Example: Change $\frac{7}{8}$ to a per cent.

Solution: Use long division to change $\frac{7}{8}$ to a decimal.

$$\begin{array}{r} .875 \\ 8\overline{)7.000} \end{array}$$

Change .875 to a per cent. The answer is 87.5%.

To change a per cent to a decimal:
1. replace the per cent with a fraction whose denominator is 100; and
2. divide the numerator by 100.

Example: Change 36% to a decimal.

Solution: Rewrite 36% as $\frac{36}{100}$. Then divide 36 by 100. The answer is .36.

Again, with familiarization, you may omit the fraction step. You simply move the decimal point two places to the left and drop the % symbol when changing from a per cent to a decimal.

To change a per cent to a fraction:
1. replace the per cent with a fraction whose denominator is 100; and
2. rewrite the resulting fraction in simplest form.

Example: Change 42% to a fraction.

Solution: Rewrite 42% as $\frac{42}{100}$. Write $\frac{42}{100}$ in simplest form.

$$\frac{42 \div 2}{100 \div 2} = \frac{21}{50}$$

The answer is $\frac{21}{50}$.

Per cent problems

There are three types of basic per cent problems:
1. Finding a per cent of a given number.
2. Finding what per cent one number is of another number.
3. Finding a number, given a per cent of that number.

Example: 36% of 75 is a certain number. Find the number.

Solution: This problem can be solved in two different ways:

Method I
1. Let x = the number sought.
2. Change the per cent to a fraction or a decimal and rewrite the word problem as an equation.

$$x \cdot \frac{36}{100} \cdot 75 \text{ or } x = (.36) \cdot 75$$

3. Solve the resulting equation.

$$x = 27$$

Method II
1. Let x = the number sought.
2. Change the per cent to a fraction and rewrite the word problem as a proportion.

$$\frac{x}{75} = \frac{36}{100}$$

3. Solve the resulting proportion.

$$\frac{x}{75} = \frac{36}{100}$$
$$100x = 2,700$$
$$x = 27$$

Example: 12% of a given number is 48. Find the number.

Solution: This problem can be solved two ways:

Method I
1. Let x = the number sought.
2. Change the per cent to a fraction or decimal and rewrite the word problem as an equation.

$$\frac{12}{100} \cdot x = 48 \qquad \text{or} \qquad (.12)x = 48$$

3. Solve the resulting equation.

$$\frac{12}{100} \cdot x = 48 \qquad \text{or} \qquad (.12)x = 48$$
$$12x = 4,800 \qquad\qquad x = 400$$
$$x = 400$$

Method II
1. Let x = the number sought.
2. Change the per cent to a fraction and rewrite the word problem as a proportion.

$$\frac{48}{x} = \frac{12}{100}$$

3. Solve the resulting proportion.

$$\frac{48}{x} = \frac{12}{100}$$
$$12x = 4,800$$
$$x = 400$$

Example: 16 is a certain per cent of 80. Find the per cent.

Solution: This problem can be solved in two ways:

Method I
1. Let x = the per cent sought.
2. Change the per cent to a fraction and rewrite the word problem as an equation.

$$16 = \frac{x}{100} \cdot 80$$

3. Solve the resulting equation.

$$16 = \frac{x}{100} \cdot 80$$

$$1,600 = x \cdot 80$$
$$20 = x$$

Method II
1. Let x = the per cent sought.
2. Change the per cent to a fraction and rewrite the word problem as a proportion.

$$\frac{x}{100} = \frac{16}{80}$$

3. Solve the resulting proportion.

$$\frac{x}{100} = \frac{16}{80}$$
$$80x = 1,600$$
$$x = 20$$

The metric system

The metric system is a system of measurement developed about 1792 during the French Revolution. In 1837, France made the metric system compulsory. In 1893, the metric system was adopted as the official system of measurement in the United States and has been used extensively in scientific circles since that time.

Metric units of length

The basic unit for measuring length in the metric system is the *meter* (abbreviated m). The other units of length are expressed in terms of the meter.

shorter than a meter

		fraction		power of 10	decimal
1 millimeter (mm)	=	$\frac{1}{1000}$ meter	=	$\frac{1}{10^3}$ meter	= .001 meter
1 centimeter (cm)	=	$\frac{1}{100}$ meter	=	$\frac{1}{10^2}$ meter	= .01 meter
1 decimeter (dm)	=	$\frac{1}{10}$ meter	=	$\frac{1}{10^1}$ meter	= .1 meter

longer than a meter

	unit	power of 10
1 decameter (dkm)	= 10 meters	= 10^1 meters
1 hectometer (hm)	= 100 meters	= 10^2 meters
1 kilometer (km)	= 1000 meters	= 10^3 meters

These units are listed horizontally below from least to greatest.

$$\overset{\div 10^1}{\underset{mm\quad cm}{\frown}}\ \overset{\div 10^1}{\underset{dm}{\frown}}\ \overset{\div 10^1}{\underset{m}{\frown}}\ \overset{\div 10^1}{\underset{dkm}{\frown}}\ \overset{\div 10^1}{\underset{hm}{\frown}}\ \overset{\div 10^1}{\underset{km}{\frown}}$$

If you move to the right one unit at a time, you divide by 10. If you move to the right more than one unit at a time, you divide by a *power* of 10.

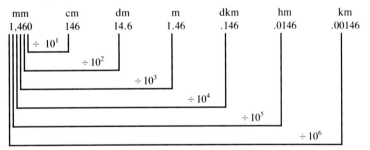

mm	cm	dm	m	dkm	hm	km
1,460	146	14.6	1.46	.146	.0146	.00146

Example: Change 4 mm to centimeters.

Solution: On the unit scale, the cm unit is the next unit to the right of the mm unit. So you divide by 10 to find the answer. This can be done by moving the decimal point one place to the left.

4 mm = .4 cm

Example: Change 721 dm to hectometers.

Solution: On the unit scale, the hm unit is three units to the right of the dm unit. So you divide 721 by 10^3 to find the answer. This can be done by moving the decimal point three places to the left.

721 dm = .721 hm.

In general, if you are changing from a shorter unit to a longer unit, you must divide by a power of 10.

If you move to the left along the horizontal scale one unit at a time, you multiply by 10. If you move to the left more than one unit at a time, you multiply by a *power* of 10.

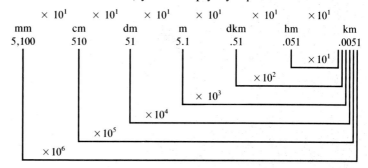

Example: Change 49 dkm to meters.

Solution: On the unit scale, the m unit is the next unit to the left of the dkm unit. So you multiply by 10 to find the answer. This can be done by moving the decimal point one place to the right.

49 dkm = 490 m

Example: Change 7.46 km to centimeters.

Solution: On the unit scale, the cm unit is five units to the left of the km unit. So you multiply by 10^5 to find the answer. This can be done by moving the decimal point five places to the right.

7.46 km = 746,000 cm

In general, if you are changing from a longer unit to a shorter unit, you must multiply by a power of 10.

Metric units of area

Area is a number associated with a two-dimensional region, such as a square or a rectangle.

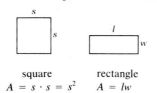

square
$A = s \cdot s = s^2$

rectangle
$A = lw$

The basic unit for measuring area in the metric system is the square meter (m^2), the area of a square whose sides are 1 m long. Area units are related as shown below.

$$\begin{array}{ccccccc}
\div 10^2 & \div 10^2 & \div 10^2 & \div 10^2 & \div 10^2 & \div 10^2 \\
mm^2 & cm^2 & dm^2 & m^2 & dkm^2 & hm^2 & km^2 \\
\times 10^2 & \times 10^2 & \times 10^2 & \times 10^2 & \times 10^2 & \times 10^2
\end{array}$$

If you move to the right on the area unit scale, you divide by a power of 10^2 or 100. If you move to the left on the scale, you multiply by a power of 10^2 or 100.

Example: Change 7 dm^2 to square decameters.

Solution: On the area unit scale, the dkm^2 unit is two units to the right of the dm^2 unit. So you divide by $(100)^2$ or 10,000. This can be done by moving the decimal point four places to the left.

7 dm^2 = .0007 dkm^2

Example: Change .05 m^2 to square millimeters.

Solution: On the area unit scale, the mm^2 unit is three units to the left of the m^2 unit. So you multiply by $(100)^3$ or 1,000,000 to find the answer. This can be done by moving the decimal point six places to the right.

.05 m^2 = 50,000 mm^2

Metric units of volume

Volume is a number associated with a three-dimensional solid, such as a cube or a rectangular solid.

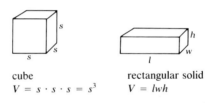

cube
$V = s \cdot s \cdot s = s^3$

rectangular solid
$V = lwh$

The basic unit for measuring volume in the metric system is the cubic meter (m^3), the volume of a cube whose sides are 1 m long. The volume units are related as shown below.

$$\overset{\div 10^3}{\underset{\times 10^3}{mm^3}} \; \overset{\div 10^3}{\underset{\times 10^3}{cm^3}} \; \overset{\div 10^3}{\underset{\times 10^3}{dm^3}} \; \overset{\div 10^3}{\underset{\times 10^3}{m^3}} \; \overset{\div 10^3}{\underset{\times 10^3}{dkm^3}} \; \overset{\div 10^3}{\underset{\times 10^3}{hm^3}} \; km^3$$

If you move to the right on the volume unit scale, you divide by a power of 10^3 or 1,000. If you move to the left on the scale, you multiply by a power of 10^3 or 1,000.

Example: Change 49,600 m^3 to cubic hectometers.

Solution: On the volume unit scale, the hm^3 unit is two units to the right of the m^3 unit. So you divide by $(1,000)^2$ or 1,000,000 to find the answer. This can be done by moving the decimal point six places to the left.

49,600 m^3 = .0496 hm^3

Example: Change .75 cm^3 to cubic millimeters.

Solution: On the volume unit scale, the mm³ unit is one unit to the left of the cm³ unit. So you multiply by 1,000 to find the answer. This can be done by moving the decimal point three places to the right.

.75 cm³ = 750 cm³

Converting metric measures of length to English measures of length

To change metric units to English units, you use a conversion table like the one below. The symbol ≐ means "approximately equal to."

1 m ≐ 39.37 in.	1 yd. ≐ .91 m
1 m ≐ 1.1 yd.	1 in. ≐ 2.54 cm
1 km ≐ .62 mi.	1 mi. ≐ 1.61 km

Example: Change 16 m to yards.

Solution: Let x = the number of yards and write a proportion.

$$\frac{1}{16} = \frac{1.1}{x}$$

Solve the resulting proportion.

$$x = 16(1.1)$$
$$x = 17.6$$
$$16 \text{ m} = 17.6 \text{ yd.}$$

The abacus has long been used to perform arithmetic problems. It can be used to add, subtract, multiply, and divide and to calculate square roots and cube roots.

Reviewing Algebra

In algebra you work with the system of *real numbers*. The set of real numbers contains the set of *natural numbers*, the set of *whole numbers*, the set of *integers*, the set of *rational numbers*, and the set of *irrational numbers*. The system of real numbers consists of the set of real numbers, certain basic operations (like addition and multiplication), and properties that apply to these operations. The basic properties are listed below. The variables a, b, and c represent real numbers.

closure property of addition:	$a + b$ is a real number
commutative property of addition:	$a + b = b + a$
associative property of addition:	$(a + b) + c = a + (b + c)$
addition property of zero:	$a + 0 = a$
inverse property of addition:	$a + (-a) = 0$
closure property of multiplication:	$a \cdot b$ is a real number
commutative property of multiplication:	$a \cdot b = b \cdot a$
associative property of multiplication:	$a \cdot (b \cdot c) = (a \cdot b) \cdot c$
multiplication property of one:	$a \cdot 1 = a$
inverse property of multiplication:	$a \cdot \dfrac{1}{a} = 1$ if $a \neq 0$
distributive property of multiplication over addition:	$a(b + c) = a \cdot b + a \cdot c$

Addition of integers and rational numbers

The set of integers contains the set of whole numbers and all of the "opposites," or negatives, of the whole numbers. A negative sign is used to indicate the opposite of a whole number. Zero is the opposite of zero.

set of integers = $\{\ldots, -3, -2, -1, 0, 1, 2, 3, \ldots\}$

The set of integers can be associated with the points of a line. If no "operation" sign is written, the number is a positive integer.

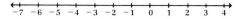

The resulting number line can be used to add integers. For example:

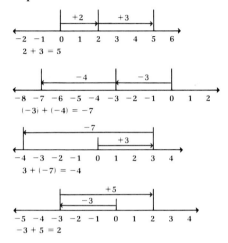

$2 + 3 = 5$

$(-3) + (-4) = -7$

$3 + (-7) = -4$

$-3 + 5 = 2$

It is not always convenient to draw number-line pictures to find sums. So, rules are usually stated. Since every integer is a rational number, and the rules for both sets are the same, you should know all of the rules for rational numbers. A rational number is any number that can be written in the form $\frac{a}{b}$, where a and b are integers and $b \neq 0$.

Before stating the rules, you must consider the idea of "absolute value." In mathematics, the symbol $|\;|$ is used to indicate absolute value. If x is any real number:

$|x| = x$ if x is greater than 0;
$|x| = 0$ if $x = 0$;
$|x| = -x$ if x is less than 0.

Example: Find the absolute value of (a) -7; (b) $\frac{2}{3}$.

Solution:
(a) Since -7 is less than 0, the absolute value of -7 is the opposite of -7.

$$|-7| = -(-7) = 7$$

(b) Since $\frac{2}{3}$ is a positive real number, the absolute value of $\frac{2}{3}$ is $\frac{2}{3}$.

Rules for addition of rational numbers

1. If the direction signs are the same (both positive or both negative), add the absolute values of the addends and use the common sign for the sum.
2. If the direction signs are different (one positive and one

negative), subtract the absolute values of the addends and use the sign of the addend with the greater absolute value.

Example: Find each sum: (a) $-21 + 13$;
(b) $-17 + (-29)$; (c) $\frac{2}{3} + (-\frac{3}{4})$.

Solution:

(a) The direction signs are not alike. Subtract the absolute values.

$$|-21| - |13| = 21 - 13 = 8$$

Since -21 has the greater absolute value, you use a negative sign for the sum. The sum is -8.

(b) The direction signs are alike. Add the absolute values.

$$|-17| + |-29| = 17 + 29 = 46$$

Use the common sign for the sum. The sum is -46.

(c) The direction signs are different. Subtract the absolute values of the addends. To subtract, it is necessary to find a common denominator.

$$\left|-\frac{3}{4}\right| - \left|\frac{2}{3}\right| = \frac{3}{4} - \frac{2}{3} = \frac{9}{12} - \frac{8}{12} = \frac{9-8}{12} = \frac{1}{12}$$

Since $-\frac{3}{4}$ has the greater absolute value, you use a negative sign for the sum. The sum is $-\frac{1}{12}$.

Rule for subtraction of rational numbers

Subtraction is defined in terms of addition. To subtract two rational numbers, add the opposite of the subtrahend to the minuend. Using symbols, this rule can be restated as follows. If x and y are any two rational numbers, then

$$x - y = x + (-y).$$

Example: Find each difference: (a) $47 - 29$;
(b) $-63 - 14$; (c) $\frac{5}{8} - (-\frac{1}{2})$; (d) $-56 - (-32)$.

Solution:

(a) Rewrite $47 - 29$ as a sum and apply the rules for adding rational numbers.

$$47 - 29 = 47 + (-29)$$

The direction signs are different. Subtract the absolute values.

$$|47| - |-29| = 47 - 29 = 18$$

Since $|47| > |-29|$, you use a positive sign for the answer. The difference is 18. (The symbol $>$ represents the phrase "is greater than.")

(b) Rewrite $-63 - 14$ as a sum and apply the rules for adding rational numbers.

$$-63 - 14 = -63 + (-14)$$

The addends have the same direction signs so you add the absolute values.

$$|-63| + |-14| = 63 + 14 = 77$$

Use the common sign for the answer. The difference is -77.

(c) Rewrite $\frac{5}{8} - (-\frac{1}{2})$ as a sum and apply the rules for adding rational numbers. The opposite of the opposite of $\frac{1}{2}$ is $\frac{1}{2}$.

$$\frac{5}{8} - \left(-\frac{1}{2}\right) = \frac{5}{8} + \frac{1}{2} = \frac{5}{8} + \frac{4}{8} = \frac{5+4}{8} = \frac{9}{8}$$

The difference is $\frac{9}{8}$ or $1\frac{1}{8}$.

(d) Rewrite $-56 - (-32)$ as a sum and apply the rules for adding rational numbers.

$$-56 - (-32) = -56 + 32$$

The direction signs of the addends are different. Subtract the absolute values.

$$|-56| - |32| = 56 - 32 = 24$$

Since $|-56| > |32|$, you use a negative sign for the answer. The difference is -24.

Rules for multiplication of rational numbers

1. If the direction signs are the same (both positive or both negative), multiply the absolute values of the factors and use a positive sign for the product.
2. If the direction signs are different (one positive and one negative), multiply the absolute values of the factors and use a negative sign for the product.

Example: Find each product: (a) $\frac{2}{3} \cdot 6$; (b) $(-12)(9)$; (c) $(-7)(-9)$.

Solution:

(a) The direction signs of the factors are alike. Multiply the absolute values of the factors and use a positive sign for the product.

$$\left|\frac{2}{3}\right| \cdot |6| = \frac{2}{3} \cdot 6 = \frac{2}{3} \cdot \frac{6}{1} = 4$$

The product is 4.

(b) The direction signs of the factors are different. Multiply the absolute values of the factors.

$$|-12| \cdot |9| = 12 \cdot 9 = 108$$

Use a negative sign for the product. The product is -108.

(c) The direction signs of the factors are the same. Multiply the absolute values of the factors and use a positive sign for the product.

$$|-7| \cdot |-9| = 7 \cdot 9 = 63$$

If you are finding the product of more than two factors, count the negative signs. If there is an odd number of negative signs, the product will be negative.

Rules for division of rational numbers

1. If the direction signs are the same (both positive or both negative), divide the absolute value of the dividend by the absolute value of the divisor. Also, use a positive sign for the quotient.
2. If the direction signs are different (one positive and one negative), divide the absolute value of the dividend by the absolute value of the divisor and use a negative sign for the quotient.

Example: Find each quotient: (a) $\frac{8}{15} \div \frac{2}{5}$; (b) $-28 \div 7$; (c) $-42 \div (-3)$.

Solution:

(a) The direction signs are the same. The quotient will be positive. Divide $\left|\frac{8}{15}\right|$ by $\left|\frac{2}{5}\right|$. To divide fractions, it is necessary to invert the divisor and multiply.

$$\left|\frac{8}{15}\right| \div \left|\frac{2}{5}\right| = \frac{8}{15} \div \frac{2}{5} = \frac{\overset{4}{\cancel{8}}}{\underset{3}{\cancel{15}}} \cdot \frac{\overset{1}{\cancel{5}}}{\underset{1}{\cancel{2}}} = \frac{4}{3}$$

The quotient is $\frac{4}{3}$ or $1\frac{1}{3}$.

(b) The direction signs are different. Divide the absolute value of -28 by the absolute value of 7.

$$|-28| \div |7| = 28 \div 7 = 4$$

Use a negative sign for the quotient. $-28 \div 7 = -4$.

(c) The direction signs are the same. The quotient will be positive. Divide $|-42|$ by $|-3|$.

$$|-42| \div |-3| = 42 \div 3 = 14$$

The quotient is 14.

Solving open sentences

In mathematics, a *statement* is a sentence that is either true or false but not both. Each of the following is a statement.

equation	inequality	inequality	equation
$5 + 3 = 10$	$4 > 0$	$-7 < -3$	$2 + 7 = 9$
false	true	true	true

An *open sentence* contains a variable and is neither true nor false until the variable is replaced with a number. Each of the following is an open sentence.

equation	inequality	equation
$x + 2 = 6$	$x - 3 > 5$	$2x + 7 = 9$

One of the primary objectives of algebra is to develop concepts for solving open sentences. Here you will only consider techniques for solving equations. To solve an equation, it is necessary to determine the number (or numbers) that will make the equation a true statement.

When solving equations, it is necessary to apply one or

more of the following properties of equality. The variables
represent real numbers.

addition property of equality:	If $a = b$, then $a + c = b + c$.
subtraction property of equality:	If $a = b$, then $a - c = b - c$.
multiplication property of equality:	If $a = b$, then $ac = bc$.
division property of equality:	If $a = b$, then $\dfrac{a}{c} = \dfrac{b}{c}$ if $c \neq 0$.

You can tell which property to apply by thinking in terms of
"opposite" operations.

Example: Solve $x + 5 = 17$ for x.

Solution: Since 5 is added to x to obtain 17, you apply the subtraction
property of equality to solve for x. The procedure can be done horizontally
or vertically.

$$x + 5 = 17$$
$$x + 5 - 5 = 17 - 5 \qquad \text{Subtract 5.}$$
$$x = 12$$

$$x + 5 = 17$$
$$\underline{-5 = -5}$$
$$x = 12$$

Example: Solve $x - 7 = 12$ for x.

Solution: Since 7 is subtracted from x to obtain 12, you apply the addition property of equality to solve for x.

$$x - 7 = 12$$
$$x - 7 + 7 = 12 + 7 \qquad \text{Add 7.}$$
$$x = 19$$

$$x - 7 = 12$$
$$\underline{+7 = +7}$$
$$x = 19$$

Later, as your skills improve, you will be able to solve
equations like these without writing the addition or subtraction step. It is always a good idea to identify the reason for
each step. For example:

$$x - 3 = 9$$
$$\qquad\qquad A_3$$
$$x = 12$$

$$x + 2 = 17$$
$$\qquad\qquad S_2$$
$$x = 15$$

A_3 means "add 3 to
both sides."

S_2 means "subtract 2
from both sides."

It is important to remember that you must always do the
same thing to *both* sides of an equation.

Example: Solve $3x = 21$ for x.

Solution: Since x is multiplied by 3 to obtain 21, you apply the division
property of equality to solve for x.

$$3x = 21$$
$$\frac{3x}{3} = \frac{21}{3} \qquad \text{Divide by 3.}$$
$$x = 7$$

Example: Solve $\frac{x}{5} = 12$ for x.

Solution: Since x is divided by 5 to obtain 12, you apply the multiplication property of equality to solve for x.

$$\frac{x}{5} = 12$$

$$5 \cdot \frac{x}{5} = 5 \cdot 12 \quad \text{Multiply by 5.}$$

$$x = 60$$

The multiplication or division step need not be shown. It is a good idea, however, to identify the property of equality that you used to solve the equation.

$$6x = 108 \qquad\qquad \frac{x}{9} = 7$$

$$\ \text{D}_6 \qquad\qquad\qquad \text{M}_9$$

$$x = 18 \qquad\qquad\ x = 63$$

D_6 means "divide both sides by 6." $\qquad$ M_9 means "multiply both sides by 9."

Each of the preceding equations could be solved in one step by applying a property of equality. It will usually take more than one step to solve an equation.

Example: Solve $\frac{2x}{3} + 5 = 17$ for x.

Solution:

showing steps $\qquad\qquad\qquad$ *short method*

$$\frac{2x}{3} + 5 = \quad 17 \qquad\qquad \frac{2x}{3} + 5 = 17$$

$$\underline{ -5 = -5}\ \text{Subtract 5.} \qquad \frac{2x}{3}\ = 12 \quad \text{S}_5$$

$$\frac{2x}{3} \quad\ = 12 \qquad\qquad\qquad 2x = 36 \quad \text{M}_3$$

$$3 \cdot \frac{2x}{3} \quad\ = \ 3 \cdot 12\ \text{Multiply by 3.} \qquad x = 18 \quad \text{D}_2$$

$$2x \quad\ = 36$$

$$\frac{2x}{2} \quad\ = \frac{36}{2}\ \text{Divide by 2.}$$

$$x = 18$$

When more than one step is involved, it is a good idea to check your solution. This is usually done by rewriting the original equation, substituting the solution for the variable, and doing the arithmetic. To understand this procedure, you can check the solution just obtained.

Check: $\dfrac{2x}{3} + 5 = 17$ if x is 18

$$\dfrac{2(18)}{3} + 5 \overset{?}{=} 17$$

$$12 + 5 \overset{?}{=} 17$$

$$17 = 17$$ The solution checks.

Example: Solve $3(2x - 7) + 5 = 14$ for x.

Solution: This equation contains parentheses. To remove parentheses, it is necessary to apply the distributive property. As a reason, write "RP" for "remove parentheses."

showing steps

$$3(2x - 7) + 5 = 14$$
$$6x - 21 + 5 = 14 \qquad \text{Remove parentheses.}$$
$$6x - 16 = 14 \qquad \text{Add.}$$
$$\underline{+ 16 = + 16} \qquad \text{Add 16.}$$
$$6x \qquad = 30$$
$$\dfrac{6x}{6} = \dfrac{30}{6} \qquad \text{Divide by 6.}$$
$$x = 5$$

short method

$$3(2x - 7) + 5 = 14$$
$$6x - 21 + 5 = 14 \qquad \text{RP}$$
$$6x - 16 = 14 \qquad \text{Add.}$$
$$6x = 30 \qquad \text{A}_{16}$$
$$x = 5 \qquad \text{D}_{6}$$

Like terms

An expression like $7y$ is called a monomial or a term. In this term, 7 is the *coefficient* of y and y is the *coefficient* of 7. Since 7 is a number, you refer to 7 as the *numerical coefficient*.

Terms like $3x$ and $5x$ are called *like terms* because they have the same variable. You combine like terms by adding or subtracting the numerical coefficients and writing the variable.

Example: Combine like terms: **(a)** $15x - 7x;$ **(b)** $21y + 16y - 7y$.

Solution:
(a) $15x - 7x = (15 - 7)x = 8x$
(b) $21y + 16y - 7y = (21 + 16 - 7)y = 30y$

The ability to combine like terms is useful when solving equations.

Example: Solve $8x + 7 - 3x = 42$ for x.

Solution: Since $8x$ and $-3x$ are like terms on the same side of the equation, they should be combined first. The sign in front of the term remains with that term. Because of the associative and commutative properties, it is possible to rewrite the equation so that like terms are side by side.

$$8x + 7 - 3x = 42$$
$$8x - 3x + 7 = 42$$
$$(8 - 3)x + 7 = 42$$

As your skills improve, you can easily omit these two steps.

$$5x + 7 = 42$$
$$5x + 7 - 7 = 42 - 7 \quad \text{Subtract 7.}$$
$$5x = 35$$
$$\frac{5x}{5} = \frac{35}{5} \quad \text{Divide by 5.}$$
$$x = 7$$

short method
$$8x + 7 - 3x = 42$$
$$5x + 7 = 42$$
$$5x = 35$$
$$x = 7$$

check
$$8x + 7 - 3x = 42$$
$$8(7) + 7 - 3(7) \overset{?}{=} 42$$
$$56 + 7 - 21 \overset{?}{=} 42$$
$$42 = 42$$

Example: Solve $7x - 4 = 2x + 11$

Solution: In this equation, terms containing variables appear on *both* sides of the equation. Our first task is to transfer all of the variables to the same side of the equation. To do this, we subtract $2x$ from both sides of the equation. Then, we solve the resulting equation for x.

$$
\begin{aligned}
7x - 4 &= 2x + 11 \\
-2x &= -2x \qquad \text{Subtract } 2x. \\
\hline
5x - 4 &= 11 \\
+4 &= +4 \qquad \text{Add 4.} \\
\hline
5x &= 15
\end{aligned}
$$

$$\frac{5x}{5} = \frac{15}{5} \quad \text{Divide by 5.}$$
$$x = 3$$

short method
$$7x - 4 = 2x + 11$$
$$5x - 4 = 11$$
$$5x = 15$$
$$x = 3$$

check
$$7x - 4 = 2x + 11$$
$$S_{2x} \quad 7(3) - 4 \overset{?}{=} 2(3) + 11$$
$$A_4 \quad 21 - 4 \overset{?}{=} 6 + 11$$
$$D_5 \quad 17 = 17$$

Formulas are equations that involve more than one variable. The same properties of equality are used to solve equations of this kind for a given variable.

Example: Solve $C = \frac{5}{9}(F - 32)$ for F.

Solution: Since we are solving the equation for F, we need to isolate F.

$$C = \frac{5}{9}(F - 32)$$

$$9 \cdot C = 9 \cdot \frac{5}{9}(F - 32) \quad \text{Multiply by 9.}$$

$$9C = 5 (F - 32)$$

$$\frac{9C}{5} = \frac{5(F - 32)}{5} \quad \text{Divide by 5.}$$

$$\frac{9C}{5} = F - 32$$

$$\frac{9C}{5} + 32 = F - 32 + 32 \quad \text{Add 32.}$$

$$\frac{9C}{5} + 32 = F$$

Exponents

Exponents are used to indicate products. In the expression 5^3, 5 is called the base and 3 the exponent. The exponent 3 indicates how many times the base 5 is used as a factor; that is, $5^3 = 5 \cdot 5 \cdot 5$. You write $5 \cdot 5 \cdot 5$ in *exponential form* as 5^3. If the bases are the same, you can find the product of two numbers written in exponential form by

1. writing the base; and
2. adding the exponents.

If x is any rational number and a and b are positive integers, this rule can be written as

$$x^a \cdot x^b = x^{a + b}.$$

Example: Multiply 3^2 and 3^4.

Solution: Rewrite the problem using symbols and apply the rule.

$$3^2 \cdot 3^4 = 3^{2 + 4} = 3^6$$

If the bases are the same, you can find the quotient of two numbers written in exponential form by

1. writing the base; and
2. subtracting the exponents.

If the exponents are the same, the quotient is 1. When applying the rule for division, you must subtract the lesser exponent from the greater exponent to keep the difference positive. If x is a non-zero rational number and both x and b are positive integers, the rule can be written as follows:

If $a > b$, then $x^a \div x^b = x^{a - b}$

If $b > a$, then $x^a \div x^b = \dfrac{1}{x^{b - a}}$

Example: Find each quotient: (a) $7^5 \div 7^2$; (b) $5^4 \div 5^6$.

Solution:

(a) The bases are the same, so you can subtract exponents to find the quotient. Because the greater exponent is in the numerator (dividend), you must subtract in the numerator.

$$7^5 \div 7^2 = \frac{7^5}{7^2} = 7^{5 - 2} = 7^3$$

(b) The bases are the same, so you can subtract exponents to find the quotient. Because the greater exponent is in the denominator, you subtract in the denominator.

$$5^4 \div 5^6 = \frac{5^4}{5^6} = \frac{1}{5^{6-4}} = \frac{1}{5^2}$$

Two other rules involving exponents are stated below. In these rules, x and y are rational numbers and a and b are positive integers.

1. $(x^a)^b = x^{ab}$ 2. $(xy)^a = x^a y^a$

Example: Find each product: **(a)** $(3^2)^4$; **(b)** $(5x)^3$.

Solution:

(a) To find this product, you must find a power. Apply Rule 1.

$$(3^2)^4 = 3^{2 \cdot 4} = 3^8$$

(b) In this situation, you have to find a power of a product. Apply Rule 2.

$$(5x)^3 = 5^3 \cdot x^3 = 5 \cdot 5 \cdot 5 \cdot x^3 = 125x^3$$

Systems of linear equations

A linear equation is any equation whose graph is a straight line. Any linear equation can be written in the form $ax + by = c$, in which x and y are variables and a, b, and c are real numbers. You are assuming that a and b are not both zero. To graph a linear equation:
1. find three ordered pairs of numbers that make the equation a true statement;
2. graph the three ordered pairs of numbers in the coordinate plane; and
3. draw the line that contains the three points.

Example: Graph $2x + y = 4$.

Solution: Make a table for the equation. The table should contain at least three entries. These entries can be found by:
1. choosing a number replacement for x (or y);
2. substituting the number for x (or y) in the equation; and
3. solving the resulting equation for the other variable.

This procedure can usually be done mentally if you choose the replacements for x and y carefully. For example, the computations are easy if you let x equal zero or y equal zero.

$$
\begin{aligned}
& 2x + y = 4 \\
\text{Let } x = 0. \quad & 2(0) + y = 4 \\
& \phantom{2(0) + {}} y = 4
\end{aligned}
$$

$$
\begin{aligned}
& 2x + y = 4 \\
\text{Let } y = 0. \quad & 2x + 0 = 4 \\
& x = 2
\end{aligned}
$$

$$2x + y = 4$$
Let $x = 3$. $\quad 2(3) + y = 4$
$$6 + y = 4$$
$$y = -2$$

table

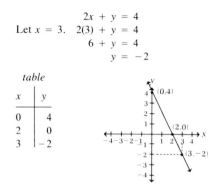

x	y
0	4
2	0
3	-2

The simplest system of linear equations contain two linear equations in two variables. To solve a system of linear equations in two variables, you must find an ordered pair of numbers that will make both equations true simultaneously. There are three basic methods for solving a system of two linear equations in two variables. The first one to be considered here is called the "graphing method."

Example: Use the graphing method to solve the following system of linear equations.

1 $\quad 2x + y = 5$
2 $\quad x - y = 4$

Solution: Graph both equations on the same coordinate axes.

$$2x + y = 5 \qquad x - y = 4$$

x	y
0	5
1	3
2	1

x	y
0	-4
4	0
2	-2

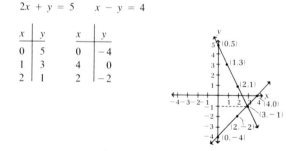

The two graphs intersect at $(3, -1)$. So, the solution set is $\{(3, -1)\}$; that is, $x = 3$ and $y = -1$.

If the two graphs were parallel (did not intersect), there would be no solution. And if both equations described the same line, there would be infinitely many solutions; every solution of one equation would automatically be a solution of the other equation.

Because it is not always convenient to develop the solution from a graph, algebraic methods have been devised for solving systems of linear equations. The first of these that you should keep in mind is called the "substitution method."

Example: Use the substitution method to solve the following system of linear equations.

$$1 \quad x - y = 2$$
$$2 \quad x + 2y = 5$$

Solution: Solve equation **1** for x.

$$1 \quad x - y = 2$$
$$x = 2 + y$$

Substitute $2 + y$ for x in equation **2** and solve the resulting equation for y.

$$2 \qquad x + 2y = 5$$
$$(2 + y) + 2y = 5$$
$$2 + y + 2y = 5$$
$$2 + 3y = 5$$
$$y = 1$$

To find x, substitute 1 for y in equation **1** and solve for x.

$$1 \quad x - y = 2$$
$$x - 1 = 2$$
$$x = 3$$

The solution set is $\{(3,1)\}$.

The second algebraic method is called the "addition/subtraction method."

Example: Use the addition/subtraction method to solve the following system of linear equations.

$$1 \quad 3x - y = 7$$
$$2 \quad 2x + y = 8$$

Solution: Look at the coefficients of the variables. If the coefficients of the x's (or y's) are the same, that variable can be eliminated by subtraction. If the coefficients of the x's (or y's) are "opposites," that variable can be eliminated by addition. In the system above, the coefficients of the y's are opposites. You can eliminate the y's by addition.

$$
\left.
\begin{array}{l}
1 \quad 3x - y = 7 \\
2 \quad 2x + y = 8
\end{array}
\right\} \quad \text{Add.}
$$
$$5x = 15$$
$$x = 3$$

To find y, substitute 3 for x in one of the original equations and solve for y.

$$2 \qquad 2x + y = 8$$
$$2(3) + y = 8$$
$$6 + y = 8$$
$$y = 2$$

The solution set is $\{(3,2)\}$.

If no pairs of coefficients are the same (or opposites), they can be made the same (or opposites) by multiplication.

Example: Solve the following system of linear equations.

1    $2x - 3y = 5$
2    $x - 2y = 3$

Solution: If equation **2** is multiplied by 2, the coefficients of the x's would be the same. Then the x's could be eliminated by subtraction. Or, if equation **2** is multiplied by -2, the coefficients of the x's would be opposites and the x's could be eliminated by addition. Similar thinking could be used to eliminate the y's. Eliminate the x's by addition, as follows:

$$\left. \begin{array}{r} \mathbf{1} \quad 2x - 3y = 5 \\ \mathbf{2} \quad -2x + 4y = -6 \end{array} \right\} \text{ Add.}$$
$$y = -1$$

To find x, substitute -1 for y in one of the equations and solve for x.

$$\begin{array}{r} \mathbf{1} \quad 2x - 3y = 5 \\ 2x - 3(-1) = 5 \\ 2x + 3 = 5 \\ x = 1 \end{array}$$

The solution set is $\{(1, -1)\}$.

Polynomials

The simplest polynomial is a monomial. A monomial is the same as a term; that is, a monomial may be a number, a variable, or a product of numbers and variables. For example, 5, $\frac{1}{2}$, x, w, $9y$, $10x^2$, $6x^6y$, and x^2y^3z are all monomials. The degree of a monomial can be found by *adding* the exponents of the variables.

The degree of 4 is 0 (no variable).
The degree of $3x^2$ is 2 (exponent of x).
The degree of $5x^2y$ is 3 (exponent of x + exponent of y).
The degree of $\frac{1}{2}xy^2z^3$ is 6 (exponent of x + exponent of y + exponent of z).

You learned to add and subtract monomials when you combined like terms. To multiply monomials, you multiply the numerical coefficients and then apply rules for exponents to multiply the variables.

Example: Find each product: **(a)** $(-2x)(3x^2)$; **(b)** $4(5y^2)(6y^3)$; **(c)** $(3xy)(5x^2y^3)$.

Solution:
(a) The commutative and associative properties of multiplication make it possible to rewrite $(-2x)(3x^2)$ as shown below.

$$(-2 \cdot 3)(x \cdot x^2)$$
multiply ⌐   ⌐ write the base; add the exponents.

The product is $-6x^3$. As your skills increase, you can find the product directly without rewriting the factors.

(b) $4(5y^2)(6y^3) = (4 \cdot 5 \cdot 6)(y^2 \cdot y^3) = 120(y^{2+3}) = 120y^5$
(c) $(3xy)(5x^2y^3) = (3 \cdot 5)(x \cdot x^2)(y \cdot y^3) = 15x^3y^4.$

To divide monomials, you divide the numerical coefficients and then apply rules for exponents to divide the variables.

Example: Find each quotient: (a) $\frac{20x^2}{4x^2}$;

(b) $40x^3y^5 \div 8xy^3$; (c) $\frac{6x^2y^3}{12x^5y^2}$.

Solution:

(a) $\frac{20x^2}{4x^2} = \left(\frac{20}{4}\right)\left(\frac{x^2}{x^2}\right)$ Since $x^2 \div x^2 = 1$, the quotient is $\frac{20}{4} \cdot 1 = 5$, if $x \neq 0$.

(b) Rewrite $40x^3y^5 \div 8xy^3$ as a fraction; then divide. Assume that $x \neq 0$.
$\frac{40x^3y^5}{8xy^3} = \left(\frac{40}{8}\right)\left(\frac{x^3}{x}\right)\left(\frac{y^5}{y^3}\right) = 5(x^{3-1})(y^{5-3}) = 5x^2y^2$

(c) $\frac{6x^2y^3}{12x^5y^2} = \left(\frac{6}{12}\right)\left(\frac{x^2}{x^5}\right)\left(\frac{y^3}{y^2}\right) = \frac{1}{2} \cdot \frac{1}{x^{5-2}} \cdot \frac{y^{3-2}}{1} = \frac{1}{2} \cdot \frac{1}{x^3} \cdot \frac{y}{1} = \frac{y}{2x^3}$

Remember, when the greater exponent is in the denominator, you must write the base in the denominator and subtract exponents in the denominator.

A polynomial is a monomial, a sum of monomials, or a difference of monomials. A polynomial with *two* terms is called a *binomial,* and a polynomial with *three* terms is called a *trinomial.* For simplicity, this discussion will concentrate on polynomials with one variable.

Adding and subtracting polynomials

You can add polynomials vertically or horizontally.

Example: Add $3x^2 + 4x - 6$, $x^2 - 2x + 4$, and $2x^2 + 5x - 1$.

Solution: To add vertically, align like terms and add the monomials in each column.

$$
\begin{array}{l}
3x^2 + 4x - 6 \\
x^2 - 2x + 4 \\
\underline{2x^2 + 5x - 1} \\
6x^2 + 7x - 3 \quad \text{sum}
\end{array}
$$

To add horizontally, rewrite the problem using symbols, remove parentheses, and combine like terms.

$(3x^2 + 4x - 6) + (x^2 - 2x + 4) + (2x^2 + 5x - 1) =$
$3x^2 + 4x - 6 + x^2 - 2x + 4 + 2x^2 + 5x - 1) =$
$6x^2 + 7x - 3$

You can subtract polynomials horizontally or vertically.

Example: Subtract $2x^2 - 3x + 5$ from $5x^2 + 4x - 7$.

Solution: To subtract horizontally, rewrite the problem using symbols, remove parentheses, and combine like terms.

$$(5x^2 + 4x - 7) - (2x^2 - 3x + 5) =$$
$$5x^2 + 4x - 7 - 2x^2 + 3x - 5 =$$
$$3x^2 + 7x - 12$$

To subtract vertically, align the like terms and subtract the monomials in each column. Remember when subtracting to add the opposite of the subtrahend to the minuend.

$$5x^2 + 4x - 7$$ Think: change the sign of
$$2x^2 - 3x + 5$$ the subtrahend and add.
$$3x^2 + 7x - 12$$

Multiplying polynomials

To multiply a monomial and a polynomial, multiply each term of the polynomial by the monomial.

Example: Multiply $2x^2 - 3x + 5$ and $7x$.

Solution: $7x(2x^2 - 3x + 5) = 7x(2x^2) - (7x)(3x) + (7x)(5) = 14x^3 - 21x^2 + 35x$

To multiply two binomials, multiply each term of one binomial by each term of the other. This can be done horizontally or vertically.

Example: Multiply $(x + 3)$ and $(x + 2)$.

Solution: To multiply horizontally, rewrite the problem using symbols. Think of one binomial as a monomial and multiply. Then remove parentheses and combine like terms.

$$(x + 3)(x + 2) = (x + 3)x + (x + 3)2 \quad \text{Think of } (x + 3)$$
$$= x^2 + 3x + 2x + 6 \quad \text{as a monomial.}$$
$$= x^2 + 5x + 6$$

To multiply vertically, rewrite the problem. Align the right-hand digits of the factors and multiply.

$$x + 3$$
$$x + 2$$

partial product $\quad 2x + 6 \longleftarrow 2(x + 3)$
partial product $\quad x^2 + 3x \longleftarrow x(x + 3)$
product $\quad\quad\quad\; x^2 + 5x + 6$

Products of trinomials and binomials are usually done vertically.

There is a technique, called the *FOIL* method, for multiplying binomials mentally.

1. Multiply the *first* terms of each binomial.
2. Multiply the two *outer* terms.
3. Multiply the two *inner* terms.
4. Multiply the *last* terms of each binomial.
5. Add the products.

$$(x + 7)(x + 5)$$

first	outer	inner	last
F	O	I	L
x^2	$5x$	$7x$	35
x^2 +	$12x$ +	35	

The *FOIL* method will be very useful later when factoring polynomials.

Dividing polynomials

To divide a polynomial by a monomial, divide each term of the polynomial by the monomial.

Example: Divide $6x^3 + 4x^2 - 18x$ by $2x$.

Solution: Rewrite the problem as a fraction. Then divide each term of the dividend by the divisor.

$$\frac{6x^3 + 4x^2 - 18x}{2x} = \frac{6x^3}{2x} + \frac{4x^2}{2x} - \frac{18x}{2x} = \left(\frac{6}{2}\right)\left(\frac{x^3}{x}\right) + \left(\frac{4}{2}\right)\left(\frac{x^2}{x}\right) - \left(\frac{18}{2}\right)\left(\frac{x}{x}\right)$$

$$= 3(x^{3-1}) + 2(x^{2-1}) - 9 \cdot 1$$

$$= 3x^2 + 2x - 9$$

When dividing a polynomial of more than two terms by a binomial, the long-division form is usually best.

Example: Divide $x^2 + 2x - 35$ by $x + 7$.

Solution: Rewrite the problem in long-division form.

$$x + 7 \overline{)x^2 + 2x - 35} \quad \overset{x}{}$$

1. Divide the first term of the dividend by the first term of the divisor to find the first term of the quotient.

$$\begin{array}{r} x - 5 \\ x + 7 \overline{)x^2 + 2x - 35} \\ x^2 + 7x \\ \hline - 5x - 35 \end{array}$$

2. Multiply the divisor and the first term of the quotient.

3. Subtract the product in step 2 from the divi-

$$\frac{-5x - 35}{0}$$

dend and bring down the next term of the dividend.
4. Repeat the procedure until the remainder is 0 or is a degree less than the degree of the divisor.

If there is a remainder, it may be left as the final difference or rewritten as a fraction in the form

$$\frac{\text{remainder}}{\text{divisor}}.$$

Sometimes not all of the powers are included in the dividend. When this occurs, zeros are used to represent missing powers.

Example: Divide $x^3 - 7x + 5$ by $x - 2$.

Solution: Rewrite the problem in long-division form. Since the x^2 term is missing in the dividend, you use $0x^2$ to represent that term.

$$
\begin{array}{r}
x^2 + 2x - 3 \\
x - 2 \overline{)x^3 + 0x^2 - 7x + 5} \\
\underline{x^3 - 2x^2} \\
2x^2 - 7x \\
\underline{2x^2 - 4x} \\
-3x + 5 \\
\underline{-3x + 6} \\
-1
\end{array}
$$

1. $\dfrac{x^3}{x} = x^2$
2. $x^2(x - 2) = x^3 - 2x^2$
3. Subtract and bring down the next term of the dividend.
4. $\dfrac{2x^2}{x} = 2x$
5. $2x(x - 2) = 2x^2 - 4x$
6. Subtract and bring down the last term of the dividend.
7. $\dfrac{-3x}{x} = -3$
8. $-3(x - 2) = -3x + 6$
9. Subtract.

The remainder may be left as is or rewritten as the fraction $\dfrac{-1}{x - 2}$.

Square roots

The symbol $\sqrt{}$, called a *radical sign*, is used to indicate "square root." The number inside a radical sign is called the *radicand*. A radicand *cannot* be a negative number. In the example $\sqrt{16}$, the number 16 is the radicand. One square root of 16 is 4 because $4^2 = 16$. Another square root of 16 is -4 because $(-4)^2 = 16$. In symbols,

$$\sqrt{16} = 4 \text{ and } -\sqrt{16} = -4.$$

The symbol $\sqrt{}$ without the negative sign indicates the *principal square root or positive square root. A perfect square,* such as 16, is a square of an integer or a rational number. The following are perfect squares.

integer perfect squares: 1, 4, 9, 16, 25, 49, 64, 81, 100

rational perfect squares: $1, \frac{1}{4}, \frac{1}{9}, \frac{4}{9}, \frac{9}{16}$

The square root of zero is zero.

Simplifying radicals

Radicals are in simplest form if
1. the radicand does not contain a whole-number factor (other than 1) that is a perfect square;
2. no radicand is a fraction; and
3. no denominator contains a radical sign.

To simplify radicals, you apply one (or both) of the following properties of radicals.

Property 1: If a and b are nonnegative real numbers, then
$$\sqrt{ab} = \sqrt{a} \cdot \sqrt{b}.$$
Property 2: If a is a nonnegative real number and b is a positive real number,
$$\sqrt{\frac{a}{b}} = \frac{\sqrt{a}}{\sqrt{b}}$$

Example: Simplify each radical: (a) $\sqrt{50}$; (b) $\sqrt{\frac{4}{9}}$; (c) $\sqrt{\frac{3}{4}}$; (d) $\sqrt{\frac{1}{5}}$.

Solution:

(a) Rewrite the radicand as a product so that one of the factors is a perfect square. Then apply Property 1 and simplify.
$$\sqrt{50} = \sqrt{25 \cdot 2} = \sqrt{25} \cdot \sqrt{2} = 5\sqrt{2}$$
$$\qquad\qquad\text{perfect square}$$

(b) The radicand is a perfect square. So $\sqrt{\frac{4}{9}} = \frac{2}{3}$.

(c) The radicand is a fraction. The denominator is a perfect square. Apply Property 2 and simplify.
$$\sqrt{\frac{3}{4}} = \frac{\sqrt{3}}{\sqrt{4}} = \frac{\sqrt{3}}{2}$$

(d) The radicand is a fraction. Multiply to make the denominator a perfect square. Apply Property 2 and simplify.
$$\sqrt{\frac{1}{5}} = \sqrt{\frac{1}{5} \cdot \frac{5}{5}} = \sqrt{\frac{5}{25}} = \frac{\sqrt{5}}{\sqrt{25}} = \frac{\sqrt{5}}{5}$$

Multiplying and dividing radicals

To multiply and divide radicals, apply Property 1 and Property 2 in reverse.

Example: Multiply: (a) $\sqrt{2} \cdot \sqrt{3}$; (b) $\sqrt{2x} \cdot \sqrt{5x}$.

Solution:
(a) Apply Property 1. $\sqrt{2} \cdot \sqrt{3} = \sqrt{2 \cdot 3} = \sqrt{6}$.
Since 6 does not contain a perfect square other than 1, $\sqrt{6}$ is in simplest form.

(b) When variables are in the radicand, you assume that they represent nonnegative real numbers.

$$\sqrt{2x} \cdot \sqrt{5x} = \sqrt{(2x)(5x)} = \sqrt{10x^2} = \sqrt{x^2} \cdot \sqrt{10} = x\sqrt{10}$$

Example: Divide: (a) $\sqrt{10} \div \sqrt{2}$; (b) $\sqrt{5} \div \sqrt{3}$.

Solution:
(a) Rewrite the problem as a fraction and apply Property 2.

$$\sqrt{10} \div \sqrt{2} = \frac{\sqrt{10}}{\sqrt{2}} = \sqrt{\frac{10}{2}} = \sqrt{5}$$

(b) Rewrite the problem as a fraction and apply Property 2. Then multiply to make the denominator a perfect square and simplify.

$$\sqrt{5} \div \sqrt{3} = \frac{\sqrt{5}}{\sqrt{3}} = \sqrt{\frac{5}{3}} = \sqrt{\frac{5}{3} \cdot \frac{3}{3}} = \sqrt{\frac{15}{9}} = \frac{\sqrt{15}}{\sqrt{9}} = \frac{\sqrt{15}}{3}$$

Adding and subtracting radicals

To add and subtract radicals, the radicands must be the same.

Example: Add $3\sqrt{2}$ and $7\sqrt{2}$.

Solution: Rewrite the problem using symbols and add.

$$3\sqrt{2} + 7\sqrt{2} = (3 + 7)\sqrt{2} = 10\sqrt{2}$$

Example: Subtract $5\sqrt{6}$ from $16\sqrt{6}$.

Solution: Rewrite the problem using symbols and subtract.

$$16\sqrt{6} - 5\sqrt{6} = (16 - 5)\sqrt{6} = 11\sqrt{6}$$

Sometimes it is necessary to simplify radicals before you can add or subtract.

Example: Add $\sqrt{18}$ and $\sqrt{50}$.

Solution: Simplify $\sqrt{18}$ and $\sqrt{50}$.

$$\sqrt{18} = \sqrt{9 \cdot 2} = \sqrt{9} \cdot \sqrt{2} = 3\sqrt{2}$$
$$\sqrt{50} = \sqrt{25 \cdot 2} = \sqrt{25} \cdot \sqrt{2} = 5\sqrt{2}$$

Since the radicands are now the same, you can now add.

$$\sqrt{18} + \sqrt{50} = 3\sqrt{2} + 5\sqrt{2} = (3 + 5)\sqrt{2} = 8\sqrt{2}$$

Factoring polynomials

Factoring polynomials is the reverse of multiplying polynomials. *To factor* a polynomial means to rewrite the polynomial as an indicated product of polynomials. The simplest kind of factoring is common monomial factoring. You already considered common monomial factoring when you applied the distributive property to express sums and differences as products.

Example: Factor each polynomial: **(a)** $5x + 20$; **(b)** $5x^3 + 35x^2 - 10x$.

Solution:

(a) You can express $5x + 20$ as $5 \cdot x + 5 \cdot 4$. By applying the distributive property, $5x + 20 = 5 \cdot x + 5 \cdot 4 = 5(x + 4)$. The common monomial factor is 5. The other factor is a binomial factor.

(b) To find the common monomial factor, you can think of $5x^3 + 35x^2 - 10x$ as $5x \cdot x^2 + 5x \cdot 7x - 5x \cdot 2$. Since $5x$ is a factor of each term, it is a common monomial factor. In factored form, $5x^3 + 35x^2 - 10x = 5x(x^2 + 7x - 2)$. Since $x^2 + 7x - 2$ has no common factor other than 1, you say that $5x$ is the *greatest common factor*. You can check the factors by multiplication.

A binomial that can be written in the form

$$\underset{\text{perfect square}}{a^2} \overset{\text{minus sign}}{-} \underset{\text{perfect square}}{b^2}$$

is called a difference of two squares. The difference of two squares can be factored as follows.

$$a^2 - b^2 = (a + b)(a - b)$$

Example: Factor $x^2 - 16$.

Solution: The polynomial is a difference of two squares. The factors are $x + 4$ and $x - 4$.

$$x^2 - 16 = (x + 4)(x - 4)$$

You can check the factors by using the *FOIL* method for multiplying binomials.

Sometimes it is necessary to remove a common monomial factor before you can recognize the difference of two squares.

Example: Factor $28x^2 - 7$.

Solution: As written, neither the first term nor the second term is a perfect square. However, there is a common monomial factor.

$$28x^2 - 7 = 7(4x^2 - 1)$$

The resulting binomial factor is a difference of two squares and can be factored.

$$28x^2 - 7 = 7(4x^2 - 1) = 7(2x + 1)(2x - 1)$$

Solving quadratic equations in one variable

A quadratic equation in one variable is any equation that can be written as $ax^2 + bx + c = 0$; in which a, b, and c are real numbers and $a \neq 0$. Simple quadratic equations like $x^2 = 16$ can be solved for x by finding the square root of both sides of the equation. $x = \sqrt{16} = \pm 4$.

Certain polynomial equations can also be solved by factoring.

Example: Solve $x^2 + 4x - 21 = 0$ for x.

Solution: $x^2 + 4x - 21 = 0$
$(x + 7)(x - 3) = 0$ Factor the left member of the equation.

When a product is equal to 0, one of the factors must be equal to 0.

either	or
$x + 7 = 0$	$x - 3 = 0$
$x = -7$	$x = 3$

The solution set is $\{-7, 3\}$. Sometimes, -7 and 3 are called solutions (or roots) of $x^2 + 4x - 21 = 0$.

Not all quadratic equations in one variable can be solved by factoring. However, every quadratic equation that has real-number solutions can be solved by using the quadratic formula. If a, b, and c are real numbers and $a \neq 0$, then the solutions for $ax^2 + bx + c = 0$ can be found by applying the following formula.

$$x = \frac{-b \pm \sqrt{b^2 - 4ac}}{2a}$$

If $b^2 - 4ac$ is less than 0, $\sqrt{b^2 - 4ac}$ is not a real number, and there are no real-number solutions of the equation.

3

Reviewing Geometry

Geometry is one of the first chances students usually have to study a mathematical system. A mathematical system contains

1. undefined terms;
2. definitions;
3. properties that are accepted as true without proof;
4. a system of logic for making decisions; and
5. statements that are proved.

The undefined terms of geometry are *point, line, plane,* and *space.*

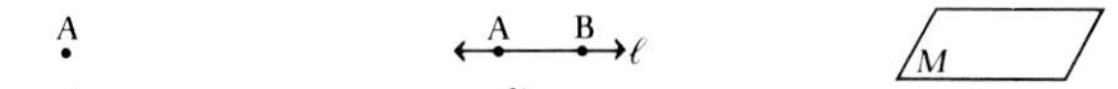

point	line	plane
Identified by a capital letter, for example, point A.	$\overrightarrow{AB}$ or ℓ	Identified by a capital script letter, for example, plane *M*.

To understand geometry, you must first understand the undefined terms. A *point* has *no* dimensions. A *line* (straight line) is a set of points and has *one* dimension—length. A *plane* is a set of points that has *two* dimensions—length and width. *Space* is the set of all points. The undefined terms are used to define other geometric terms like line segment, ray, angle, triangle, circle, and solid, as will be shown below.

The study of logic for geometry could comprise an entire unit. However, most geometric statements are "if, then" statements or "conditionals." For example:

if $2x = 6$,   then $x = 3$.

hypothesis   conclusion

The "if" part of an "if, then" statement is assumed to be true, whereas the "then" part of the statement must be proved. The most common logical reasoning pattern used in geometric proof is called the law of detachment, or modus ponens. (Three dots $\therefore$ represent the word "therefore.")

law of detachment

If p, then q. (general statement)
    p is true. (specific statement)
$\therefore$ q is true. (conclusion)

In a geometric proof, the form is somewhat different:

statements	reasons
p (specific statement) $\therefore$ q (conclusion)	Given. If p, then q (general statement).

Example: Prove: If $2x = 6$, then $x = 3$.

Solution:

statements	reasons
1. $2x = 6$	1. Given.
2. $x = 3$	2. If equals are divided by equals, the quotients are equal.

The properties that function as general statements in geometric proofs are definitions, assumed statements (called axioms, postulates, or simply assumptions), or previously proved statements (called theorems). Some of the more common introductory axioms of geometry are listed below.

Axioms:
1. A line contains at least two distinct points.
2. Given two distinct points, there is exactly one line that contains them.
3. A plane contains at least three points that are not collinear (in line).
4. Given three distinct points not on the same line, there is exactly one plane that contains them.
5. Space contains at least four points that are not coplanar (on the same plane).
6. If a plane contains two points of a line, the plane contains the line.
7. If two distinct planes intersect, the intersection is a line.

In addition to these axioms, all of the properties of real numbers (from Section 2) are assumed. Other axioms are necessary as you progress through geometry and will be stated as you proceed through this section.

Distance

In geometry, distance is a *positive* real number.

Axiom: Given any two distinct points, there is a positive real number that represents the distance from one to the other.

The distance from A to B (AB) can be found by counting or by subtracting the coordinates of the points (-3 is the co-ordinate of point A and 5 is the coordinate of point B). Since distance is a positive number, you must always subtract the lesser coordinate from the greater or use absolute value symbols. The distance from A to B is 8.

Betweenness

The concept of "between" for points is included in most modern geometry textbooks. This concept was introduced to eliminate dependence on figures in geometric proof.

Definition: Point Q is between points P and R whenever (1) points P, Q, and R are collinear; and (2) the distance from P to Q plus the distance from Q to R is equal to the distance from P to R; that is, $PQ + QR = PR$.

Q is *not* between P and R.
(P, Q, and R are not collinear.)

Q is *not* between P and R.
($PQ + QR \neq PR$)

The idea of "betweenness" lends itself to rather easy geometric proofs. There are two types of geometric proof—direct and indirect. Direct proof is the most common. A direct proof consists of

1. a figure;
2. given information (in terms of the figure);
3. a statement of what to prove (in terms of the figure):
4. a plan; and
5. statements and reasons.

A direct proof is usually organized as follows. Mathematical symbols are often used to abbreviate key words in the reasons in a proof.

Given:
Prove:
Proof:

| statements | reasons |

Example: Write statements and reasons to complete the following proof. Given: P, Q, and R are points of line ℓ and Q is between P and R.

Prove: QR = PR − PQ.

$$\ell \xleftarrow{\qquad \overset{P}{\bullet} \quad \overset{Q}{\bullet} \qquad \overset{R}{\bullet} \qquad} \rightarrow$$

Solution: Plan: We can use the fact that Q is between P and R (given) and the definition of "between" for points to prove that PQ + QR = PR. Then, by applying the subtraction property of equality, we can subtract PQ from both sides of the equation to obtain QR = PR − PQ. The proof can be written as follows:

Proof:

statements	reasons
1. P, Q, and R are points of line ℓ.	1. Given.
2. Q is between P and R.	2. Given.
3. PQ + QR = PR	3. Definition of "between" for points.
4. QR = PR − PQ	4. Subtraction property of equality.

When writing a proof, it is a good idea to list one statement per step. All of the given information must be included in the proof. The first step contains information about the figure. Statement 2 and statement 3 comprise a basic reasoning pattern (law of detachment).

2. Q is between P and R (specific statement).	2. Given.
3. PQ + QR = PR (conclusion).	3. If Q is between P and R, then PQ + QR = PR (general statement).

The conclusion of this reasoning pattern becomes the specific statement in the next reasoning pattern.

3. PQ + QR = PR	
4. QR = PR − PQ	4. If equals are subtracted from equals, then the differences are equal.

Line segments and rays

A *line segment* is a set of points in a plane—a subset of a line.

Definition: If P and Q are distinct points, line segment PQ is the set whose elements are P, Q, and all points of line PQ between P and Q.

$$\xleftarrow{\qquad \overset{P}{\bullet} \qquad \overset{Q}{\bullet} \qquad} \rightarrow$$

line segment PQ
symbol: $\overline{PQ}$

P and Q are the endpoints of $\overline{PQ}$.

The measure of a line segment is the distance from one endpoint to the other. Each line segment has exactly *one* measure.

Example: Find the measure (symbol m) of each line segment: (a) $\overline{AB}$: (b) $\overline{CD}$.

Solution:
(a) The distance from A to B is 6. So, $m(\overline{AB}) = 6$.
(b) The distance from C to D is 7. So, $m(\overline{CD}) = 7$.

If two line segments have the same measure, we say that the line segments are *congruent*. The symbol $\cong$ is used to indicate *congruence*.

Example: Tell which two segments are congruent.

Solution: Find the measures of the segments $m(\overline{AB}) = 3$; $m(\overline{AC}) = 5$; $m(\overline{AD}) = 10$; $m(\overline{BC}) = 2$; $m(\overline{CD}) = 5$; $m(\overline{BD}) = 7$. Since $m(\overline{CD}) = m(\overline{AC}) = 5$, you can conclude that $\overline{CD} \cong \overline{AC}$.

A *ray* is also a subset of a line.

Definition: If P and Q are distinct points, ray PQ is the union of $\overline{PQ}$ and the set of all points R such that Q is between P and R.

ray PQ
symbol: $\overrightarrow{PQ}$

P is the endpoint of $\overrightarrow{PQ}$.

The endpoint of a ray is always named first. If two collinear rays have the same endpoint and extend in opposite directions, they are called "opposite" rays.

$\overrightarrow{PR}$ and $\overrightarrow{PQ}$ are opposite rays.

Angles

An *angle* is a set of points in a plane.

Definition: An angle is the union of two noncollinear rays that have a common endpoint.

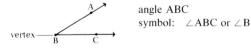

angle ABC
symbol: $\angle ABC$ or $\angle B$

$\overline{BA}$ and $\overline{BC}$ are called *sides*. When three letters are used to name an angle, the vertex letter of the angle is always given in the center.

Axiom: To every angle there corresponds a unique real number greater than 0 and less than 180. The angle measures most commonly used are degree measures. Angles are classified according to "size."

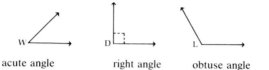

| acute angle | right angle | obtuse angle |
| $0 < m \angle W < 90$ | $m \angle D = 90$ | $90 < m \angle L < 180$ |

Example: Classify each angle, given that
(a) m $\angle A = 37$; (b) m $\angle X = 126$; (c) m$\angle B = 90$.

Solution:
(a) Since 37 is greater than 0 and less than 90, $\angle A$ is an acute angle.

(b) Since 126 is greater than 90 and less than 180, $\angle X$ is an obtuse angle.

(c) Since m $\angle B = 90$, $\angle B$ is a right angle.

If two angles have the same measure, the angles are congruent.

Lines and planes

Two lines in the same plane are either *parallel* or *intersecting*.

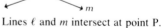

Line ℓ is parallel to line m ($\ell \parallel m$).   Lines ℓ and m intersect at point P.

If two lines intersect, they are either *oblique* or *perpendicular*.

oblique lines   perpendicular lines

Angles formed by perpendicular lines are right angles. Angles formed by oblique lines are either acute or obtuse angles.

If two lines intersect, there is exactly one plane that contains both lines.

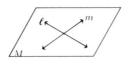

If two planes intersect, the intersection is a line.

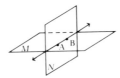

The intersection of plane M and plane N is $\overline{AB}$.

A line can be parallel to a plane or can intersect the plane.

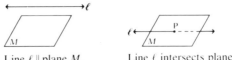

Line $\ell \parallel$ plane M.   Line ℓ intersects plane M at P.

Remember from the list of axioms that if a plane contains two points of a line, it contains the line.

If two planes do not intersect, they are parallel.

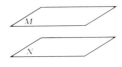

Plane $M \parallel$ plane N.

Circles, line segments, and lines

A *circle* is a set of points in a plane.

Definition: A circle is the set of all points in a plane that are a given distance from a given point of the plane.

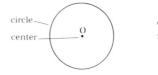

circle O

symbol: $\odot$O

Three line segments are associated with every circle.

$\overline{OA}$ is a radius.
$\overline{EF}$ is a chord.
$\overline{BC}$ is a diameter.

One endpoint of a *radius* is the center of the circle and the other endpoint is a point of the circle. Both endpoints of a *chord* are points of the circle. A *diameter* is a chord that contains the center of the circle.

There are two lines associated with a circle.

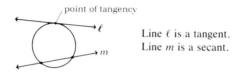

point of tangency

Line ℓ is a tangent.
Line m is a secant.

A *tangent* intersects a circle in exactly one point. The radius drawn to the point of tangency is perpendicular to the tangent. A *secant* contains a chord of the circle. As a result, it intersects the circle in two points.

Pairs of angles

If the measures of two angles are added and
1. the sum is 90, the angles are *complementary angles.*
2. the sum is 180, the angles are *supplementary angles.*

Example: Two complementary angles have measures of $x + 40$ and $2x - 10$. Find the measure of each angle.

Solution: Since the angles are complementary, the sum of their measures is 90. You can use this fact to write an equation and then solve it for x.

$$(x + 40) + (2x - 10) = 90$$
$$3x + 30 = 90$$
$$3x = 60$$
$$x = 20$$

Now, by substituting 20 for x, you can find the measure of each angle.

$$x + 40 = 20 + 40 = 60 \qquad 2x - 10 = 2(20) - 10 = 30$$

Example: Angles A and B are supplementary angles. If the measure of $\angle B$ is 20 more than 3 times the measure of $\angle A$, find the measure of each angle.

Solution: You begin by representing the measures of both angles.

Let: x = the measure of $\angle A$.
$3x + 20$ = the measure of $\angle B$.

Because the two angles are supplementary, the sum of their measures is 180.

$$x + (3x + 20) = 180$$
$$4x + 20 = 180$$
$$4x = 160$$
$$x = 40$$
$$3x + 20 = 140$$

Adjacent angles are *two* angles that (1) are coplanar; (2) have the same vertex; (3) have a common side; and (4) have no common interior points.

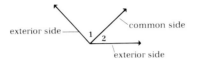

exterior side ———

common side

exterior side

∠1 and∠2 are adjacent angles.

If the exterior sides of two adjacent angles are opposite rays, the angles are supplementary.

Example: Refer to the figure below. Find the measure of ∠1 given that m ∠2 = 72.

Solution: The two angles are adjacent and the exterior sides are opposite rays. So, the angles are supplementary.

m ∠1 + m ∠2 = 180

Now if you substitute 72 for m ∠2, you can solve for m ∠1.

m ∠1 + 72 = 180
m ∠1 = 108

The nonadjacent angles formed by two intersecting lines are called *vertical angles.*

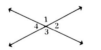

∠1 and ∠3 are vertical angles.
∠2 and ∠4 are vertical angles.

If two angles are vertical angles, they are congruent.

Triangles

A triangle is a set of points in a plane.

Definition: If A, B, and C are three distinct noncollinear points, triangle ABC is the union of $\overline{AB}$, $\overline{BC}$, and $\overline{AC}$.

triangle ABC
symbol: △ABC
angles: ∠A, ∠B, ∠C
sides: $\overline{AB}$, $\overline{AC}$, $\overline{BC}$

Triangles can be classified by side.

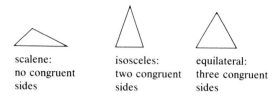

scalene: isosceles: equilateral:
no congruent   two congruent   three congruent
sides   sides   sides

Or they can be classified by angle.

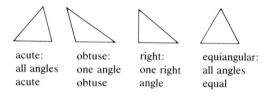

acute: obtuse: right: equiangular:
all angles   one angle   one right   all angles
acute   obtuse   angle   equal

The sides of a right triangle are given special names.

The sum of the measures of the angles of a triangle is always 180.

Triangles and congruence

Congruence of triangles is an important geometric concept. In general terms, two triangles are congruent if they have the same *size* and *shape*. In modern geometry courses, however, congruence of triangles is developed by using the idea of one-to-one correspondence.

There are six different ways to match the vertices of △ABC with those of △PQR. One of them is given below.

A ↔ P, B ↔ Q, C ↔R

This correspondence automatically pairs angles and sides of the two triangles.

corresponding angles   corresponding sides

∠A ↔ ∠P $\overline{AB} \leftrightarrow \overline{PQ}$
∠B ↔ ∠Q $\overline{BC} \leftrightarrow \overline{QR}$
∠C ↔ ∠R $\overline{AC} \leftrightarrow \overline{PR}$

Now, if corresponding angles *and* corresponding sides are congruent, that is, if

$\angle A \cong \angle P$		$\overline{AB} \cong \overline{PQ}$
$\angle B \cong \angle Q$	and	$\overline{BC} \cong \overline{QR}$
$\angle C \cong \angle R$		$\overline{AC} \cong \overline{PR}$

the correspondence is a congruence of triangles. You can indicate that the triangles are congruent by writing $\triangle ABC \cong \triangle PQR$.

The order in which the vertices are named indicates the corresponding parts of congruent triangles.

Example: Given that $\triangle WDL \cong \triangle SRO$, identify the congruent corresponding parts.

Solution: Because of the order in which the letters are written:

$\angle W \cong \angle S$		$\overline{WD} \cong \overline{SR}$
$\angle D \cong \angle R$		$\overline{DL} \cong \overline{RO}$
$\angle L \cong \angle O$		$\overline{WL} \cong \overline{SO}$

Once you know that two triangles are congruent, you know automatically that all six corresponding parts are congruent. To prove that two triangles are congruent, it is necessary to accept new axioms.

Axiom: Two triangles are congruent if three sides of one triangle are congruent to three sides of the other triangle (abbreviated SSS).

Axiom: Two triangles are congruent if two sides and the included angle of one triangle are congruent to two sides and the included angle of the other triangle (abbreviated SAS).

Axiom: Two triangles are congruent if two angles and the included side of one triangle are congruent to two angles and the included side of the other triangle (abbreviated ASA).

Axiom: Two right triangles are congruent if the hypotenuse and leg of one right triangle are congruent to the hypotenuse and leg of the other right triangle (abbreviated HL).

Example: Given: $\triangle PQS$ and $\triangle RSQ$ with common side $\overline{SQ}$; $\overline{PQ} \cong \overline{RS}$; $\overline{PS} \cong \overline{RQ}$.
Prove: $\angle P \cong \angle R$.

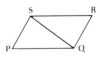

Solution: Plan: We will prove that $\triangle PQS$ is congruent to $\triangle RSQ$. Then $\angle P$ will be congruent to $\angle R$ because they are corresponding parts of congruent triangles. To help yourself decide which congruence axiom to use, mark the congruent segments on the figure. Since $\overline{SQ}$ is in both triangles, three sides of one triangle are congruent to three sides of the other triangle.

Proof:

statements	reasons
1. $\triangle$ PQS and $\triangle$ RSQ with common side $\overline{SQ}$.	1. Given.
2. $\overline{PQ} \cong \overline{RS}$	2. Given.
3. $\overline{PS} \cong \overline{RQ}$	3. Given.
4. $\overline{SQ} \cong \overline{SQ}$	4. A line segment is congruent to itself.
5. $\triangle$ PSQ $\cong$ $\triangle$ RSQ	5. SSS congruence axiom.
6. $\therefore \angle P \cong \angle R$	6. Corresponding parts of congruent triangles are congruent.

Parallel lines

Two lines in the same plane that do not intersect are *parallel*. A line that intersects two coplanar lines at distinct points is called a *transversal*. Line *t* in the following diagrams is a transversal.

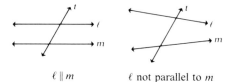

$\ell \parallel m$ ℓ not parallel to *m*

A transversal and two coplanar lines form eight angles.

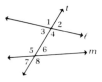

The four angles outside the given lines are called *exterior* angles. The four angles inside the given lines are called *interior* angles.

exterior angles: $\angle 1$, $\angle 2$, $\angle 7$, $\angle 8$
interior angles: $\angle 3$, $\angle 4$, $\angle 5$, $\angle 6$

Certain pairs of these angles have special names. *Alternate interior angles* are two interior angles, like $\angle 3$ and $\angle 6$, that
   1. have different vertices; and
   2. are on opposite sides of the transversal.

Alternate exterior angles are two exterior angles, like $\angle 1$ and $\angle 8$, that
1. have different vertices; and
2. are on opposite sides of the transversal.

Corresponding angles are two angles, like $\angle 1$ and $\angle 5$, that
1. have different vertices;
2. are on the same side of the transversal; and
3. comprise one interior angle and one exterior angle.
    alternate interior angles
      $\angle 3$ and $\angle 6$
      $\angle 4$ and $\angle 5$
    alternate exterior angles
      $\angle 1$ and $\angle 8$
      $\angle 2$ and $\angle 7$
    corresponding angles
      $\angle 1$ and $\angle 5$; $\angle 3$ and $\angle 7$
      $\angle 2$ and $\angle 6$; $\angle 4$ and $\angle 8$

To develop ideas concerning these angles and parallel lines, you accept two axioms.

Axiom 1: If two parallel lines are cut by a transversal, each pair of corresponding angles is congruent.

Once this axiom has been accepted, it is possible to prove two useful theorems.

Theorem 1: If two parallel lines are cut by a transversal, each pair of alternate interior angles is congruent.

Theorem 2: If two parallel lines are cut by a transversal, each pair of alternate exterior angles is congruent.

Example: Prove Theorem 1 for one pair of alternate angles.

Solution: Draw a figure that accurately depicts the conditions described in the theorem. Write the "given" and "prove" in terms of the figure.
Given: Lines ℓ and m cut by transversal t; $\ell \| m$.
Prove: $\angle 1 \cong \angle 2$.

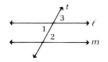

Plan: We will use the axiom to prove that $\angle 2 \cong \angle 3$ and the fact that $\angle 1$ and $\angle 3$ are vertical angles to prove that $\angle 1 \cong \angle 3$. Then, the transitive property guarantees that $\angle 1 \cong \angle 2$.

Proof:

statements	reasons
1. Lines ℓ and m cut by transversal t.	1. Given.
2. $\angle 2$ and $\angle 3$ are corresponding angles.	2. Definition of corresponding angles.
3. $\ell \| m$	3. Given.
4. $\angle 2 \cong \angle 3$	4. If two parallel lines are cut by a transversal, each pair of corresponding angles are congruent.
5. $\angle 1$ and $\angle 3$ are vertical angles.	5. Definition of vertical angles.
6. $\angle 1 \cong \angle 3$	6. If two angles are vertical angles, they are congruent.
7. $\therefore \angle 1 \cong \angle 2$	7. Steps 4 and 6 and the transitive property of equality (if $\angle 1 \cong \angle 3$ and $\angle 3 \cong \angle 2$, then $\angle 1 \cong \angle 2$).

Axiom 2: If two lines are cut by a transversal so that a pair of corresponding angles is congruent, the lines are parallel.

This axiom makes it possible to prove the following theorems.

Theorem: If two lines are cut by a transversal so that a pair of alternate interior angles is congruent, the lines are parallel.

Theorem: If two lines are cut by a transversal so that a pair of alternate exterior angles is congruent, the lines are parallel.

Indirect proof

An indirect proof uses the following types of reasoning:
1. assume the opposite of the statement you are trying to prove;
2. show that this assumption leads to a statement that contradicts a known fact; and
3. so the assumption must be false and its opposite (the statement you wanted to prove) is true.

Example: Given: Lines ℓ and m cut by transversal t; $\angle 1 \not\cong \angle 2$.
Prove: ℓ is not parallel to m.

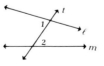

Solution: Plan: Assume that ℓ is parallel to m. Then show that $\angle 1 \cong \angle 2$, which contradicts the given statement.

Indirect Proof: Assume $\ell \parallel m$. Since $\angle 1$ and $\angle 2$ are alternate interior angles (definition of alternate interior angles), they are congruent. If two parallel lines are cut by a transversal, each pair of alternate interior angles is congruent, so $\angle 1 \cong \angle 2$. But this contradicts the fact that $\angle 1 \not\cong \angle 2$ (given). Therefore, the assumption must be false, and ℓ is not parallel to m.

Polygons

The simplest polygon is a triangle. The sum of the measures of the angles of a triangle is 180.

Polygons are named by the number of sides.

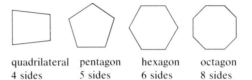

| quadrilateral | pentagon | hexagon | octagon |
| 4 sides | 5 sides | 6 sides | 8 sides |

Each polygon has interior angles and exterior angles.

$\angle 1$ is an interior angle
$\angle 2$ is an exterior angle

The number of interior angles of a polygon is equal to the number of its sides. To find the sum of the measures of the *interior* angles of a polygon, you apply the formula $I = 180(n - 2)$, in which the variable n represents the number of sides. The sum of the measures of the *exterior* angles of a polygon is always 360.

Example: Find the sum of the measures of the interior angles of a pentagon.

Solution: A pentagon has 5 sides. Write the formula, substitute 5 for n, and solve the resulting equation for I. $I = 180(n - 2) = 180(5 - 2) = 540$. The sum of the measures of the interior angles of a pentagon is 540.

You can also use this formula to find the number of sides (or interior angles) a polygon has, given the sum of the measures of the interior angles. Write the formula, substitute the sum of the measures of the interior angles for I, and solve for n.

A regular polygon is a polygon that has all of its interior angles congruent and all of its sides congruent. Since the angles of a regular polygon are congruent, it is possible to find the measure of one interior angle (or one exterior angle) by dividing the sum of the measures of the interior angles (or exterior angles) by the number of sides in the polygon.

The measure of one exterior angle of a regular polygon with n

$$sides = E_1 = \frac{360}{n}$$

The measure of one interior angle of a regular polygon with n

$$sides = I_1 = \frac{180(n-2)}{n}$$

Example: Find the number of degrees in (a) one exterior angle of a regular hexagon; (b) one interior angle of a regular pentagon.

Solution:

(a) A regular hexagon has 6 sides. To find the number of degrees in each exterior angle, we divide 360 by 6.

$$E_1 = \frac{360}{n} = \frac{360}{6} = 60$$

(b) A regular pentagon has 5 sides. To find the number of degrees in each interior angle, you write the formula, substitute 5 for n and solve for I_1.

$$I_1 = \frac{180(n-2)}{n} = \frac{180(5-2)}{5} = 108.$$

These formulas can also be used to determine the number of sides a regular polygon has, given the measure of one interior (or exterior) angle. Write the appropriate formula, substitute the measure of one interior (or exterior) angle for E_1, and solve the resulting equation for n.

Quadrilaterals

A *quadrilateral* is a polygon with four sides. If both pairs of opposite sides are parallel, the quadrilateral is a *parallelogram*.

quadrilateral ABCD
symbol: Quad ABCD

parallelogram PQRS
symbol: ▱ PQRS

A line segment that joins two nonadjacent vertices of a quadrilateral is called a *diagonal* of the quadrilateral.

$\overline{BD}$ and $\overline{AC}$ are diagonals of Quad ABCD.

$\overline{PR}$ and $\overline{SQ}$ are diagonals of ▱ PQRS.

By using diagonals and ideas from parallel lines, you can prove four important theorems about parallelograms.

Theorem 1: Either diagonal of a parallelogram separates the parallelogram into two congruent triangles.

Theorem 2: The opposite angles of a parallelogram are congruent.

Theorem 3: The opposite sides of a parallelogram are congruent.

Theorem 4: The diagonals of a parallelogram bisect each other.

The definition of parallelogram or one of the following theorems can be used to prove that a quadrilateral is a parallelogram.

Theorem 5: A quadrilateral is a parallelogram if one pair of opposite sides is both congruent and parallel.

Theorem 6: A quadrilateral is a parallelogram if both pairs of opposite sides are congruent.

Theorem 7: A quadrilateral is a parallelogram if the diagonals bisect each other.

The following quadrilaterals are special parallelograms.

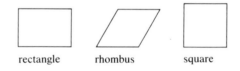

rectangle   rhombus   square

A *rectangle* is a parallelogram that has four right angles. A *rhombus* is a parallelogram that has four congruent sides. A *square* is a rectangle that has four congruent sides and four right angles.

Since rectangles, rhombuses, and squares are parallelograms, all of the theorems proved for parallelograms apply to these figures. There are some special theorems, however, that apply only to rectangles, rhombuses, and squares.

Theorem 8: The diagonals of a rectangle (square) are congruent line segments.

Theorem 9: The diagonals of a rhombus (square) are perpendicular to each other.

If only two sides of a quadrilateral are parallel, the quadrilateral is a *trapezoid*.

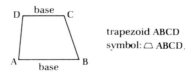

trapezoid ABCD
symbol: ⌁ ABCD.

The two parallel sides of a trapezoid are called its bases. A trapezoid has three important line segments associated with it—two diagonals and the line segment joining the midpoints of the nonparallel sides, called the *median*.

 $\overline{PQ}$ is the median of $\triangle$ ABCD.

The median of any trapezoid is a line segment that
1. is parallel to both bases ($\overline{PQ} \parallel \overline{AB}$ and $\overline{PQ} \parallel \overline{CD}$); and
2. has a measure that is one-half the sum of the measures of the two bases [PQ = $\frac{1}{2}$(AB + CD)].

Example: Find the measure of the median of a trapezoid if one base is 9 inches long and the other base is 15 inches long.

Solution: The measure of the median is one-half the sum of the measures of the bases. In symbols, the median = $\frac{1}{2}$(9 + 15) = $\frac{1}{2}$(24) = 12. The median is 12 inches long.

In an isosceles trapezoid, the nonparallel sides are congruent.

Similarity

Two polygons are similar if they have the same shape. By definition, two polygons are similar if
1. the corresponding angles are congruent; and
2. the lengths of corresponding sides are proportional.
To prove that two triangles are similar (symbol~), we use the following axiom.

Axiom: Two triangles are similar if two angles of one triangle are congruent to two angles of the other triangle (abbreviated AA).

Example: Given: $\triangle$ABC with $\overline{BD} \perp \overline{AC}$; $\angle$ABC is a right angle.

Prove: $\triangle$ADB ~ $\triangle$ABC.

Solution: Plan: Prove that two angles of $\triangle$ABC are congruent to two angles of $\triangle$ADB.

Proof:

statements	reasons
1. $\triangle$ABC; $\overline{BD} \perp \overline{AC}$	1. Given.
2. $\angle$BDA is a right angle.	2. If two lines are perpendicular, they intersect to form right angles.

3. ∠ABC is a right angle.	3. Given.
4. ∠BDA ≅ ∠ABC	4. All right angles are congruent.
5. ∠A ≅ ∠A	5. An angle is congruent to itself.
6. ∴ △ADB ~ △ABC	6. AA axiom.

By using the same procedure, it is possible to prove that △BDC ~ △ABC and that △ADB ~ △BDC. Hence, it becomes possible to prove the following theorem.

Theorem: The altitude to the hypotenuse of a right triangle forms two other right triangles that are similar to the given right triangle and to each other.

Once this theorem has been proved, three algebraic relationships can easily be established.

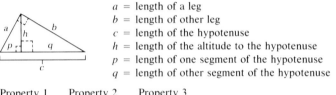

a = length of a leg
b = length of other leg
c = length of the hypotenuse
h = length of the altitude to the hypotenuse
p = length of one segment of the hypotenuse
q = length of other segment of the hypotenuse

Property 1	Property 2	Property 3
$\dfrac{p}{h} = \dfrac{h}{q}$	$\dfrac{c}{a} = \dfrac{a}{p}$	$\dfrac{c}{b} = \dfrac{b}{q}$

In Property 1, the length of the altitude to the hypotenuse is the *mean proportional* between the lengths of the segments of the hypotenuse. In Property 2 and Property 3, the length of a leg is the *mean proportional* between the length of the hypotenuse and the length of one segment of the hypotenuse (the one that shares an endpoint with that leg).

Example: The altitude to the hypotenuse of a right triangle separates the hypotenuse into two segments whose lengths are 4 and 9. Find the length of the altitude.

Solution: You know the lengths of the segments of the hypotenuse and you want to find the length of the altitude. Apply Property 1.

$$\frac{p}{h} = \frac{h}{q}$$

$$\frac{4}{h} = \frac{h}{9}$$

$$h^2 = 36$$

$$h = \pm 6$$

$$h = 6 \qquad \text{Measures are always positive.}$$

Pythagorean theorem	The Pythagorean theorem is probably the best-known theorem of high school geometry. More than one hundred ''proofs'' are known for this theorem, including one submitted by U.S. President James A. Garfield.

Pythagorean Theorem: **If** c **is the measure of the hypotenuse of a right triangle and** a **and** b **are the measures of the legs, then** $a^2 + b^2 = c^2$.

Example: Refer to the figure below. Find x.

Solution: Apply the Pythagorean theorem.

$$a^2 + b^2 = c^2$$
$$5^2 + 12^2 = x^2$$
$$25 + 144 = x^2$$
$$169 = x^2$$
$$\pm 13 = x$$
$$13 = x \quad \text{Measures are always positive.}$$

If the answer is not a perfect square, it should be left in simplest radical form.

Example: Refer to the figure below. Find x.

Solution: Apply the Pythagorean theorem.

$$a^2 + b^2 = c^2$$
$$x^2 + 4^2 = 10^2$$
$$x^2 + 16 = 100$$
$$x^2 = 84$$
$$x = \pm\sqrt{84}$$
$$x = \sqrt{84}$$

Since 84 is not a perfect square, you express $\sqrt{84}$ in simplest radical form.

$$\sqrt{84} = \sqrt{4 \cdot 21} = \sqrt{4} \cdot \sqrt{21} = 2\sqrt{21}$$

Special right triangles	There are two special right triangles. One is a 30-60-90 triangle.

The side opposite the 60° angle is the longer leg.

The side opposite the 30° angle is the shorter leg.

The lengths of the sides of a 30-60-90 triangle are related algebraically.

1. The length of the shorter leg is one-half the length of the hypotenuse.
2. The length of the longer leg is $\sqrt{3}$ times the length of the shorter leg.

These relationships are summarized in the following reference triangle.

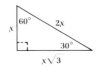

Hence, if you know the length of one side of a 30-60-90 triangle, you can readily find the length of the other two sides.

The other special right triangle is a 45-45-90 triangle, shown below. In such a triangle, both legs are the same length.

The lengths of the sides of a 45-45-90 triangle are related as follows:

1. The length of either leg can be found by dividing the length of the hypotenuse by $\sqrt{2}$.
2. The length of the hypotenuse can be found by multiplying the length of either leg by $\sqrt{2}$.

The reference triangle for a 45-45-90 triangle is shown below.

Example: Find the length of the diagonal of a square if the length of one side of the square is 4.

Solution: The diagonal of a square bisects two right angles of the square, forming a 45-45-90 triangle. If the length of one side of the square is 4, then the length of the diagonal is $4\sqrt{2}$.

4

Reviewing
Trigonometry

The word "trigonometry" comes from the Greek words for
"triangle measurement." The ancient Greeks invented trigonometry to help them in their study of astronomy. Since ancient times, the study of trigonometry has broadened until
now trigonometry is essential in such fields as engineering,
physics, and navigation. It is one high school mathematics
course that has a great number of practical applications.

Angles

An angle is the union of two rays that have the same endpoint.

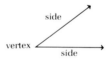

A number called the *measure* is associated with each angle.
The number depends on the choice of unit. Angles are usually
measured in *degrees* or *radians*.

degrees   radians

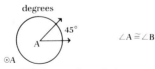

$\angle A \cong \angle B$

⊙A   ⊙B

There are 360 degrees in a circle.   There are 2π radians in a circle.
One degree is $\frac{1}{360}$ of a circle.   One radian is $\frac{1}{2\pi}$ of a circle.

one degree   one radian

An angle of 1° has the same meas-   An angle of 1 radian has the same
ure as an angle of $\frac{\pi}{180}$ radians.   measure as an angle of $\frac{180}{\pi}$ degrees.

To change from radian measure to degree measure, you multiply the radian measure by $\frac{180}{\pi}$.

$$m_{\text{degree}} \angle A = \frac{180}{\pi} m_{\text{radian}} \angle A$$

Example: Change $\frac{5\pi}{6}$ radians to degree measure.

Solution: To change radian measure to degree measure, you multiply by $\frac{180}{\pi}$.

$$m_{\text{degree}} \angle A = \frac{180}{\pi} m_{\text{radian}} \angle A = \frac{180}{\pi} \left(\frac{5\pi}{6}\right) = 150$$

To change from degree measure to radian measure, you multiply by $\frac{\pi}{180}$.

$$m_{\text{radian}} \angle A = \frac{\pi}{180} m_{\text{degree}} \angle A$$

Example: Change 120° to radian measure.

Solution: To change from degree measure to radian measure, you must multiply the degree measure by $\frac{\pi}{180}$.

$$m_{\text{radian}} \angle A = \frac{\pi}{180} m_{\text{degree}} \angle A = \frac{\pi}{180} (120) = \frac{2\pi}{3}$$

A table of common degree/radian equivalences is given below.

degree measure:	360°	180°	150°	120°	90°	60°	45°	30°
radian measure:	2π	π	$\frac{5\pi}{6}$	$\frac{2\pi}{3}$	$\frac{\pi}{2}$	$\frac{\pi}{3}$	$\frac{\pi}{4}$	$\frac{\pi}{6}$

Right triangles

A *right triangle* is any triangle that has a right angle. Triangle ACB is a right triangle.

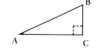

$\angle A$ and $\angle B$ are acute angles.
$\angle C$ is a right angle.

The sum of the measures of the angles of any triangle is 180°. In a right triangle, the sum of the measures of the acute angles is 90°. Whenever the sum of the measures of two angles is 90°, you can say that the angles are *complementary*. Thus, the acute angles of a right triangle are complementary. The sides of a right triangle have special names.

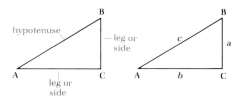

Lower-case letters are used to represent the measures of the sides of a triangle. If the vertices are A, B, and C, then *a,* *b,* and *c* would be used to represent the measures of the sides opposite A, B, and C respectively. It is customary to let C represent the right angle.

The Pythagorean theorem relates the measures of the sides of a right triangle.

Pythagorean Theorem: If *c* is the measure of the hypotenuse of a right triangle and *a* and *b* are the measures of the legs, then $a^2 + b^2 = c^2$.

If the measures of any two sides of a right triangle are given, the measure of the third side can be found easily by substituting the known values in the Pythagorean theorem and then solving the resulting equation for the unknown quantity.

Trigonometric ratios

Six trigonometric ratios can be defined for each acute angle of a right triangle. These definitions are made in terms of the measures of the sides of the right triangle. The names of the trigonometric ratios and their abbreviations are given below.

sine   cosine   tangent   cotangent   cosecant   secant
sin   cos   tan   cot   csc   sec

To define the trigonometric ratios, the following right triangle will be used as an example:

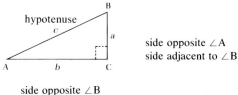

side opposite ∠A
side adjacent to ∠B

side opposite ∠B
side adjacent to ∠A

The sine ratio and the cosine ratio are usually defined first.

$$\sin A = \frac{\text{length of the side opposite } \angle A}{\text{length of the hypotenuse}} = \frac{a}{c}$$

$$\cos A = \frac{\text{length of the side adjacent to } \angle A}{\text{length of the hypotenuse}} = \frac{b}{c}$$

The other four trigonometric ratios are defined in terms of sin and cos.

$$\tan A = \frac{\sin A}{\cos A} = \frac{\text{length of the side opposite } \angle A}{\text{length of the side adjacent to } \angle A} = \frac{a}{b}$$

$$\cot A = \frac{\cos A}{\sin A} = \frac{\text{length of the side adjacent to } \angle A}{\text{length of the side opposite } \angle A} = \frac{b}{a}$$

$$\csc A = \frac{1}{\sin A} = \frac{\text{length of the hypotenuse}}{\text{length of the side opposite } \angle A} = \frac{c}{a}$$

$$\sec A = \frac{1}{\cos A} = \frac{\text{length of the hypotenuse}}{\text{length of the side adjacent to } \angle A} = \frac{c}{b}$$

If the product of two numbers is 1, the numbers are reciprocals. Notice that sin A and csc A are reciprocals; cos A and sec A are reciprocals; and tan A and cot A are reciprocals.

The trigonometric ratios for ∠B of right triangle ACB are similar to those stated for ∠A.

$$\sin B = \frac{\text{length of the side opposite } \angle B}{\text{length of the hypotenuse}} = \frac{b}{c}$$

$$\cos B = \frac{\text{length of the side adjacent to } \angle B}{\text{length of the hypotenuse}} = \frac{a}{c}$$

$$\tan B = \frac{\text{length of the side opposite } \angle B}{\text{length of the side adjacent to } \angle B} = \frac{b}{a}$$

$$\cot B = \frac{\text{length of the side adjacent to } \angle B}{\text{length of the side opposite } \angle B} = \frac{a}{b}$$

$$\csc A = \frac{\text{length of the hypotenuse}}{\text{length of the side opposite } \angle B} = \frac{c}{b}$$

$$\sec B = \frac{\text{length of the hypotenuse}}{\text{length of the side adjacent to } \angle B} = \frac{c}{a}$$

Example: Refer to the 30-60-90 triangle below. Find the trigonometric ratio for each acute angle.

Solution: To find the trigonometric ratios for the acute angles, you simply apply the definitions stated for ∠A and ∠B of right triangle ACB.

$$\sin 30° = \frac{1}{2}$$

$$\cos 30° = \frac{\sqrt{3}}{2}$$

$$\tan 30° = \frac{1}{\sqrt{3}} = \frac{\sqrt{3}}{3}$$

$$\sin 60° = \frac{\sqrt{3}}{2}$$

$$\cot 30° = \frac{\sqrt{3}}{1} = \sqrt{3}$$

$$\csc 30° = \frac{2}{1} = 2$$

$$\sec 30° = \frac{2}{\sqrt{3}} = \frac{2\sqrt{3}}{3}$$

$$\cot 60° = \frac{1}{\sqrt{3}} = \frac{\sqrt{3}}{3}$$

$$\cos 60° = \frac{1}{2} \qquad\qquad \csc 60° = \frac{2}{\sqrt{3}} = \frac{2\sqrt{3}}{3}$$

$$\tan 60° = \frac{\sqrt{3}}{1} = \sqrt{3} \qquad\qquad \sec 60° = \frac{2}{1} = 2$$

In the previous example, it is interesting to notice that

$$\left(\frac{1}{2}\right)^2 + \left(\frac{\sqrt{3}}{2}\right)^2 = \frac{1}{4} + \frac{3}{4} = \frac{4}{4} = 1.$$

Since $\sin 30° = \frac{1}{2}$ and $\cos 30° = \frac{\sqrt{3}}{2}$, it follows that $\sin^2 30° + \cos^2 30° = 1$. It is also true that $\sin^2 60° + \cos^2 60° = 1$. In fact, it can be shown that this relationship holds for any angle A.

$$\sin^2 A + \cos^2 A = 1$$

A relationship of this kind, one that holds for any replacement of a variable, is called an *identity*. This particular trigonometric identity is called a *Pythagorean Identity*. Although there are several trigonometric identities, the one stated above is one of the most useful.

Special right triangles (30-60-90 and 45-45-90) occur quite often in mathematics. In the following table, you will find the trigonometric ratios associated with these triangles.

angle	sin	cos	tan	cot	csc	sec
$\frac{\pi}{6}$ or 30°	$\frac{1}{2}$	$\frac{\sqrt{3}}{2}$	$\frac{1}{\sqrt{3}}$ or $\frac{\sqrt{3}}{3}$	$\sqrt{3}$	2	$\frac{2}{\sqrt{3}}$ or $\frac{2\sqrt{3}}{3}$
$\frac{\pi}{4}$ or 45°	$\frac{1}{\sqrt{2}}$ or $\frac{\sqrt{2}}{2}$	$\frac{1}{\sqrt{2}}$ or $\frac{\sqrt{2}}{2}$	1	1	$\sqrt{2}$	$\sqrt{2}$
$\frac{\pi}{3}$ or 60°	$\frac{\sqrt{3}}{2}$	$\frac{1}{2}$	$\sqrt{3}$	$\frac{1}{\sqrt{3}}$ or $\frac{\sqrt{3}}{3}$	$\frac{2}{\sqrt{3}}$ or $\frac{2\sqrt{3}}{3}$	2

Solving right triangles

Trigonometry is used to "solve" right triangles. To solve a right triangle, it is necessary to find the lengths of the three sides and the measures of the three angles.

Example: Solve right triangle ACB if m $\angle$B = 30° and c = 4.

Solution: First draw a sketch and label the resulting triangle. To solve the triangle, you must find m $\angle$A, a, and b. First, you will use the definition of sine to find b.

$$\sin 30° = \frac{b}{c} = \frac{b}{4}$$

From the table, sin 30° = $\frac{1}{2}$. So, you can substitute $\frac{1}{2}$ for sin 30° and solve the resulting equation for b.

$$\frac{1}{2} = \frac{b}{4}$$
$$b = 2$$

You can now find a by using either the Pythagorean theorem or a trigono-metric ratio.

Pythagorean theorem	*trigonometry*

$$a^2 + b^2 = c^2 \qquad\qquad \cos 30° = \frac{a}{c} = \frac{a}{4}$$
$$a^2 + 2^2 = 4^2 \qquad\qquad \frac{\sqrt{3}}{2} = \frac{a}{4}$$
$$a^2 + 4 = 16 \qquad\qquad 2\sqrt{3} = a$$

$$a^2 = 12$$
$$a = \pm\sqrt{12}$$
$$a = \sqrt{12}$$
$$a = 2\sqrt{3}$$

You can use the fact that the acute angles of a right triangle are comple-mentary to find m $\angle$A.

$$\text{m} \angle A + \text{m} \angle B = 90°$$
$$\text{m} \angle A + 30° = 90°$$
$$\text{m} \angle A = 60°$$

Not all right triangles are special right triangles. To solve most right triangles, it is necessary to use a trigonometric ta-ble. A portion of a trigonometric table has been reproduced at right. The values of the trigonometric ratios in this table are approximate. The symbol $\approx$ is used to indicate that an ap-proximate number is being used.

To find the trigonometric ratios associated with acute an-gles whose measures are less than or equal to 45°,
1. read *down* the angle column on the left-hand side of the table to the correct angle; and
2. read *across* the row to the desired trigonometric-ratio column (labeled at the top).

Example: Find sin 39° 20′.

Solution: Since 39° 20′ is less than 45°, we can find sin 39° 20′ by
1. reading down the angle column of the left-hand side of the table to 39° 20′; and

Partial Trigonometric Table

angle	sin	cos	tan	cot	sec	csc	
38° 00′	.6157	.7880	.7813	1.280	1.269	1.624	52° 00′
10′	.6180	.7862	.7860	1.272	1.272	1.618	50′
20′	.6202	.7844	.7907	1.265	1.275	1.612	40′
30′	.6225	.7826	.7954	1.257	1.278	1.606	30′
40′	.6248	.7808	.8002	1.250	1.281	1.601	20′
50′	.6271	.7790	.8050	1.242	1.284	1.595	10′
39° 00′	.6293	.7771	.8098	1.235	1.287	1.589	51° 00′
10′	.6316	.7753	.8146	1.228	1.290	1.583	50′
20′	.6338	.7735	.8195	1.220	1.293	1.578	40′
30′	.6361	.7716	.8243	1.213	1.296	1.572	30′
40′	.6383	.7698	.8292	1.206	1.299	1.567	20′
50′	.6406	.7679	.8342	1.199	1.302	1.561	10′
40° 00′	.6428	.7660	.8391	1.192	1.305	1.556	50° 00′
10′	.6450	.7642	.8441	1.185	1.309	1.550	50′
20′	.6472	.7623	.8491	1.178	1.312	1.545	40′
30′	.6494	.7604	.8541	1.171	1.315	1.540	30′
40′	.6517	.7585	.8591	1.164	1.318	1.535	20′
50′	.6539	.7566	.8642	1.157	1.322	1.529	10′
	cos	sin	cot	tan	csc	sec	angle

2. reading across the 39° 20′ row to the sin column (labeled at the top). The resulting number is .6338. Therefore, sin 39° 20′ ≈ .6338.

Similarly, to find the trigonometric ratios associated with acute angles whose measures are greater than 45°,

1. read *up* the angle column on the right-hand side of the table to the correct angle; and
2. read *across* the row to the desired trigonometric-ratio column (labeled at the bottom).

Example: Find tan 51° 30′.

Solution: Since 51° 30′ is greater than 45°, you can find tan 51° 30′ by
1. reading up the angle column on the right-hand side of the table to 51° 30′ (you must read above 51°); and
2. reading across the 51° 30′ row to the tan column (labeled at the bottom).

The resulting number is 1.257. Therefore, tan 51° 30′ ≈ 1.257.

When using the table to solve right triangles, it is important to remember that the answers you obtain will only be approximate.

Example: Solve △ACB if m ∠A = 50° 40′, m ∠C = 90°, and b = 20.

Solution: First draw a sketch and label the resulting triangle. To solve this triangle, you must find m ∠B, a, and c.
First, use the definition of tangent to find a.

$$\tan = \frac{a}{b}$$

$$\tan 50° \ 40' = \frac{a}{20}$$

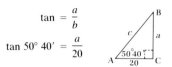

From the table, tan 50° 40′ ≈ 1.220. To find a, you can substitute 1.220 for tan 50° 40′ and solve the resulting equation.

$$1.220 \approx \frac{a}{20}$$

$$24.40 \approx a$$

To find c, you could use the Pythagorean theorem, the cosine ratio, or the secant ratio. The Pythagorean theorem would be quite involved and the cosine ratio involves division. So, you should use the secant ratio.

$$\sec 50° \ 40' = \frac{c}{b} = \frac{c}{20}$$

$$1.578 \approx \frac{c}{20}$$

$$31.56 \approx c$$

You can use the fact that ∠A and ∠B are complementary to find m ∠B.

m ∠A + m ∠B = 90°
50° 40′ + m ∠B = 90°

To subtract 50° 40′ from 90°, it is necessary to think of 90° as 89° 60′.

89° 60′
50° 40′
─────
39° 20′

The measure of ∠B is 39° 20′.

Solving oblique triangles

Trigonometry can also be used to solve *oblique* triangles; *i.e.*, triangles that are not right triangles. There are two kinds of oblique triangles, acute and obtuse. An *acute triangle* is a triangle with three acute angles. An *obtuse triangle* is a triangle with one obtuse angle and two acute angles.

To solve an oblique triangle, we use the *law of sines* or the *law of cosines*. In any triangle ABC, in which a, b, and c are the measures of the sides opposite ∠A, ∠B, and ∠C respectively:

law of sines

$$\frac{\sin A}{a} = \frac{\sin B}{b} = \frac{\sin C}{c}$$

law of cosines

$$a^2 = b^2 + c^2 - 2bc \cos A$$
$$b^2 = a^2 + c^2 - 2ac \cos B$$
$$c^2 = a^2 + b^2 - 2ab \cos C$$

The law of sines can be applied whenever you are given
1. the measures of two angles and the measure of a side opposite one of them; or
2. the measures of two sides and the measure of an angle opposite one of them.

The second set of conditions may determine *two* triangles. For this reason, it is often called the ambiguous case.

Example: Refer to the triangle below. Find *b*.

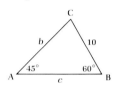

Solution: You are given m ∠A, m ∠B, and the length of the side opposite ∠A. You can find *b* by applying the law of sines.

$$\frac{\sin A}{a} = \frac{\sin B}{b}$$

$$\frac{\sin 45°}{10} = \frac{\sin 60°}{b}$$

$$\frac{\left(\frac{\sqrt{2}}{2}\right)}{10} = \frac{\left(\frac{\sqrt{3}}{2}\right)}{b}$$

$$\frac{\sqrt{2}}{2}b = 5\sqrt{3}$$

$$b = \frac{10\sqrt{3}}{\sqrt{2}} = 5\sqrt{6}$$

The law of cosines can be applied whenever you are given
1. the measure of three sides of a triangle; or
2. the measures of two sides of a triangle and the measure of the angle included by those sides.

Example: Refer to the triangle below. Find *b*.

Solution: You are given the measures of two sides of the triangle and the measure of the included angle. You can find *b* by applying the law of cosines.

$$b^2 = a^2 + c^2 - 2ac \cos B$$
$$b^2 = 2^2 + 3^2 - 2(2)(3) \cos 60°$$
$$b^2 = 2^2 + 3^2 - 2(2)(3)\tfrac{1}{2} = 4 + 9 - 6 = 7$$
$$b = \pm\sqrt{7}$$
$$b = \sqrt{7}$$

Example: Refer to the triangle below. Find m ∠A.

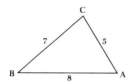

Solution: You are given the measures of three sides of △ABC. You can find m ∠A by applying the law of cosines.

$$a^2 = b^2 + c^2 - 2bc \cos A$$
$$7^2 = 5^2 + 8^2 - 2(5)(8) \cos A$$
$$49 = 25 + 64 - 80 \cos A$$
$$49 = 89 - 80 \cos A$$
$$-40 = -80 \cos A$$
$$\tfrac{1}{2} = \cos A$$

The angle whose cosine is $\tfrac{1}{2}$ has a measure of 60°. Therefore, m ∠A = 60°.

Areas of triangles

Trigonometry can be used to find the area of a triangle if you are given the measures of two sides of the triangle and the measure of the angle included by those sides.

Area formulas
$A = \tfrac{1}{2}bc \sin A$
$A = \tfrac{1}{2}ab \sin C$
$A = \tfrac{1}{2}ac \sin B$

Example: Refer to the triangle below. Find the area of △ABC.

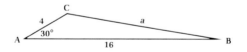

Solution: Since you are given m ∠A, *b*, and *c*, you can find the area of △ABC by applying the formula $A = \tfrac{1}{2}bc \sin A$. $A = \tfrac{1}{2}bc \sin A = \tfrac{1}{2}(4)(16) \sin 30° = \tfrac{1}{2}(4)(16)\tfrac{1}{2} = 16$.

5

Reviewing "New Math"

"Modern mathematics" or "new math" is an approach to mathematics that is designed to
  1. clarify mathematical concepts by using careful language; and
  2. broaden your understanding by incorporating unifying ideas.

In this unit, some of these fundamental ideas will be illustrated and discussed. Anyone who studies a "new math" course will need to be familiar with four basic concepts—sets, relations, functions, and logic.

Sets

A *set* is a collection of things. Each of the things that belong to a set is an *element*, or *member*, of the set. Braces { } are used to indicate a set. For example:

$A = \{a, b, c\}$ A is the name of the set. The letters a, b, and c are the elements of the set.
   read: "The set whose elements are a, b, and c."

When each element of a set is listed, the set has been described using *roster notation*. Set A was described using roster notation. Each of the following sets is also described using roster notation. The order in which the elements of a set are listed is *not* important.

$B = \{\square, \bigcirc, \triangle, \square\}$ $C = \{3, w, \triangle, \bigcirc, 7, \pi\}$

When using roster notation, it is easy to determine which things belong to a set and which things do not. The symbol $\in$ means "is an element of" and the symbol $\notin$ means "is not an element of." For example:

$\square \in B$ $\square \notin C$

$\square$ is an element of set B $\square$ is not an element of set C

A set described using roster notation is always a *finite* set because it is possible to count all of the elements. There are two other notations for describing sets—partial roster and rule. Instances of each are illustrated below.

partial roster:
example of a finite set: {1, 2, 3, ⋯, 100} read: "The set whose elements are 1, 2, 3, *and so on until* 100."

rule:
example of a finite set: {x | x is a whole number less than 7}
read: "The set of all *x such that x* is a whole number less than 7."

These two notations can also be used to describe *infinite* sets. An infinite set is any set that is not finite. Examples are given below.

partial roster:
example of an infinite set: {1, 2, 3,. . .}
read: "The set whose elements are 1, 2, 3, *and so on.*"

rule:
example of an infinite set: {x | x is a whole number}
read: "The set of all *x such that x* is a whole number."

When using partial roster notation or a rule, you must be certain that the set is *well defined;* that is, you must be certain that you can tell exactly which elements belong to the set and which do not.

The *empty set* (or *null set*] has no elements. The symbol for the empty set is ∅. By agreement, the empty set is a finite set.

Example: Use roster notation to describe each set:
(a) {x | x is a whole number less than 7};
(b) {1, 2, 3, ⋯, 10}; (c) ∅.

Solution: (a) {0, 1, 2, 3, 4, 5, 6}
(b) {1, 2, 3, 4, 5, 6, 7, 8, 9, 10}
(c) { }

Set relationships

Two sets are equal if they have exactly the same elements.

Example: Suppose that A = {1, 3, 5} and B = {5, 1, 3}. Is set A equal to set B?

Solution: Since 1 ∈ A and 1 ∈ B, 3 ∈ A and 3 ∈ B, 5 ∈ A and 5 ∈ B, and there are no other elements in either set, you can conclude that A = B.

Another set relationship is the subset relationship. Set *A* is a *subset* of set *B* if every element of *A* is an element of *B*. You use the symbol ⊆ to mean "is a subset of." If set *B* contains elements that are not in set *A*, then *A* is a *proper subset* of *B*. You use the symbol ⊂ to mean "is a proper subset of." The empty set is a subset of every set.

Example: Suppose that $A = \{1, 2, 3\}$ and $B = \{1, \triangle, 2, \square, 3, \bigcirc, \pi\}$. Is set *A* a subset of set *B*? A proper subset of set *B*?

Solution: Since $1 \in A$ and $1 \in B$, $2 \in A$ and $2 \in B$, and $3 \in A$ and $3 \in B$, you can conclude that $A \subseteq B$. And, because *B* contains elements other than 1, 2, and 3, $A \subset B$.

In any discussion, the *universal set* is the set of all things being considered. For example, if you designate the set of integers as the universal set, you have restricted your considerations to integers. The letter *U* is generally used for the universal set.

The *complement* of a given set is the set of all elements in the universal set that do not belong to the given set. For example, if the universal set is the set of integers and set *A* is the set of odd integers, then the complement of set *A*, denoted by A' (read *A* prime) is the set of all integers that are *not* odd. Thus,

$A' = \{x \mid x \text{ is an even integer}\}.$

Example: If $U = \{2, 4, 7, 8, 11, 16\}$ and $A = \{4, 11, 16\}$, find A'.

Solution: The complement of set *A* contains all elements of *U* that are not in *A*.

$A' = \{2, 7, 8\}$

Pictures are often used to represent set ideas. Pictures that show a universal set and depict set relationships are called *Venn diagrams*. The following Venn diagram shows the relationship between set *A*, its complement A' and the universal set *U* to which both belong.

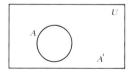

Set operations

There are three set operations—union, intersection, and Cartesian product.

Definition: The *union* of set A and set B is the set whose elements belong to set A, set B, or both.

The symbol $A \cup B$ is used to represent the union of set A and set B. The shaded portion of the Venn diagram below identifies the union of A and B.

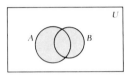

Example: If $A = \{a, b, c\}$ and $B = \{1, a, 2\}$, find $A \cup B$.

Solution: You must find all elements that are in set A or set B or both. It is not necessary to name an element more than once.

$A \cup B = \{a, b, c, 1, 2\}$

Definition: The *intersection* of set A and set B is the set whose elements are in both A and B.

The symbol $A \cap B$ is used to represent the intersection of set A and set B. The shaded portions of the following Venn diagrams represent the intersection of A and B.

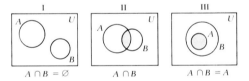

If the intersection of two sets is the empty set (diagram I), you say that the two sets are *disjoint*. In diagram III, set A is a subset of set B.

Example: Suppose that $A = \{2, 4, 6\}$; $B = \{2, a, 3, b, 4, c\}$; and $C = \{1, 3\}$. Find **(a)** $A \cap B$; **(B)** $A \cap C$.

Solution:
(a) To find $A \cap B$, you must find all the elements that are in both sets. $2 \in A$ and $2 \in B$; $4 \in A$ and $4 \in B$. $A \cap B = \{2, 4\}$
(b) Set A and set C have *no* common elements. Set A and set C are disjoint.

$A \cap C = \emptyset$

Definition: The *Cartesian product* of set A and set B is the set whose elements are ordered pairs of the form (x, y), in which $x \in A$ and $y \in B$.

You use the symbol $A \times B$ to represent the Cartesian product of set A and set B. In an ordered pair, the first term is called the *first component* and the second term is called the *second component*.

second component

(x, y)

first component

Example: Suppose that $A = \{1, 2\}$ and $B = \{a, b\}$. Find $A \times B$.

Solution: You must find all possible ordered pairs of the form (x, y) where $x \in A$ and $y \in B$.

$A \times B = \{1,a), (1,b), (2,a), (2,b)\}$

Relations

A *relation* is a subset of a Cartesian product of two sets. As a result, a relation is always a set of ordered pairs. For example:

$R = \{(1,a), (2,b), (3c)\}$.

R is the name of the relation and the elements enclosed in braces comprise the set of ordered pairs.

The set of all first components of the ordered pairs of a relation is called the *domain* of the relation and the set of all second components is called the *range* of the relation. For instance, in the relation $R = \{(1,a), (2,b), (3,c)\}$, the domain is $\{1, 2, 3\}$ and the range is $\{a, b, c\}$.

Example: If $R = \{(2,3), (1,0), (4,5)\}$ determine: **(a)** the domain; **(b)** the range.

Solution:

(a) The domain is the set of all first components of the ordered pairs of R.

$D_R = \{2, 1, 4\}$

(b) The range is the set of all second components of the ordered pairs of R.

$R_R = \{3, 0, 5\}$

Function

A *function* is a special kind of relation. In a function, no two ordered pairs have the same first component.

Example: Determine which relations are functions:
(a) $R = \{(2,3), (3,4), (2,5)\}$; **(b)** $S = \{(1,2), (2,2), (3,2), (4,2)\}$; **(c)** $T = \{1, 2, 3\}$.

Solution:

(a) Both (2,3) and (2,5) have the same first component. So relation R is not a function.

(b) Set S is a relation because it is a set of ordered pairs. No two ordered pairs have the same first component. Therefore, S is a function.

(c) Set T is not a set of ordered pairs. Therefore set T cannot be a function.

A lower-case letter (like f) is usually used to represent a function. Since a function is a relation, a function has a domain and a range. If x is an element of the domain, $f(x)$ is the element of the range that corresponds to it.

Example: If $f = \{(1,3), (2,5), (3,7)\}$, find $f(1)$.

Solution: $f(1)$ is the range element of function f that corresponds to domain element 1. Since $(1,3) \in f$, 3 corresponds to domain element 1. Therefore, $f(1) = 3$. Similarly, $f(2) = 5$ and $f(3) = 7$.

In many functions, each domain element is related to its corresponding range element by a rule. For example, assume that the universal set is the set of integers (each variable represents an integer), and

$f = \{(x,y) \mid y = x + 3\}$.

A rule for this function is $y = x + 3$. You can use the rule to find ordered pairs of function f.

If $x = 0$, then $y = 0 + 3 = 3$.
If $x = 1$, then $y = 1 + 3 = 4$.
If $x = 2$, then $y = 2 + 3 = 5$.
$f = \{\cdots, (0,3), (1,4), (2,5), \cdots\}$

Example: If $f(x) = 2x - 1$ is a rule for a function, find the range element that corresponds to each domain element: (a) -3; (b) 5.

Solution:

(a) To find the range element that corresponds to -3, you substitute -3 for x in the rule $f(x) = 2x - 1$.

$f(x) = 2x - 1$
$f(-3) = 2(-3) - 1 = -7$

The required range element is -7. The ordered pair $(-3, -7)$ is an element of the function.

(b) Substitute 5 for x in $f(x) = 2x - 1$.

$f(x) = 2x - 1$
$f(5) = 2(5) - 1 = 9$

The required range element is 9. The ordered pair $(5,9)$ is an element of the function.

Logic

"Modern mathematics" emphasizes proof. Before a statement can be proved, it is necessary to develop a system of logic so that the "truth value" of a statement can be determined.

Definition: A *statement* is a sentence that is either true or false but not both.

There are two kinds of statements—simple statements and compound statements. A *simple statement* expresses a single complete thought. A *compound statement* is formed by joining at least two simple statements with a "connective." The connectives that are generally considered in mathematics are listed below with their symbols.

name	connective	symbol
negation	not	$\sim$
conjunction	and	$\wedge$
disjunction	or	$\vee$
conditional	if, then	$\rightarrow$
biconditional	if and only if	$\leftrightarrow$

Negation

The *negation* of a simple statement is formed by using the word "not" or the phrase "it is not true that." For example:

simple statement: Sara is a beautiful girl.
negation: Sara is not a beautiful girl.
It is not true that Sara is a beautiful girl.

Negation is often defined by using a *truth table*. In the following truth table, p represents a simple statement; $\sim p$ represents its negation.

p	$\sim p$
T	F
F	T

This table indicates the truth value of the negation of any simple statement represented by p. The negation of a true statement is a false statement and the negation of a false statement is a true statement.

Example: Form the negation of the statement "Tim has red hair."

Solution: "Tim does *not* have red hair."

"*It is not true that* Tim has red hair."

Conjunction

A *conjunction* is a compound statement formed by joining two simple statements with the connective "and."

Example: Form the conjunction of the following two simple statements: "John is tall." "Martha is short."

Solution: "John is tall *and* Martha is short."

The conjunction of any two statements p and q is represented symbolically as $p \wedge q$. The truth table for conjunction is given below. This table indicates the truth value of the conjunction of any pair of simple statements represented by p and q.

p	q	$p \wedge q$
T	T	T
T	F	F
F	T	F
F	F	F

The conjunction of two simple statements is true if both simple statements are true; it is false in all other cases.

Example: Determine the truth value of the statement "$3 \neq 2$ and $5 > 4$."

Solution: The simple statement "$3 \neq 2$" is true and the simple statement "$5 > 4$" is true. The first row of the truth table for conjunction tells you that when both simple statements are true, the conjunction of the two simple statements is true. Therefore, "$3 \neq 2$ and $5 > 4$" is true.

Disjunction

A *disjunction* is a compound statement formed by joining two simple statements with the connective "or." The "or" you are using is the "inclusive or," which means *one or the other or both*.

Example: Form the disjunction of the following two simple statements: "Carl plays chess." "Carl plays football."

Solution: To form the disjunction, you join the two simple statements with "or."
"Carl plays chess *or* Carl plays football."

The disjunction of any two simple statements p and q is represented symbolically as $p \vee q$. The truth table for disjunction is given at right. This table indicates the truth value of the disjunction of any pair of simple statements represented by p and q.

p	q	$p \vee q$
T	T	T
T	F	T
F	T	T
F	F	F

The disjunction of two simple statements is false if both simple statements are false; it is true in all other cases.

Example: Determine the truth value of the statement "3 > 1 or 5 = 2."

Solution: The simple statement "3 > 1" is true and the simple statement "5 = 2" is false. The second row of the truth table for disjunction tells us that a disjunction is true under these conditions. Therefore, "3 > 1 or 5 = 2" is true.

Conditional

A *conditional* is a compound statement formed by joining two simple statements with the connective "if, then."

Example: Form the conditional of the following two simple statements. "It is windy today." "The fishing is good."

Solution: To form the conditional, you join the two simple statements with "if, then."
"*If* it is windy today, *then* the fishing is good."

The conditional of any two simple statements p and q is represented symbolically as p→q. The "if" part of a conditional is often called the *hypothesis* and the "then" part is called the *conclusion*. If the hypothesis and conclusion of a true conditional are interchanged, the resulting conditional *need not* be true. The truth table for conditional statements is given below. This table indicates the truth value of the conditional of any two simple statements represented by p and q.

p	q	p → q
T	T	T
T	F	F
F	T	T
F	F	T

The conditional of two simple statements is false if the hypothesis is true and the conclusion is false; it is true in all other cases.

Example: Determine the truth value of the statement "If 3 = 5, then 7 > 2."

Solution: The simple statement "3 = 5" is false and the simple statement "7 > 2" is true. The third row of the truth table for conditional tells you that the conditional is true under these conditions. Therefore, "If 3 = 5, then 7 > 2" is true.

Biconditional

A *biconditional* is a compound statement formed by joining two simple statements with the connective "if and only if."

> **Example:** Form the biconditional of the following two simple statements. "Jane can win the race." "It is snowing."

> **Solution:** To form the biconditional, you join the two simple statements with "if and only if."
> "Jane can win the race *if and only if* it is snowing."

The biconditional of any two simple statements p and q can be represented symbolically as $p \leftrightarrow q$. A biconditional has two parts—the "if" part (p if q) and the "only if" part (p only if q). The "if" part of a biconditional can be replaced by $q \leftrightarrow p$ and the "only if" part can be replaced by $p \rightarrow q$. So, it is possible to rewrite a biconditional as a *conjunction of two conditionals*.

> $p \leftrightarrow q$ means $(p \rightarrow q)$ and $(q \rightarrow p)$.

The truth table for biconditional statements is given below. This table indicates the truth value of the biconditional of any two simple statements represented by p and q.

p	q	$p \leftrightarrow q$
T	T	T
T	F	F
F	T	F
F	F	T

The biconditional of two simple statements is true whenever both simple statements are true or both simple statements are false; it is false in all other cases.

> **Example:** Determine the truth value of the statement "5 < 3 if and only if 7 = 2."

> **Solution:** The simple statement "5 < 3" is false and the simple statement "7 = 2" is false. The fourth row of the truth table for biconditional tells you that the biconditional is true under these conditions. Therefore, "5 < 3 if and only if 7 = 2" is true.

acute angle An angle whose degree measure is greater than 0 and less than 90.

adjacent angles Two angles that are coplanar, have the same vertex, share a common side, and have interiors that are disjoint sets.

alternate angles Angles formed by a transversal and two parallel lines. The angles are on opposite sides of the transversal and have different vertices.

angle The union of two noncollinear rays that have the same end point.

area A number associated with a region of a plane determined by a polygon or a circle.

axiom A statement in mathematics that is accepted as true without proof.

biconditional A compound statement formed by joining two simple statements with the connective "if and only if."

binomial A polynomial with two terms.

centimeter A unit of length in the metric system of measurement equal to one-hundredth of a meter.

chord A line segment whose end points are points of a circle.

circle A set of points in a plane that are a given distance from a given point of the plane called the center.

circumference The length of any given circle.

complement The set of all elements of a universal set that are not elements of a given set.

complementary angles Two angles whose degree measures add up to 90.

composite number Any number that is not a prime number.

conditional A compound statement that is formed by joining two simple statements with the connective "if, then."

congruent angles Two angles that have the same measure.

congruent segments Two segments that have the same measure.

conjunction A compound statement that is formed by joining two simple statements with the connective "and."

constant function A function that has a single range element.

convergent sequence A sequence that has a limit.

coordinate system A one-to-one correspondence between the set of real numbers and the set of points of a line or plane.

coplanar points Points of the same plane.

corresponding angles A pair of angles formed by a transversal and two parallel lines. Both angles are on the same side of the transversal, they have different vertices, and one is an interior angle while the other is an exterior angle.

cosine A trigonometric ratio defined for an acute angle of a right triangle.

degree A unit of angle measure.

diameter of a circle A chord that contains the center of a circle.

disjoint sets Two sets whose intersection is an empty set.

disjunction A compound statement formed by joining two simple statements with the connective "or."

distance The length of the line segment that joins two points.

divergent sequence A sequence that does not converge, that is, an infinite sequence that does not have a limit.

domain The set of all first components of the ordered pairs of a relation or function.

element A member of a set.

empty set A set that has no elements.

equal sets Two sets that have exactly the same elements.

equation A statement in mathematics that two expressions are equal.

exponent A number that indicates how many times another number, called the base, is used as a factor.

extremes The first and fourth terms of a proportion.

factor One of the numbers you multiply to obtain a product.

finite set A set that has a countable number of elements.

formula An open sentence that expresses a general rule in mathematics.

function A set of ordered pairs no two of which have the same first component.

hypotenuse The side of a right triangle that is opposite the right angle.

improper fraction A fraction in which the numerator is greater than the denominator.

inequality A statement that two mathematical expressions are not equal.

infinite set A set that is not finite.

inverse A conditional formed by negating the hypothesis and conclusion of a given conditional.

inverse operation An operation that undoes a given operation.

isosceles triangle A triangle with at least two sides congruent.

least common denominator The least common multiple of the denominators of two or more fractions.

least common multiple Given two or more numbers, the least positive integer that is divisible by these given numbers.

linear function A function whose graph is a line.

means The second and third terms of a proportion.

measure of an angle A real number greater than zero and less than 180, associated with an angle.

meter The standard unit of length in the metric system. A meter is about 39.37 inches.

millimeter A unit of length in the metric system equal to one-thousandth of a meter.

monomial A polynomial with one term.

negation of a statement A statement formed by inserting the phrase "it is not true that" before a given simple statement.

number line A line to which a coordinate system has been assigned.

obtuse angle An angle whose degree measure is greater than 90 and less than 180.

octagon A polygon with eight sides.

parallel lines Two or more lines in the same plane that do not intersect.

parallelogram A quadrilateral that has both pairs of opposite sides parallel.

pentagon A polygon with five sides.

per cent A ratio of some number to 100.

perpendicular lines Any two lines that intersect to form right angles.

pi The ratio of the circumference of a circle to the measure of a diameter of that circle.

postulate A mathematical statement that is accepted as true without proof.

prime number A positive integer greater than 1 whose only factors are 1 and the number itself.

proportion An equation in which both numbers of the equation are ratios.

quadrilateral A polygon with four sides.

radian A unit of measure for angles.

radius of a circle A line segment that joins the center of a circle to any point of the circle.

range The set of all second components of the ordered pairs of a relation or function.

ratio An indicated quotient of two numbers.

ray The subset of a line.

real number Any rational or irrational number.

rectangle A parallelogram that has four right angles.

relation Any set of ordered pairs.

right angle An angle whose degree measure is 90.

secant A line that intersects a given circle in two points.

semicircle An arc of a circle determined by the end points of a diameter of the circle.

set A collection of things.

similar triangles Two triangles whose corresponding angles are congruent and the measures of whose corresponding sides are in proportion. Similar triangles have the same shape but not necessarily the same size.

sine A trigonometric ratio defined for an acute angle of a right triangle.

skew lines Lines in space that are not coplanar and do not intersect.

slope The measure of the steepness of a line.

solution set The set that contains all of the numbers which make a given open sentence, or system of open sentences, true.

square A rectangle that has four congruent sides.

square root One of two equal factors of any given number.

supplementary angles Two angles whose degree measures add up to 180.

tangent A trigonometric ratio defined for an acute angle of a right triangle.

theorem A statement in mathematics that must be proved.

transversal A line that intersects two or more lines at distinct points.

triangle A polygon with three sides.

trinomial A polynomial with three terms.

universal set The set whose elements are under consideration in a given situation.

value of a function The range element of the function that is associated with a given domain element.

Venn diagram A diagram in which regions are used to represent set ideas.

vertex of an angle The common end point of the rays that determine an angle.

vertical angles Two nonadjacent angles formed by two intersecting lines.

x-axis The horizontal axis in a coordinate plane; the abscissa.

y-axis The vertical axis in a coordinate plane; the ordinate.

Basic Information from the Physical Sciences

What is the distance between the Earth and the Sun? What is the atomic weight of copper? How does a laser work? Physical science classes are concerned with this kind of information every day.

This unit provides you with the answers to these and many similar physical science questions. And the unit presents you with a review of some basic information from the physical sciences.

Chemists conduct scientific experiments, investigations, and tests in laboratories.

Facts about Astronomy

Astronomy is the study of the universe. The universe consists of numerous *galaxies*—star clusters of up to a trillion stars revolving around the core of the galaxy. Gases and tiny dust particles make up the galaxies and the universe. The size and temperature of a star determine how much energy it gives off. However, the star's apparent brightness, or *magnitude,* depends not only on its size and temperature but also on its distance from the viewer. In this section, you can review important facts about astronomy, including facts about the *solar system* in which you live.

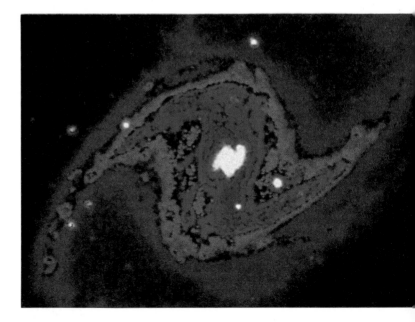

This computer-generated false-color image of the galaxy NGC 1365 vividly reveals its spiral structure. Computer analysis is a modern technique applied to images and data from astronomical telescopes that greatly extends their information value.

Eclipses of the Sun and Moon

Fairly rare, eclipses can be seen from only a limited number of places on earth. Lunar eclipses take place when the moon's slightly tilted orbit takes it to a point where the earth lies directly between the sun and moon. The earth then shadows the moon's surface. The darkest part of the shadow, called the *umbra,* causes a total lunar eclipse. As the moon's orbit swings out of the umbra, the moon becomes only partially shadowed as it enters a cone-shaped area, called the *penumbra.* In a solar eclipse, the moon's shadow is cast on the earth when it passes directly between the sun and earth. The umbra causes the sky to blacken during a total eclipse. Only the sun's corona can be seen to protrude beyond the moon's edges. (Never look directly at a total solar eclipse because of possible eye damage.) The penumbra, the area of partial solar eclipse, extends over a larger area than the umbra and can often be seen by many more people.

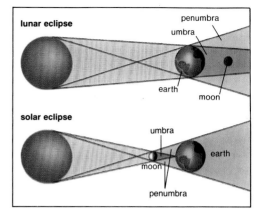

Constellations in the Sky

Constellations are imaginary figures traced in the sky by ancient observers. By assigning shapes of familiar objects to star patterns, they mapped the stars in the year-round skies. Ursa Major and Ursa Minor were especially important constellations because Ursa Minor contains the North Star—an ancient guide for travelers—and the North Star can be found by its relation to the easily seen Big Dipper portion of Ursa Major. Other important constellations included Leo the Lion (in the southern spring sky), Cygnus the Swan (part of the Northern Cross), Scorpius (The Scorpion), and Orion the Hunter.

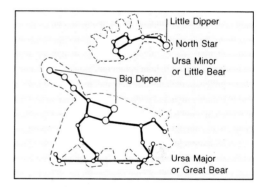

Table: The 20 Brightest Stars

Star	Distance (light-years)	Star	Distance (light-years)
1. Sirius	8.8	11. Beta Centauri	490
2. Canopus	98	12. Altair	16
3. Alpha Centauri	4.3	13. Alpha Crucis	370
4. Arcturus	36	14. Aldebaran	68
5. Vega	26	15. Spica	300
6. Capella	46	16. Antares	400
7. Rigel	900	17. Pollux	35
8. Procyon	11	18. Formalhaut	23
9. Betelgeuse	300	19. Deneb	1,600
10. Archernar	114	20. Beta Crucis	490

Table: Distances in the Universe

Planet	Mean distance from the sun*	
	In miles	**In kilometers**
Mercury	36,000,000	57,900,000
Venus	67,230,000	108,200,000
Earth	92,960,000	149,600,000
Mars	141,700,000	228,000,000
Jupiter	483,700,000	778,400,000
Saturn	885,200,000	1,424,600,000
Uranus	1,781,000,000	2,866,900,000
Neptune	2,788,000,000	4,486,100,000
Pluto	3,660,000,000	5,890,000,000

*The mean between the farthest distance from the sun and the closest.

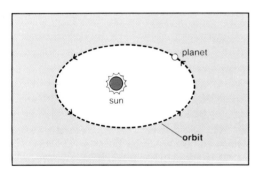

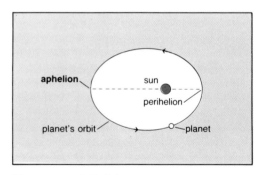

Planetary Orbits

The planets and asteroids of the solar system revolve around the sun in elliptical orbits, as shown. The sun's gravity keeps the planets and asteroids in their orbital paths. Though orbits are generally the same shape, they of course occur in different sizes.

In the table (above), note that the mean distance of the planet Pluto from the sun is 3,660,000,000 mi. (5,890,000,000 km). This means that Pluto has a much larger orbit around the sun than does Venus, for example. The planet Venus, as you will note, has a mean distance from the sun of "only" 67,230,000 mi. (108,200,000 km).

The speed at which a particular planet or astral body moves is affected by its distance from the sun in that part of its orbit. It moves faster when closer to the sun, slower when farther away.

Features of Orbits

The closest point to the sun during an orbital swing is called the *perihelion*. The farthest point in the orbital swing is called the *aphelion*. As each planet revolves around the sun, the planet also rotates around its own imaginary axis. On earth, this results in day and night. Man-made objects can be placed into orbit, too; spacecraft have been put into orbit around the Earth and other planets.

The Moon—Earth's Natural Satellite

Though bright in the sky at varying times of the month, the moon does not produce its own light; it merely reflects sunlight. The moon travels around the earth once every 27⅓ days. It is about 222,000 miles (357,000 kilometers) from the earth at the closest part of its elliptical orbit—the *perigee.* At the farthest, the *apogee,* the moon is about 253,000 miles (407,153 kilometers) away. Half of the moon's surface is always exposed to sunlight. However, you cannot always see the illuminated side fully because the moon's orbit places it in different viewing positions during the month, thus creating the eight phases of the moon. The amount of moonlight visible on the earth ranges from very little during a new moon (when the moon lies almost between the sun and earth) to a full moon (when the moon rises in the east as the sun sets).

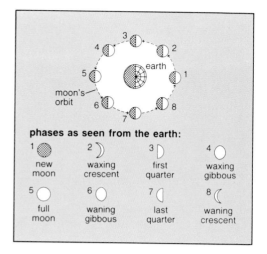

phases as seen from the earth:

1 new moon
2 waxing crescent
3 first quarter
4 waxing gibbous
5 full moon
6 waning gibbous
7 last quarter
8 waning crescent

The Sun's Composition

The sun has three outer layers—*corona, chromosphere,* and *photosphere.* Usually invisible, the corona is the extremely hot outer atmosphere of the sun. The average temperature there is about 4,000,000° F. (2,200,000° C). The chromosphere is the reddish layer above the sun's surface. At its outer edge, temperatures can rise to 50,000° F. (27,800° C). The photosphere, the sun's surface, is a textured area with an average temperature of 10,000° F. (5,500° C). The interior of the sun is a violent furnace fueled by thermonuclear reactions. As the nuclei of atoms in the sun's *core* fuse, they release huge amounts of high-energy radiation. The radiation passes through the *radiative zone* and triggers hot gas currents in the *convection zone,* which rise to the photosphere. The sun's energy then shoots into space. The sun has a diameter of about 865,000 mi. (1,392,000 km).

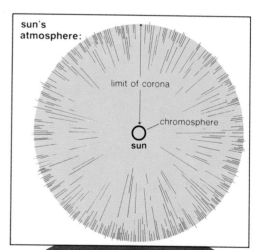

sun's atmosphere:

limit of corona

chromosphere

sun

convection zone
Temperature, about 2,000,000° F. (1,100,000° C). Density, about $\frac{1}{10}$ that of water.

radiative zone
Temperature, about 4,500,000° F. (2,500,000° C). Density, about equal to that of water.

core
Temperature, about 27,000,000° F. (15,000,000° C). Density, about 100 times that of water.

photosphere
Temperature, about 10,000° F. (5500° C). Density, between $\frac{1}{1,000,000}$ and $\frac{10}{1,000,000}$ that of water.

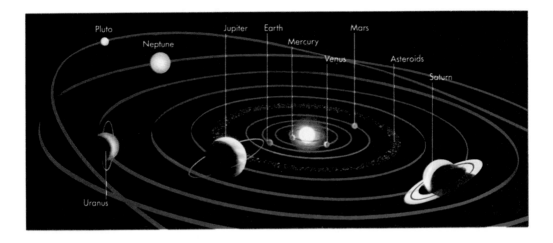

Table: The Planets at a Glance*

	Mercury	Venus	Earth	Mars
Distance from the sun:				
Mean	36,000,000 mi. (57,900,000 km)	67,230,000 mi. (108,200,000 km)	92,960,000 mi. (149,600,000 km)	141,700,000 mi. (228,000,000 km)
Shortest	28,600,000 mi. (46,000,000 km)	66,800,000 mi. (107,500,000 km)	91,400,000 mi. (147,100,000 km)	128,500,000 mi. (206,800,000 km)
Greatest	43,000,000 mi. (69,200,000 km)	67,700,000 mi. (108,900,000 km)	94,500,000 mi. (152,100,000 km)	154,900,000 mi. (249,200,000 km)
Closest approach to Earth	57,000,000 mi. (91,700,000 km)	25,700,000 mi. (41,400,000 km)	_____ _____	48,700,000 mi. (78,390,000 km)
Length of year (earth-days)	88	225	365	687
Average orbital speed	30 mi. per sec. (48 km per sec.)	22 mi. per sec. (35 km per sec.)	19 mi. per sec. (31 km per sec.)	15 mi. per sec. (24 km per sec.)
Diameter at equator	3,031 mi. (4,878 km)	7,520 mi. (12,100 km)	7,926 mi. (12,756 km)	4,200 mi. (6,790 km)
Rotation period	59 earth-days	243 earth-days	23 hrs. 56 min.	24 hrs. 37 min.
Tilt of axis (degrees)	about 0	175	23½	25
Temperature	−315° to 648° F. (−193° to 342° C)	850° F. (455° C)	−126.9° to 136° F. (−88.29° to 58° C)	−191° to −24° F. (−124° to −31° C)
Atmosphere:				
Pressure	0.00000000003 lb. per sq. in. (0.000000000002 kg per cm^2)	1.5 to 1,323 lbs. per sq. in. (0.1 to 93 kg per cm^2)	14.7 lbs. per sq. in. (1.03 kg per cm^2)	0.1 lbs. per sq. in. (0.007 kg per cm^2)
Gases	Sodium, helium, hydrogen, oxygen	Carbon dioxide, nitrogen, water vapor, argon, carbon monoxide, neon, sulfur dioxide	Nitrogen, oxygen, carbon dioxide, water vapor	Carbon dioxide, nitrogen, argon, oxygen, carbon monoxide, neon, krypton, xenon, water vapor
Mass (Earth = 1)	0.06	0.82	1	0.11
Density (g/cm^3)	5.44	5.27	5.52	3.95
Gravity (Earth = 1)	0.38	0.9	1	0.38
Number of satellites	0	0	1	2

*All figures are approximate.

The Solar System

Our solar system consists of the sun, nine planets, and a ring of minor planets called *asteroids*. Most scientists believe the sun formed more than 4.5 billion years ago from a disk of hot, swirling gases. As the sun was forming, dense regions on its edges spun off and condensed as planets, moons, and asteroids. Jupiter is the largest of the planets, with a diameter 11 times greater than the Earth's. Pluto is the smallest, about a fourth of the Earth's diameter. The planets and asteroids revolve around the sun in paths called orbits. The orbits vary in their distances from the sun—Mercury is closest to the sun, with a mean distance of 36 million miles (57.9 million kilometers); Pluto is farthest from the sun, as you will note.

Jupiter	Saturn	Uranus	Neptune	Pluto
483,700,000 mi. (778,400,000 km)	885,200,000 mi. (1,424,600,000 km)	1,781,000,000 mi. (2,866,900,000 km)	2,788,000,000 mi. (4,486,100,000 km)	3,660,000,000 mi. (5,890,000,000 km)
460,000,000 mi. (740,000,000 km)	838,000,000 mi. (1,349,000,000 km)	1,700,000,000 mi. (2,740,000,000 km)	2,754,000,000 mi. (4,432,500,000 km)	2,748,000,000 mi. (4,423,200,000 km)
507,000,000 mi. (816,000,000 km)	932,000,000 mi. (1,500,000,000 km)	1,860,000,000 mi. (2,999,000,000 km)	2,821,000,000 mi. (4,539,800,000 km)	4,571,200,000 mi. (7,356,000,000 km)
390,700,000 mi. (628,760,000 km)	762,700,000 mi. (1,277,400,000 km)	1,700,000,000 mi. (2,720,000,000 km)	2,700,000,000 mi. (4,350,000,000 km)	3,583,000,000 mi. (5,765,500,000 km)
4,333	10,759	30,685	60,188	90,700
8 mi. per sec. (13 km per sec.)	6 mi. per sec. (10 km per sec.)	4 mi. per sec. (6 km per sec.)	3 mi. per sec. (5 km per sec.)	3 mi. per sec. (5 km per sec.)
88,700 mi. (142,700 km)	74,600 mi. (120,000 km)	31,570 mi. (50,800 km)	30,200 mi. (48,600 km)	1,900 mi. (3,000 km)
9 hrs. 55 min.	10 hrs. 39 min.	16 to 28 hrs.	18 to 20 hrs.	6 earth-days
3	27	98	29	90
−236° F. (−149° C)	−285° F. (−176° C)	−357° F. (−216° C)	−360° F. (−218° C)	−342° to −369° F. (−208° to −223° C)
2.35 to 1,470 lbs. per sq. in. (0.17 to 103 kg per cm²)	1.5 to 15 lbs. per sq. in. (0.1 to 1 kg per cm² or higher)	?	?	?
Hydrogen, helium, methane, ammonia, ethane, acetylene, phosphine, water vapor, carbon monoxide	Hydrogen, helium, methane, ammonia, ethane, phosphine (?)	Hydrogen, helium, methane, acetylene	Hydrogen, helium, methane, ethane(?)	Methane
318	95	14.6	17.2	0.0017 (?)
1.31	0.704	1.21	1.66	1.0 (?)
2.87	1.32	0.93	1.23	0.03 (?)
16	23	15	2	1

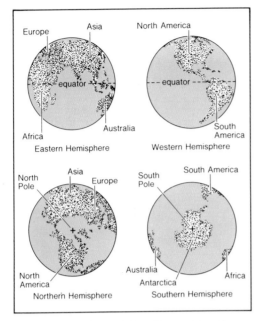

Eastern Hemisphere
Western Hemisphere
Northern Hemisphere
Southern Hemisphere

Characteristics of the Planet Earth

Third closest planet to the sun, the earth is the only planet on which life is known to exist. Densest of all the planets, it has a density about 5.5 times greater than water. In its yearly revolution around the sun, the earth travels at an average speed of 19 miles (31 kilometers) a second. As it revolves, it also rotates on an imaginary axis through the North and South poles. This axis tilts slightly, positioning the Northern Hemisphere away from the sun in winter and toward it in summer. The opposite happens to the Southern Hemisphere. The earth is essentially a rocky ball with a hot interior, as hot as 9,000°F. (5,000°C). But the earth is not perfectly round; it has a slight bulge at the equator. Water covers much of its surface. The earth's land areas are in the form of seven continents.

Table: The Earth at a Glance

Age: 4,500,000,000 (4½ billion) years.

Weight: 6,600,000,000,000,000,000,000,000 (6.6 sextillion) short tons (6.0 sextillion metric tons).

Motion: *Rotation* (spinning motion around an imaginary line connecting the North and South poles)—once every 23 hours, 56 minutes, 4.09 seconds. *Revolution* (motion around the sun)—once every 365 days, 6 hours, 9 minutes, 9.54 seconds.

Size: *Polar Diameter* (distance through the earth from North Pole to South Pole)—7,899.83 miles (12,713.54 kilometers). *Equatorial Diameter* (distance through the earth at the equator)—7,926.41 miles (12,756.32 kilometers). *Polar Circumference* (distance around the earth through the poles)—24,859.82 miles (40,008.00 kilometers). *Equatorial Circumference* (distance around the earth along the equator)—24,901.55 miles (40,075.16 kilometers).

Area: *Total Surface Area*—196,951,000 square miles (510,100,000 square kilometers). *Land Area*—approximately 57,259,000 square miles (148,300,000 square kilometers), about 30 per cent of total surface area. *Water Area*—approximately 139,692,000 square miles (361,800,000 square kilometers), about 70 per cent of total surface area.

Surface features: *Highest Land*—Mount Everest, 29,028 feet (8,848 meters) above sea level. *Lowest Land*—shore of Dead Sea, 1,310 feet (399 meters) below sea level.

Ocean depths: *Deepest Part of Ocean*—Challenger Deep in Pacific Ocean southwest of Guam, 36,198 feet (11,033 meters) below surface. *Average Ocean Depth*—12,450 feet (3,795 meters).

Temperature: *Highest*, 136° F. (58° C) at Al Aziziyah, Libya. *Lowest*, −127° F. (−88° C) at Vostok in Antarctica. *Average Surface Temperature*, 57° F. (14° C).

Atmosphere: *Height*—99 per cent of the atmosphere is less than 50 miles (80 kilometers) above the earth's surface, but particles of the atmosphere are 1,000 miles (1,600 kilometers) above the surface. *Chemical Makeup of Atmosphere*—78 per cent nitrogen, 21 per cent oxygen, 1 per cent argon with small amounts of other gases.

Chemical makeup of the earth's crust (in per cent of the crust's weight): oxygen 46.6 silicon 27.7, aluminum 8.1, iron 5.0, calcium 3.6, sodium 2.8, potassim 2.6, magnesium 2.0, and other elements totaling 1.6.

The Earth's Radiation Belts

Two doughnut-shaped bands of charged particles, called the *Van Allen belts* after their discoverer, ring the earth at the equator—trapped by the earth's magnetic field. The belts consist mainly of protons and electrons, supplied by cosmic rays, sun radiation, and high-altitude nuclear explosions. The Van Allen belts are part of the magnetic region surrounding the earth called the *magnetosphere*. The magnetosphere has a tearlike shape because the force of the *solar wind*, a stream of high-energy particles from the sun, pushes the earth's magnetic field away from the sun. Fluctuations in the Van Allen belts cause protons and electrons from them to rain the earth, producing such vivid nightly displays as the aurora borealis and aurora australis.

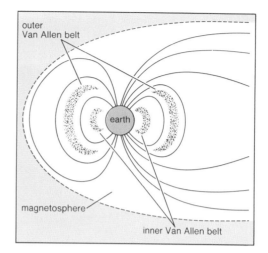

Distances and Contents of Space

The light-year is a unit of astronomical measurement. Light spans 5,880,000,000,000 miles (9,460,000,000,000 kilometers) in a calendar year. Light from the sun, the nearest star, takes about 8 minutes 20 seconds to reach earth; from Alpha Centauri, a nearby star cluster, 4.3 years; from the center of our galaxy, the Milky Way, many thousands of years. Measurement of the earth's atmosphere and the makeup of cis- and translunar space have been made through instrument-bearing space probes. Spectrum analysis, using the imprint from the wavelengths of energy emitted or absorbed by chemical elements and compounds, is used to detect space matter. Radiation instruments also enable astronomers to uncover the X rays, gamma rays, and other radiation in space.

Interplanetary space consists of solar wind radiation, large rocks called meteoroids, and dust called micrometeorites, tons of which fall to earth each day. Comets—masses of metal, rock, and vapors of icy gases—also circle the sun in interplanetary space. Interstellar space consists of such cosmic rays as protons and some atomic nuclei, as well as hydrogen, helium, and other gases.

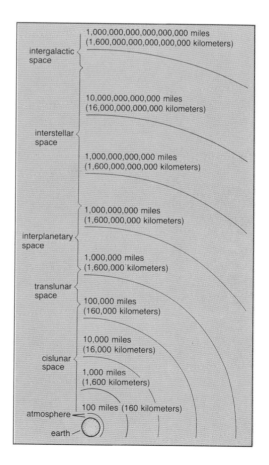

2

Facts about Chemistry

Chemistry is the study of matter and its changes. Matter consists of chemical elements, their mixtures, or their compounds. Chemists have accepted 103 elements so far; 3 others have been claimed but not verified.

Elements share some characteristics. They have measurable physical properties, such as boiling point, melting point, hardness, mass, and density. Their chemical properties are determined by their electron configuration. An element's chemical properties enable a reaction with other elements to form compounds. Reactivity depends on the stability of an element's outer shell of electrons. Neon, xenon, and others have their outer electrons stably locked. Lithium, sodium, and others have their outer electrons bound so unstably that they can fly away and leave a gap in the shell. When an atom loses an electron and becomes a positively charged ion while another gains that electron and becomes a negatively charged ion, the two are attracted into an *ionic bond*. A more stable linkage occurs in a *covalent bond,* when the outer shells of two or more atoms merge and the combined electrons become "thick" enough to prevent the positively charged nuclei of the atoms from repelling the electrons.

Certain elements share chemical properties. They are grouped in the *periodic table of the elements* (see pages 112–113). The vertical groups relate to common physical traits.

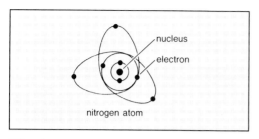

nitrogen atom

The Atom

The atom is the basic unit of an element. The atom consists of a nucleus and one or more electrons orbiting the nucleus. The nucleus contains protons with positive (+) charges and neutrons with no charges. Electrons have negative (−) charges. The force of electron motion around the nucleus keeps them from being attracted by the oppositely charged protons. An atom's *atomic number* is determined by the number of protons in its nucleus. Its mass, or *atomic weight,* is the sum of its protons and neutrons. Nitrogen, for example, has an atomic number of 7 and an atomic weight of 14.0067, or $_7N^{14}$. The proton, electron, and neutron are types of particles.

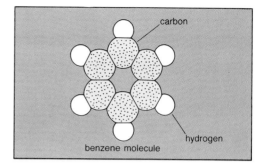

benzene molecule

Atoms Form Molecules

Molecules are combinations of atoms. They can be of the same element, such as the molecules of hydrogen gas, H_2, or they can form from atoms of different elements, as when hydrogen and oxygen combine to form a molecule of water, H_2O.

Each atom has a *valence* number that shows its ability to combine with others to form molecules. Hydrogen has a valence of 1, and oxygen has a valence of 2. The outer shell of an oxygen atom can share space with the electrons of two hydrogen atoms. In a complex molecule like benzene, six carbon atoms link together in ringlike covalent bonds, while each carbon atom also forms a covalent bond with a hydrogen atom.

Carbon is a unique atom; it can bond with many other elements. Molecules containing carbon are found in living things and are thus called *organic compounds.* Organic chemistry is the study of these carbon compounds.

Ionic Bonding

When atoms lose or gain electrons, they become electrically charged *ions.* Each electron shell, or layer, accommodates a maximum number of electrons.

A filled shell is stable; it does not readily give up or attract other electrons. Sodium (atomic number 11) has 11 protons to hold 11 electrons. Those electrons orbit in three shells—the first has two electrons (stable), the second has eight electrons (stable), and the third has one electron (unstable).

Sodium can gain stability by losing an electron, leaving the stable eight-electron shell as the outer one. When it does this, sodium becomes a positively charged *cation.* In contrast, chlorine (atomic number 17) can achieve a stable eight-electron outer shell by gaining an electron. When it does so, it becomes a negatively charged chloride *anion.*

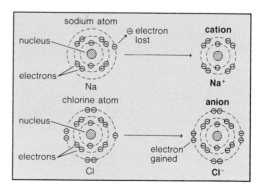

Ionically bound sodium and chloride ions form Na^+Cl^-, or common table salt. However, an ionic bond is broken easily; sodium and chloride ions constantly *dissociate* in solution and seek others to bond with.

Radioactive Decay

Some elements are *radioactive*. This term describes the process by which certain nuclei that are unstably bound together will spontaneously release particles of mass and radiation. When this happens, the nucleus loses some mass and may even become a different element. Radioactive decay is measured by half-life—the time it takes for one-half of a radioactive element to decay. One common radioactive substance is radium isotope 226. When the nucleus of this isotope breaks up, an alpha particle made of two protons and two neutrons is set free, and an atom of radon-222 is then formed. It takes approximately 1,660 years for one half of a given amount of radium 226 to decay to radon-222.

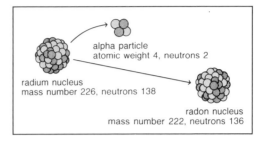

alpha particle
atomic weight 4, neutrons 2

radium nucleus
mass number 226, neutrons 138

radon nucleus
mass number 222, neutrons 136

The Bunsen Burner

Many chemical experiments call for heating a solution or finding its boiling point, which is a physical property of a compound. The high heat needed to bring a substance to its boiling point quickly is usually furnished by a *Bunsen burner*. Ports in the base of the burner tube allow air to mix with the fuel gas for maximum combustion. The spark of a flint lighter is used to ignite the flame. The temperature at the tip of the hottest part of the flame—the middle, *reducing* cone—is some 2,700°F. (1,480°C). Flasks containing solutions for heating are supported on wire meshes over the flame. The mesh spreads the flame evenly over the base of the flask. Obviously, a Bunsen burner should be handled with the utmost concern for safety.

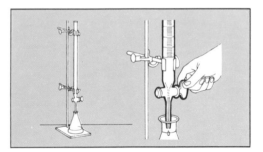

Use of the Burette in Titration

In chemical analysis by *titration*, drop-by-drop amounts of a measured amount of reagent are released from a calibrated burette until an *end point* is reached—usually a color change. For example, a known amount of silver nitrate is slowly added to an unknown amount of a chloride solution mixed with potassium chromate to find the chloride concentration. When the last chloride ions combine with silver ions, the solution turns reddish brown. This is because silver ions now combine with chromate ions from the potassium chromate to form reddish-brown silver chromate. Calculations using the amount of silver nitrate titrated can then be used to determine the amount of chloride in the test solution.

Electrolytic Action

When an electric current passes through an ionic substance, a chemical reaction can occur. The process is called *electrolysis*. Acids, bases, and salts largely dissociate into ions in water solution and permit large electric currents to pass through the solution. They are called *strong electrolytes*. *Weak electrolytes* can carry little current because they dissociate only slightly. When the electric current is supplied by some outside source, electrons are supplied to the electrolyte at the cathode and accepted from the electrolyte at the anode. Positively charged hydrogen ions (H^+) are attracted electrically to the cathode, where they pick up electrons to form molecules of hydrogen gas. Oxygen-containing (OH^-) ions are drawn to the anode and release electrons and form oxygen gas. Electrolysis results in separating the hydrogen and oxygen of water and combining them into two molecules of hydrogen gas and one molecule of oxygen gas. The chemical shorthand way of describing this is:

$$2\ H_2O \xrightarrow{\text{electric current}} 4\ H^+ + 2\ O \quad 2\ H_2^\uparrow + O_2^\uparrow$$

When the electrolyte is water-free, other reactions occur.

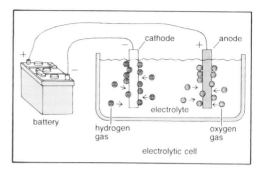

electrolytic cell

Electrolytic Action of a Dry Cell

A dry cell is one means of generating an electric current by electrolysis. The cell consists of a positive anode of carbon, a pasty mixture of manganese dioxide and carbon grains, cardboard soaked with ammonium chloride (the electrolyte), and a negative cathode of zinc.

The top is sealed to keep the cell dry. When the electrodes of the dry cell are connected, an electric current flows between the cathode and the anode; this is because carbon attracts electrons better than zinc. The electrons come from the zinc, which breaks down into positively charged zinc ions. They then combine with the negatively charged ions of the ammonium chloride electrolyte to form zinc chloride. Meanwhile, electrons flow back to the carbon anode. There, they combine with hydrogen ions from the ammonium component of the electrolyte and form hydrogen gas.

Ordinarily, hydrogen gas would act as an insulator, *polarize* the cell, and stop the current (electron flow). However, the hydrogen gas is absorbed by the pasty mix of manganese dioxide and carbon grains.

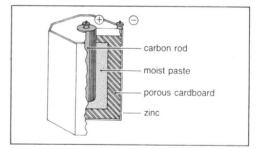

Chemical Reactions   Chemical elements can combine to form compounds when they share electrons or when their ions or ionlike groups, called *radicals,* electrically attract each other. Water is an example of electron sharing or *covalence.* Two atoms of hydrogen share one atom of oxygen in a water molecule. This can be written as H–O–H, where each – represents two electrons shared by each atom in the molecule. Sodium chloride, common table salt, is an example of the electrical combining power of ions. The sodium ion has an electrical charge, or *electrovalence,* of $+1$; the chloride ion has an electrovalence of -1. The two ions are attracted and combined as Na^+Cl^-.

Oxidation and Reduction   An atom is said to be *oxidized* when it loses electrons. Once, oxidation meant merely that oxygen combined with a substance during combustion. Now, it means any chemical reaction in which an atom increases its positive charge by losing electrons. By contrast, an atom is *reduced* when it gains electrons and thus increases its negative charge. Oxidation-reduction activity, or a *redox* reaction, features substance A losing electrons (being oxidized) while substance B picks them up (becomes reduced). The degree to which a substance can be oxidized is indicated by its *oxidation number.* Electrovalent elements have identical oxidation and electrovalence numbers. For example, the oxidation number of sodium is $+1$, as is its electrovalence number. However, covalent elements do not always have identical oxidation and covalence numbers. Sometimes, they combine in molecular groups called *radicals.* The hydroxyl radical, OH, is an example. The charge on each atom of the radical accounts for the oxidation number of a radical ($O^{-2} H^{+1} = OH^{-1}$). A free element (uncombined with others) has an oxidation number of 0.

   Oxidation-reduction reactions always involve a change in the oxidation numbers of the chemical participants. For example, the formation of zinc chloride and hydrogen gas from free zinc and hydrochloric acid is an oxidation-reduction reaction:
$$Z^0n + 2H^{+1}Cl^{-1} \longrightarrow Zn^{+2}Cl^{-1}_2 + H^0_2.$$
Zinc is oxidized (loses electrons) and hydrogen is reduced (gains electrons).

Catalysts   Chemical reactions can be sped or slowed by *catalysis.* Catalysts are chemicals that affect the reaction rate without being changed in the reaction. Chemical compound formation needs *activation energy* to loosen the chemical bonds of the reactants. Catalysts function by altering the amount of activation energy needed.

States of Matter

Matter ordinarily exists in one of three interchangeable forms—solid, liquid, or gas. The rate of molecular vibration and movement determines the physical state of a substance. It is a solid if its molecules are arranged in an orderly, closely bound sequence. Some molecular vibration occurs but only in a tight area. As more energy acts on a solid, its molecules move more easily around each other until they assume a liquid flow. Liquids can take the shape of their containers. As still more energy acts on a liquid, its molecules begin to fly apart in all directions as a gas. Gases fill up their containers.

Effects of Temperature and Pressure

Each element or compound needs a certain amount of heat energy at a given amount of pressure to enter the next physical state. For example, at sea level where the atmosphere pressure is 14.7 pounds per square inch (1.03 kilograms per square centimeter), water boils at 212°F. (100°C); that is, it changes from the liquid to the gaseous state at that temperature and pressure. However, as the elevation above sea level increases, the pressure decreases, so that at mountainous altitudes, water boils at lower temperatures.

Boyle's Law and Charles's (Gay-Lussac's) Law

Temperature and pressure affect gases considerably. According to *Boyle's law,* a change in the volume occupied by a gas produces an opposite change in the pressure exerted by the gas as long as the temperature remains the same. When pressure decreases, the gas volume increases, and vice versa. According to *Charles's law* or *Gay-Lussac's law* (two-pre-19th century scientists observed the same principle), a gas increases by 1/273 of its original volume for each degree of temperature rise above 0°C as long as the pressure remains the same. The Kelvin temperature scale starts at a point where molecular motion ceases—*absolute zero* (0°K or -273.15°C). Kelvin temperatures are found by adding 273 to the Celsius reading (10°C $=$ 283°K). *A general gas law* has been formulated to account for all the natural forces that affect the behavior of gases—$pv = RT$. Pressure *(p)* multiplied by volume *(v)* equals Kelvin temperature *(T)* multiplied by a constant number *(R)*.

Avogadro's Law

Early in the 19th century, the Italian chemist Amedeo Avogadro proposed that the atoms of gases join in pairs to form molecules, such as H_2 (hydrogen), O_2 (oxygen), and N_2 (nitrogen). He also suggested all gases behaved alike and that equal amounts of gases (having the same pressure and temperature) would contain the same number of molecules. The number of molecules in a gram-molecular weight of a gas is called *Avogadro's number*—$6.02 \times 10.^{23}$

Determining Molecular Weight

The molecular weight of a substance is the sum of its weights. Because of the extreme tininess of atoms, any expression of their weight must be a relative measure. The atomic weight of an atom is its heaviness or lightness compared with the weight of a standard isotope of carbon—carbon-12. Atomic weights, or *mass numbers,* for each element are listed in the periodic table. When using the table's atomic weights, round off the figures. For example, the atomic weight of chlorine is 35.453. When determining the molecular weight of a chlorine-containing molecule, use 35.5 for chlorine's atomic weight. As an example, the molecular weight of calcium chloride, $CaCl_2$, is 111. The molecule contains one atom of calcium (atomic weight $= 40$) and two atoms of chlorine (atomic weight $= 35.5$). Adding them up, we get $40 + 35.5 + 35.5 = 111$. Unit weights of molecular substances are expressed in *gram-moles.* A mole of calcium chloride contains 111 grams. Using Avogadro's number, a mole of $CaCl_2$(111 grams) contains 6.02×10^{23} calcium chloride molecules.

Strengths of Solutions

Solutions consist of substances dissolved in other substances. The chemical mixing of the two substances in solution is so complete that they cannot be separated by filtration or through settling. A solution is comprised of a *solute* and a *solvent.* The solute is the chemical that dissolves in the solvent. Solutes can be solids, liquids, or gases. *Solubility* is the measure of how much solute can dissolve in a given amount of solvent. A solid usually becomes more soluble when the solvent is heated. By contrast, the solubility of a gas lessens when the solvent is heated.

Percentages sometimes indicate the concentration of a solute in a solvent. A 10% sugar solution, for instance, has 10 parts of sugar (by weight) to 90 parts of water (by weight).

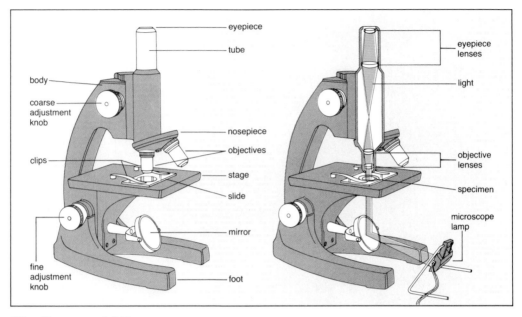

The Compound Microscope

The compound microscope is used in both bio-chemical and chemical research. Chemists some-times study the crystal patterns of compounds through a microscope. The magnifying power of a microscope is the power of each objective multi-plied by the power of the eyepiece. For example, if the eyepiece is $10\times$ and the objective is $10\times$, then the magnifying power is $100\times$, or 100 diameters. A viewing object is placed on a glass slide on the stage, and light is reflected off the mirror and through the object. The object is brought into fo-cus by the adjustment knobs. To avoid breaking the slide when viewing something under high mag-nification, move the objective downward carefully until it barely touches the slide, then adjust upward while looking through the eyepiece.

Distillation

Distillation separates liquid compounds with differ-ent boiling points from each other in solution. The compounds having the lowest boiling points will separate first; those with the highest, last. To sepa-rate compound A having a boiling point of 150°F. (65°C) and compound B having a boiling point of 250°F. (121°C), heat the solution in the distillation flask to compound A's boiling point and maintain the heat. (Distillation apparatuses ordinarily have a thermometer in the stopper of the distillation flask.) Compound A will vaporize and flow as a gas out of the flask outlet and into the condenser tube. Cool water circulating in a jacket around the con-denser will lower the vapor temperature of com-pound A until it liquefies and collects as distillate

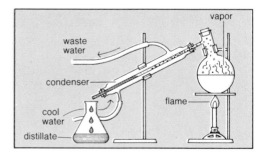

in a flask under the condenser outlet. After distil-late no longer accumulates, raise the flame under the distillation flask until the boiling point of com-pound B is reached.

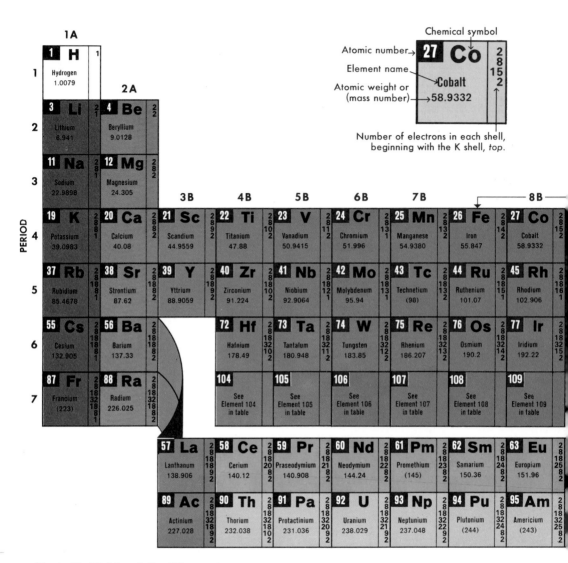

Periodic Table of the Elements

This table gives basic information about the known chemical elements. Eight major classes of elements are shown, differentiated by color. Hydrogen stands alone, in that it does not clearly belong to any one class.

A key to understanding the information about each element is found in the enlarged sample square for Cobalt at the top of this page. This key will help you identify the chemical symbol, the atomic number, atomic weight, and other important information about each element.

An alphabetical table of the elements, with information about their discovery, is found on pages 114–116.

Legend:

- Alkali metals
- Alkaline earth metals
- Transition metals
- Lanthanide series
- Actinide series
- Other metals
- Nonmetals
- Noble gases

8 A

| 2 He | Helium | 4.00260 | 2 |

| 3 A | 4 A | 5 A | 6 A | 7 A |

5 B	Boron	10.81	2 3
6 C	Carbon	12.011	2 4
7 N	Nitrogen	14.0067	2 5
8 O	Oxygen	15.9994	2 6
9 F	Fluorine	18.9984	2 7
10 Ne	Neon	20.179	2 8

13 Al	Aluminum	26.9815	2 8 3
14 Si	Silicon	28.0855	2 8 4
15 P	Phosphorus	30.9738	2 8 5
16 S	Sulfur	32.06	2 8 6
17 Cl	Chlorine	35.453	2 8 7
18 Ar	Argon	39.948	2 8 8

1B   2B

28 Ni	Nickel	58.69	2 8 16 2
29 Cu	Copper	63.546	2 8 18 1
30 Zn	Zinc	65.39	2 8 18 2
31 Ga	Gallium	69.72	2 8 18 3
32 Ge	Germanium	72.59	2 8 18 4
33 As	Arsenic	74.9216	2 8 18 5
34 Se	Selenium	78.96	2 8 18 6
35 Br	Bromine	79.904	2 8 18 7
36 Kr	Krypton	83.80	2 8 18 8

46 Pd	Palladium	106.42	2 18 18 0
47 Ag	Silver	107.868	2 8 18 1
48 Cd	Cadmium	112.41	2 8 18 2
49 In	Indium	114.82	2 8 18 3
50 Sn	Tin	118.71	2 8 18 4
51 Sb	Antimony	121.75	2 8 18 5
52 Te	Tellurium	127.60	2 8 18 6
53 I	Iodine	126.905	2 8 18 7
54 Xe	Xenon	131.29	2 8 18 8

78 Pt	Platinum	195.08	2 8 32 17 1
79 Au	Gold	196.967	2 8 32 18 1
80 Hg	Mercury	200.59	2 8 32 18 2
81 Tl	Thallium	204.383	2 8 32 18 3
82 Pb	Lead	207.2	2 8 32 18 4
83 Bi	Bismuth	208.980	2 8 18 32 18 5
84 Po	Polonium	(209)	2 8 18 32 18 6
85 At	Astatine	(210)	2 8 32 18 7
86 Rn	Radon	(222)	2 8 18 32 18 8

64 Gd	Gadolinium	157.25	2 8 18 25 9 2
65 Tb	Terbium	158.925	2 8 18 27 8 2
66 Dy	Dysprosium	162.50	2 8 18 28 8 2
67 Ho	Holmium	164.930	2 8 18 29 8 2
68 Er	Erbium	167.26	2 8 18 30 8 2
69 Tm	Thulium	168.934	2 8 18 31 8 2
70 Yb	Ytterbium	173.04	2 8 18 32 8 2
71 Lu	Lutetium	174.967	2 8 18 32 9 2

96 Cm	Curium	(247)	2 8 18 32 25 9 2
97 Bk	Berkelium	(247)	2 8 18 32 26 9 2
98 Cf	Californium	(251)	2 8 18 32 28 8 2
99 Es	Einsteinium	(252)	2 8 18 32 29 8 2
100 Fm	Fermium	(257)	2 8 18 32 30 8 2
101 Md	Mendelevium	(258)	2 8 18 32 31 8 2
102 No	Nobelium	(259)	2 8 18 32 32 8 2
103 Lr	Lawrencium	(260)	2 8 18 32 32 9 2

Table: The Elements and Their Discoverers

Name	Symbol	Atomic weight*	Atomic number	Density (g/cm³) at 20° C	Discoverer	Country of discovery	Date of discovery
Actinium	Ac	227.028	89	10.07†	André Debierne	France	1899
Aluminum	Al	26.9815	13	2.70	Hans Christian Oersted	Denmark	1825
Americium	Am	[243]	95	13.67	G. T. Seaborg; R. A. James; L. O. Morgan; A. Ghiorso	United States	1945
Antimony	Sb	121.75	51	6.691		Known to ancients	
Argon	Ar	39.948	18	0.00166	Sir William Ramsay; Baron Rayleigh	Scotland; Eng.	1894
Arsenic	As	74.9216	33	5.73		Known to ancients	
Astatine	At	[210]	85	0.0175†	D. R. Corson; K. R. MacKenzie; E. Segrè	United States	1940
Barium	Ba	137.33	56	3.5	Sir Humphry Davy	England	1808
Berkelium	Bk	[247]	97	14.0**	G. T. Seaborg; S. G. Thompson; A. Ghiorso	United States	1949
Beryllium	Be	9.0128	4	1.848	Friedrich Wöhler; A. A. Bussy	Germany; Fr.	1828
Bismuth	Bi	208.980	83	9.747		Known to ancients	
Boron	B	10.81	5	2.34	H. Davy; J. L. Gay-Lussac; L. J. Thenard	England; Fr.	1808
Bromine	Br	79.904	35	3.12	Antoine J. Balard; Carl J. Löwig	France; Germany	1826
Cadmium	Cd	112.41	48	8.65	Friedrich Stromeyer	Germany	1817
Calcium	Ca	40.08	20	1.55	Sir Humphry Davy	England	1808
Californium	Cf	[251]	98	————	G. T. Seaborg; S. G. Thompson; A. Ghiorso; K. Street, Jr.	United States	1950
Carbon	C	12.011	6	2.25		Known to ancients	
Cerium	Ce	140.12	58	6.768	W. von Hisinger; J. Berzelius; M. Klaproth	Sweden; Germany	1803
Cesium	Cs	132.905	55	1.873	Gustav Kirchhoff, Robert Bunsen	Germany	1860
Chlorine	Cl	35.453	17	0.00295	Carl Wilhelm Scheele	Sweden	1774
Chromium	Cr	51.996	24	7.19	Louis Vauquelin	France	1797
Cobalt	Co	58.9332	27	8.9	Georg Brandt	Sweden	1737
Copper	Cu	63.546	29	8.96		Known to ancients	
Curium	Cm	[247]	96	13.51†	G. T. Seaborg; R. A. James; A. Ghiorso	United States	1944
Dysprosium	Dy	162.50	66	8.550	Paul Émile Lecoq de Boisbaudran	France	1886
Einsteinium	Es	[252]	99	————	Argonne; Los Alamos; U. of Calif.	United States	1952
Element 104	————	————	104	————	Claimed by G. Flerov and others	Russia	1964
					Claimed by A. Ghiorso and others	United States	1969
Element 105	————	————	105	————	Claimed by G. Flerov and others	Russia	1968
					Claimed by A. Ghiorso and others	United States	1970
Element 106	————	————	106	————	Claimed by G. Flerov and others	Russia	1974
					Claimed by A. Ghiorso and others	United States	1974
Element 107	————	————	107	————	Claimed by G. Flerov; Y. Oganessian and others	Russia	1976
					Claimed by P. Armbruster and others	Germany	1981
Element 108	————	————	108	————	Claimed by P. Armbruster and others	Germany	1984
Element 109	————	————	109	————	Claimed by P. Armbruster and others	Germany	1982
Erbium	Er	167.26	68	9.15	Carl Mosander	Sweden	1843
Europium	Eu	151.96	63	5.245	Eugène Demarçay	France	1901
Fermium	Fm	[257]	100	————	Argonne; Los Alamos; U. of Calif.	United States	1953
Fluorine	F	18.9984	9	0.00158	Henri Moissan	France	1886
Francium	Fr	[223]	87	————	Marguerite Perey	France	1939
Gadolinium	Gd	157.25	64	7.86	Jean de Marignac	Switzerland	1880
Gallium	Ga	69.72	31	5.907	Paul Émile Lecoq de Boisbaudran	France	1875
Germanium	Ge	72.59	32	5.23	Clemens Winkler	Germany	1886
Gold	Au	196.967	79	19.32		Known to ancients	
Hafnium	Hf	178.49	72	13.31	Dirk Coster; Georg von Hevesy	Denmark	1923

*A number in brackets indicates the mass number of the most stable isotope.
†The density is calculated and not based on an actual measurement.
**Estimated.

Name	Symbol	Atomic weight*	Atomic number	Density (g/cm³) at 20° C	Discoverer	Country of discovery	Date of discovery
Helium	He	4.00260	2	0.0001664	Sir William Ramsay; Nils Langlet; P. T. Cleve	Scotland; Sweden	1895
Holmium	Ho	164.930	67	8.79	J. L. Soret	Switzerland	1878
Hydrogen	H	1.00797	1	0.00008375	Henry Cavendish	England	1766
Indium	In	114.82	49	7.31	Ferdinand Reich; H. Richter	Germany	1863
Iodine	I	126.905	53	4.93	Bernard Courtois	France	1811
Iridium	Ir	192.22	77	22.65	Smithson Tennant	England	1804
Iron	Fe	55.847	26	7.874		Known to ancients	
Krypton	Kr	83.80	36	0.003488	Sir William Ramsay; M. W. Travers	Great Britain	1898
Lanthanum	La	138.906	57	6.89	Carl Mosander	Sweden	1839
Lawrencium	Lr	[260]	103	————	A. Ghiorso; T. Sikkeland; A. E. Larsh; R. M. Latimer	United States	1961
Lead	Pb	207.2	82	11.35		Known to ancients	
Lithium	Li	6.941	3	0.534	Johann Arfvedson	Sweden	1817
Lutetium	Lu	174.967	71	9.849	Georges Urbain	France	1907
Magnesium	Mg	24.305	12	1.738	Sir Humphry Davy	England	1808
Manganese	Mn	54.9380	25	7.3	Johann Gahn	Sweden	1774
Mendelevium	Md	[258]	101	————	G. T. Seaborg; A. Ghiorso; B. Harvey; G. R. Choppin; S. G. Thompson	United States	1955
Mercury	Hg	200.59	80	13.546		Known to ancients	
Molybdenum	Mo	95.94	42	10.22	Carl Wilhelm Scheele	Sweden	1778
Neodymium	Nd	144.24	60	7.0	C. F. Auer von Welsbach	Austria	1885
Neon	Ne	20.179	10	0.0008387	Sir William Ramsay; M. W. Travers	England	1898
Neptunium	Np	237.048	93	20.25	E. M. McMillan; P. H. Abelson	United States	1940
Nickel	Ni	58.69	28	8.902	Axel Cronstedt	Sweden	1751
Niobium	Nb	92.9064	41	8.57	Charles Hatchett	England	1801
Nitrogen	N	14.0067	7	0.001165	Daniel Rutherford	Scotland	1772
Nobelium	No	[259]	102	————	A. Ghiorso; G. T. Seaborg; T. Sikkeland; J. R. Walton	United States	1958
Osmium	Os	190.2	76	22.48	Smithson Tennant	England	1804
Oxygen	O	15.9994	8	0.001332	Joseph Priestley; Carl Wilhelm Scheele	England; Sweden	1774
Palladium	Pd	106.42	46	12.02	William Wollaston	England	1803
Phosphorus	P	30.9738	15	1.83	Hennig Brand	Germany	1669
Platinum	Pt	195.08	78	21.45	Julius Scaliger	Italy	1557
Plutonium	Pu	[244]	94	19.86	G. T. Seaborg; J. W. Kennedy; E. M. McMillan; A. C. Wahl	United States	1940
Polonium	Po	[209]	84	9.24	Pierre and Marie Curie	France	1898
Potassium	K	39.0983	19	0.862	Sir Humphry Davy	England	1807
Praseodymium	Pr	140.908	59	6.769	C. F. Auer von Welsbach	Austria	1885
Promethium	Pm	[145]	61	7.22	J. A. Marinsky; Lawrence E. Glendenin; Charles D. Coryell	United States	1945
Protactinium	Pa	231.036	91	15.37†	Otto Hahn; Lise Meitner; Frederick Soddy; John Cranston	Germany; England	1917
Radium	Ra	226.025	88	5.0	Pierre and Marie Curie	France	1898
Radon	Rn	[222]	86	0.00923	Friedrich Ernst Dorn	Germany	1900
Rhenium	Re	186.207	75	21.02	Walter Noddack; Ida Tacke; Otto Berg	Germany	1925
Rhodium	Rh	102.906	45	12.41	William Wollaston	England	1803
Rubidium	Rb	85.4678	37	1.532	R. Bunsen; G. Kirchhoff	Germany	1861
Ruthenium	Ru	101.07	44	12.41	Karl Klaus	Russia	1844
Samarium	Sm	150.36	62	7.49	Paul Émile Lecoq de Boisbaudran	France	1879
Scandium	Sc	44.9559	21	2.989	Lars Nilson	Sweden	1879
Selenium	Se	78.96	34	4.79	Jöns Berzelius	Sweden	1817

*A number in brackets indicates the mass number of the most stable isotope.
†The density is calculated and not based on an actual measurement.

The Elements and Their Discoverers (*Continued*)

Name	Symbol	Atomic weight*	Atomic number	Density (g/cm³) at 20° C	Discoverer	Country of discovery	Date of discovery
Silicon	Si	28.0855	14	2.33	Jöns Berzelius	Sweden	1823
Silver	Ag	107.868	47	10.50		Known to ancients	
Sodium	Na	22.9898	11	0.971	Sir Humphry Davy	England	1807
Strontium	Sr	87.62	38	2.60	A. Crawford	Scotland	1790
Sulfur	S	32.06	16	2.07		Known to ancients	
Tantalum	Ta	180.948	73	16.6	Anders Ekeberg	Sweden	1802
Technetium	Tc	[98]	43	11.50†	Carlo Perrier; Émilio Segrè	Italy	1937
Tellurium	Te	127.60	52	6.24	Franz Müller von Reichenstein	Romania	1782
Terbium	Tb	158.925	65	8.25	Carl Mosander	Sweden	1843
Thallium	Tl	204.383	81	11.85	Sir William Crookes	England	1861
Thorium	Th	232.038	90	11.66	Jöns Berzelius	Sweden	1828
Thulium	Tm	168.934	69	9.31	Per Theodor Cleve	Sweden	1879
Tin	Sn	118.71	50	7.2984		Known to ancients	
Titanium	Ti	47.88	22	4.507	William Gregor	England	1791
Tungsten	W	183.85	74	19.3	Fausto and Juan José de Elhuyar	Spain	1783
Uranium	U	238.029	92	19.07	Martin Klaproth	Germany	1789
Vanadium	V	50.9415	23	6.1	Nils Sefströni	Sweden	1830
Xenon	Xe	131.29	54	0.005495	Sir William Ramsay; M. W. Travers	England	1898
Ytterbium	Yb	173.04	70	6.959	Jean de Marignac	Switzerland	1878
Yttrium	Y	88.905	39	4.472	Johann Gadolin	Finland	1794
Zinc	Zn	65.39	30	7.133	Andreas Marggraf	Germany	1746
Zirconium	Zr	91.224	40	6.506	Martin Klaproth	Germany	1789

*A number in brackets indicates the mass number of the most stable isotope.
†The density is calculated and not based on an actual measurement.

Simple Chemical Procedures

Certain simple experiments show chemical reactions or illustrate the chemical characteristics of some common substances. Most can be performed with the materials available in a school science laboratory. All should be performed cautiously and carefully.

Finding Starch in Foods

Starch is a chemical called a carbohydrate. Iodine turns starch bluish-black. Moisten a small piece of each of the following foods separately and test for starch: an apple; a potato; flour; bread; crumbled cornflakes; and cheese. Drop the moistened food sample into a test tube and add a few drops of iodine solution from a medicine dropper. If the food turns bluish-black, it contains starch; if it turns rusty brown, it does not. Foods with large concentrations of starch turn the darkest; those with small amounts turn light blue.

Testing for Acids and Bases

Mix the following solutions in five test tubes: sugar dissolved in water; sodium bicarbonate (baking soda) in water; acetic acid (vinegar) in water; lemon juice in water; and corn starch in water. Place five strips of red litmus paper in a row, then five strips of blue litmus paper in another row. Using a clean medicine dropper, put one drop of the first solution on one of the red and the blue litmus papers. Rinse the dropper and repeat the process with the remaining solutions. Acids turn blue litmus paper red; bases turn red litmus paper blue; neutral substances do not affect the color of the test papers. Judging from the color changes, which of the test solutions was acidic, basic, neutral?

Neutralizing an Acid with a Base

Place 30 ml of an acetic acid solution in a 100-ml beaker, and place 10 ml of an ammonium hydroxide solution in a 50-ml. beaker. Put a piece of blue litmus paper into the beaker of acetic acid. What color does the litmus paper turn? Using a clean medicine dropper, add the ammonium hydroxide drop by drop to the acetic acid, stirring after each drop. Continue adding the ammonium hydroxide until the litmus is no longer red. This is the neutralization point. How many drops of base were needed to neutralize the acid? If you continue to add ammonium hydroxide after the neutralization point, the solution will become basic and the litmus will turn blue.

Heat of Solution

Heat energy is released in many chemical reactions or when the state of a substance (solid, liquid, or gas) changes. The following experiment, which illustrates heat of solution, should take place in a supervised school laboratory because a strong base is used.

Place 10 ml of water in three test tubes and put them in a rack. Fill a 200-ml beaker with 100 ml of water and place it in a box containing insulation. Record its temperature and keep the thermometer in the beaker of water. Into the first test tube, *carefully* put two pellets of sodium hydroxide (NaOH). Place the test tube into the beaker of water, gently swirl it in the water, and record the water temperature. Carefully put four NaOH pellets in the second test tube containing 10 ml of water and place it in the beaker containing a new batch of water, again recording the temperature rise. Repeat the procedure a third time, using six pellets of NaOH in the 10 ml of water. How much heat was released in each case? This can be determined by computing the before-and-after temperatures and knowing that 1 calorie of heat energy is needed to raise 1 ml of water 1°C.

Precipitation

In certain chemical reactions that take place in solution, insoluble solids called *precipitates* form and fall out of solution to the bottom of the container. Using three test tubes, place 1 ml of silver nitrate ($AgNO_3$) solution into each. Add 1 ml of sodium bromide (NaBr) to the first test tube, 1 ml of sodium iodide (NaI) to the second, and 1 ml of sodium chloride (NaCl) to the third. Note the precipitation that occurs in each case. The precipitates are silver bromide (AgBr), silver iodide (AgI), and silver chloride (AgCl), respectively.

Forming a Gas

Formation of gas can be evidence that a chemical reaction has taken place. To a large beaker half filled with dilute acetic acid (vinegar), add a teaspoon of sodium bicarbonate (baking soda). Note the bubbles forming in the solution. Carbon dioxide is the gas escaping from it. Light a match and hold it over the beaker while the gas continues to bubble. What happens to the flame? What can you say about the ability of carbon dioxide to support combustion?

Acids and Bases

Acids and bases are two important groups of compounds that react easily with each other. An *acid* is a compound containing hydrogen that gives up hydrogen ions (H^+) when it dissociates in water. An acid is also a compound that can replace its hydrogen ions with a metal. Sulfuric acid, hydrochloric acid, and nitric acid are strong acids. This means that they tend to give up their hydrogen ions easily.

A *base* is a compound containing either a hydroxyl ion (OH^-) or a hydroxyl group (OH) that will give up hydroxyl ions when it dissociates in water. Many metals have hydroxyl compounds. Sodium hydroxide and potassium hydroxide are strong bases. The reactiveness between acids and bases is evident—acids want to replace their hydrogen ions with metals, and bases have metals to exchange for hydrogen ions. The hydrogen ion concentration of a substance in solution determines its pH (the logarithm of the reciprocal of the hydrogen ion concentration).

Pure water has an H^+ concentration of 0.0000001; it has a "neutral" pH of 7. Substances at the low end of the pH scale are strong acids, like lemons.

common pH values:

	common substances	pH	concentration of H^+ ions in moles per liter at 25°C	
		0		
acid solution		1	0.1	(10^{-1})
	lemons	2	.01	(10^{-2})
	apples	3	.001	(10^{-3})
	tomatoes	4	.0001	(10^{-4})
		5	.00001	(10^{-5})
	bread	6	.000001	(10^{-6})
neutral solution	cow's milk	7	.0000001	(10^{-7})
	blood plasma	8	.00000001	(10^{-8})
	seawater	9	.000000001	(10^{-9})
basic solution		10	.0000000001	(10^{-10})
	milk of magnesia	11	.00000000001	(10^{-11})
		12	.000000000001	(10^{-12})
		13	.0000000000001	(10^{-13})
		14	.00000000000001	(10^{-14})

3

Facts about Physics

Physics deals with matter and energy, and how they interact. Energy forms include light, heat, sound, magnetism, and electricity. Gravitation, a pervasive force in the universe, influences the orbits of planets around the sun, as well as a gymnast's movements. One part of physics called *mechanics* is concerned with forces and motion. Another deals with the electromagnetic spectrum of radiation. Nuclear physics studies the particles and energy exchanges in atoms of matter.

Physics begins by examining the information that people sense about the world around them. Objects are seen to move from place to place, and when completely free of contact with other objects, they move in straight lines at a steady speed. Being at rest is moving at a steady zero speed. Whenever objects do not behave this way, they are said to be accelerated, and a *force* is said to act on them.

Different objects may accelerate differently with the same force, and their relative sluggishness is related to the internal quality of the object called mass. When forces act on objects, the accelerations produce changes in such things as position, size, shape, and chemical nature. The kind and size of any change is judged by use of a quantity called *energy*. Energy is generally subdivided into types by the form of the change that is seen. Thus, an increase in speed is linked to an increase in *kinetic* (motion) energy.

Energy can change from one type to another. But any total batch of energy cannot be changed in amount—though it may be spread around, changed in form, or moved from one place to another. This "savings" plan is called the *law of conservation of mass-energy,* to allow for some of a system's energy being converted into matter and some of the matter being converted into energy.

Center of Gravity

The science of *mechanics* studies the forces dormant in bodies at rest and the working forces in bodies in motion. Civil engineers use information from *statics*—how bodies behave at rest—to prevent disastrous movement in stable structures, such as bridges and buildings. Aeronautical engineers use the principles of *dynamics*—how bodies behave in motion—to design flyable airplanes and rockets.

One of the mechanical principles important to both those studies is *center of gravity*. Solid objects have one of many configurations, such as the hexagon, cylinder, or pyramid shown at the right. All of the weight of a solid body is considered to be centered at one point (represented by the dot in each solid). At this point, the downward pull of gravity is counteracted by equal forces pushing upward to keep the center at rest. However, if the upward or supporting forces are overcome by grav-

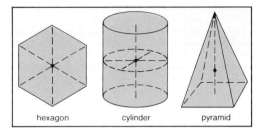

hexagon   cylinder   pyramid

ity at the object's center, the object becomes unstable and can topple in some cases. In other cases, the forces rotate the object when the force acts along a line that does not pass through the object's gravitational center.

Turning forces are called *torques*. They make an object rotate around an axis that supports the center of gravity. All torques acting on an object's center of gravity must be balanced for the object to remain in *equilibrium*.

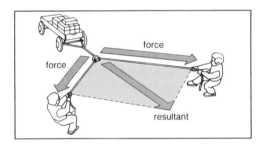

force

force

resultant

Dimensions of Forces

A *force* is anything of the same nature as a human push or pull. It has both size and direction, and is expressed as *newtons* in the metric system or *pounds* in the English system. Force is a *vector* quantity because it is always associated with direction. Different, or *concurrent,* forces will act as a single force with a single magnitude on an object if they act in the same direction. For instance, a 40 newton force and a 30 newton force pushing an object 45 degrees northeast have the effect of a 70 newton force. However, if they act in opposite directions, the total force on the object would be only 10 newtons. When the concurrent forces act on an object from different directions (as in the illustration), the magnitude and direction of the *resultant* force can be found by drawing a parallelogram using the two concurrent forces as sides of the parallelogram.

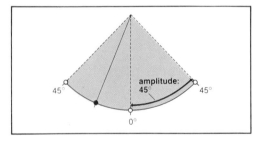

amplitude:
45°

45°   45°

0°

Swing of a Pendulum

The swing of a pendulum is simple *harmonic motion*. It is the circular counterpart of the back-and-forth *oscillating* motions of a spring when stretched and released. The bob (mass) of a pendulum is suspended from the center of an imaginary circle and held at rest by the downward pull of gravity (0°). When the bob is moved 45 degrees to the right along the arc of the circle and then released, it will swing past the 0° centerline and to a point 45 degrees to the left of centerline. The *amplitude* of the swing is 45°. During the swing, *potential* and *kinetic* energies are continually exchanged. Potential energy is stored energy, or energy that is ready for work. Kinetic energy is the energy of motion. Eventually, the pendulum will stop swinging because its energy has been expended working to overcome the friction of air resistance.

Centripetal and Centrifugal Forces

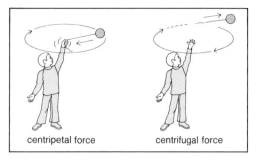

centripetal force   centrifugal force

Centripetal and centrifugal forces are counteracting forces. *Centripetal force* keeps an object accelerating in a circular path while it tries to pull the object toward the center of the circle. *Acceleration* occurs when an object's direction continually and uniformly changes, as it does in a circular path. Centripetal acceleration can be found from the formula *a* equals v^2 over *r*, where *a* is the centripetal acceleration, *v* is the velocity (speed) in meters per second, and *r* is the radius of the circle in meters.

An equal but opposite force called *centrifugal force* keeps the object from being pulled to the circle's center. For example, a ball being swung in a circle by a string exhibits centripetal acceleration. The string supplies centripetal force; it pulls in on the ball. However, the ball itself reacts to the pull and exerts an outward pull on the string—the centrifugal force.

If the string should break, both forces would be canceled out and the ball would fly away at a tangent to its circular path. Centripetal force accelerates the planets as they revolve around the sun.

Table: The Laws of Thermodynamics

Law	Formal statement	What it means	Example
First law of thermodynamics	The change in a system's internal energy equals the heat absorbed by the system minus the work done by the system.	All the universe's energy is constant. Even when energy forms are interchanged, energy is not destroyed. Heat is a form of energy, and it can do work.	In a heat engine, 5 units of heat energy are converted into 5 units of mechanical energy.
Second law of thermodynamics	A reversible, isothermal change occurs when the entropy increase in a system absorbing a given amount of heat at a given temperature equals the ratio of heat absorbed by the system to its absolute temperature.	Outside energy must be applied to lessen the amount of natural disorder, or entropy, in a system. This law explains why heat flows from hotter substances (losing entropy, gaining order) to colder substances (gaining entropy, losing order), and not vice versa.	A beaker of water over a Bunsen burner flame does not freeze while the flame gets increasingly hotter. Instead, the water temperature rises.
Third law of thermodynamics	The entropy of ordered solids is nil at the absolute zero of temperature.	No disorder exists in a system where there is no molecular movement (absolute zero). Though substances can get near absolute zero, they can never reach it.	There is hardly any electrical resistance in a metal conductor cooled almost to absolute zero ($-273.16°C$) because its molecules scarcely move.

A Gasoline Engine in Operation

A two-stroke cycle *internal combustion engine* performs work through the conversion of the chemical energy in gasoline into the mechanical energy needed to spin the engine's crankshaft. The engine has a hard metal cylinder capable of withstanding great heat and pressure, a spark plug, a piston, a connecting rod, and a crankshaft in the engine crankcase. During the intake-compression stroke, a mixture of vaporized gasoline and air is compressed as the piston head pushes it toward the top of the combustion chamber in the cylinder. A series of rings seal the piston with the wall of the cylinder during the stroke to prevent gas from escaping into the crankcase. At maximum compression, the spark plug electrically ignites the fuel-air mixture, causing the mixture to burn. The combustion temperature is between 3,000°–4,000°F (1,500°–2,200°C). The explosive expansion of the heated gases produces pressure large enough to force the piston downward. This starts the power-exhaust stroke, in which the expanding gases do mechanical work. The downward motion of the piston also forces the connecting rod downward. As it does, the connecting rod turns the crankshaft, which then transmits torque to anything attached to it. The base of the connecting rod makes a circular swing around the bottom of the crankcase, and the rod's upward motion forces the piston upward too. This starts another intake-compression stroke. A fuel-air mixture drawn into the crankcase during the preceding stroke is not admitted into the combustion chamber through an intake valve, while the burned gases exit through an exhaust valve. The fresh charge of fuel and air undergoes compression and will be ignited by another spark. The cycle continues until the fuel is used up.

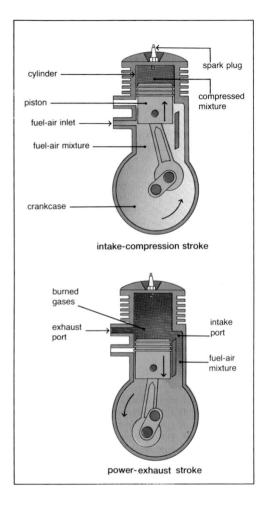

intake-compression stroke

power-exhaust stroke

Effects of Lenses on Light Rays

Rays of light travel in a vacuum at the speed of 186,282 miles per second (299,792 kilometers per second). However, when light rays strike an *optically dense* medium, such as glass, they slow down. The speed of light through glass is 124,000 miles per second (200,000 kilometers per second). As a light ray passes through glass, it is *refracted,* or bent. Whether the light rays converge or not at a point in back of the lens after being refracted depends on the shape of the glass surface. Converging lenses are *convex*. They are thicker in the center than at the edges. An imaginary line called the *principal axis* passes through the centers of the lens's curved surfaces. As light rays are refracted through a convex lens, they cross at a common point along the principal axis called the *principal focus*. The distance between the lens center and the principal focus is called the *focal length* by scientists.

When an object is more than one focal length away, a convex lens forms a *real image* of it; that is, an image that can be formed on a screen on the eye's retina. The real image is always *inverted* (upside down). It is enlarged when the object is between one and two focal lengths away and reduced when more than two focal lengths distant. A *virtual image* is formed when the object is less than one focal length away from a convex lens; we see the image as through it was formed in front of the lens. This is always the case of images formed by *diverging lenses*. *Concave* lenses are diverging lenses. They are thinner at the center than at the edges. Light rays passing through a concave lens

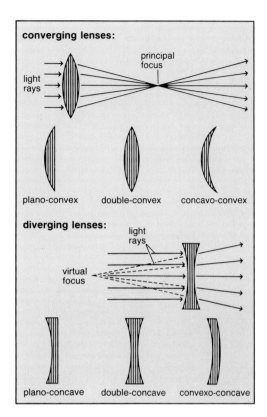

do not cross, but when they enter the eye, they seem to come from a point in front of the lens.

A virtual image is right side up. It is the result of the brain's interpretation of where it "thinks" the light rays meet in front of the lens.

Measuring Light Intensity

The *candela* (also called *candle*) is the measuring unit of light, the visible part of the electromagnetic spectrum. One candela equals the light intensity given off by a 0.0167-square-centimeter piece of platinum while melting (or 1/60 of the light intensity of a nonreflecting surface heated to the solidification temperature of platinum).

The amount of light emitted from a luminous source in a given period of time is measured in *lumens*. If a point of light emitting one candela (candle) is located in the center of a sphere having a one-foot radius, the intensity of light on a one-square-foot section of the sphere's surface has an *illuminance* of one foot-candle. The intensity of illumination at any distance from a light source can

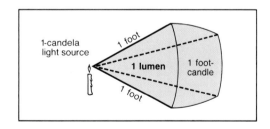

be determined from the *inverse-square law*.

This law states that a surface's illumination intensity is inversely proportional to the square of its distance from the light source. The formula is: $E = l/d^2$, where E is the illuminance in lumen/feet^2 or lumen/meter^2, l is the light intensity in lumens, and d is the distance in feet or meters.

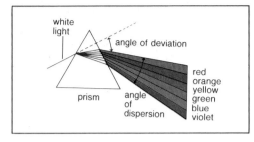

The Spectrum of Visible Light

Light is considered to have the properties of a wave. Every wave has *wavelength,* the distance between one crest of the wave and the next. Sunlight is *polychromatic*—it is a mixture of light waves having different wavelengths. It is also considered *whitelight* because it contains different wavelengths of colored light mixed in right proportions. An incandescent light bulb emits white light.

The rays in a beam of white light travel through the air at about the same speed. However, when a beam of white light strikes the face of a glass prism, the beam is bent and dispersed into its seven component colors through refraction. Dispersion occurs because the varying wavelengths of white light are refracted differently. Red light, having the longest wavelength, is slowed the least by the prism and thus is bent the least. Violet light, having the shortest wavelength, is slowed the most and therefore bent the most.

The *angle of deviation* is between the path of refraction and the path the beam of white light would have traveled unrefracted. The *angle of dispersion* is the amount of spread of the different colors as they disperse into the *color spectrum.* Another prism can refract the dispersed colors back into a beam of white light.

Generating a Laser Beam

A laser is a device that generates a light wave. Its wave flow is *coherent*—steadily rippling—instead of being interrupted and patchy like that of incandescent light, and *monochromatic*—having a single wavelength. The ruby laser's beam is red. The laser has an artificial ruby rod with chromium impurities, a heavily silvered mirror end, a lightly silvered mirror end, and a flash tube. As the energy of the flash tube pumps the chromium atoms to a high level of excitation, energy packets called photons bounce back and forth between the mirrors until they finally emerge as a unified red wave.

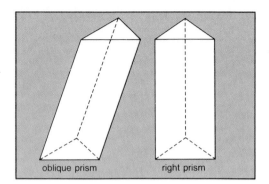

oblique prism   right prism

Prisms Refract Light Rays

Prisms can *refract,* or bend, light rays. Viewed from all around, an *oblique prism* has no equal sides. A *right prism* viewed from all around has three equal sides. Prisms have different abilities to bend light.

The bending ability of any refracting substance is its *index of refraction*—the ratio of the speed of light in a vacuum and the speed of light in the refracting substance. For example, water has an index of refraction of 1.33; ice, 1.5; and flint glass, 1.61. When a light ray strikes the surface of a refracting substance, it is bent at a certain angle, the *angle of refraction.*

At the border where air (the incident medium) and a prism's glass (the refracting medium) meet, there is a perpendicular line called the *normal.* The *angle of incidence* exists between the path of the incident light ray and the normal. The angle of refraction, on the other hand, exists between the path of the refracted light ray and the normal. Its size depends on the prism's index of refraction. Two right prisms on top of each other refract light like a convex lens.

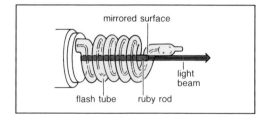

Measuring the Angle of Light Rays

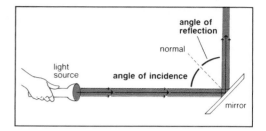

Light can *reflect*, or bounce off a surface. Light rays travel in a straight line, and when they encounter a reflecting surface, they bounce off in straight lines. Before they strike the surface, the light rays are called *incident rays;* after they bounce off, they are called *reflected rays.*

The amount of reflection is measured from a *normal* line that is perpendicular to the reflecting surface. The angle between the incident rays and the normal line is the *angle of incidence.* The angle between the normal line and the reflected rays is the *angle of reflection.* The angle of incidence always equals the angle of reflection. For example, if the angle of incidence is 45°, the angle of reflection will be 45°.

A beam of light actually contains a number of parallel incident rays. If the beam strikes a very shiny surface, the normal lines will all be parallel and all the incident rays will be reflected at equal angles, allowing the reflected rays to keep the same spatial pattern. This is why a mirror produces a true image of what the eye sees. However, when the incident rays strike a rough surface, the normal lines will not be parallel, and the reflected rays will be scattered.

Holograms—Laser Photographs

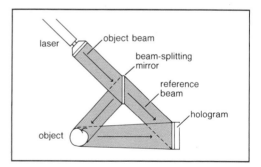

Holography is a way of producing a three-dimensional image. A *hologram* is a pattern of interference lines cast on a reflective surface. The pattern is formed from the interference caused when reflected laser light strikes a *reference beam* of non-reflected laser light. The two beams are out of *phase* (step) and thus interfere with each other. The portion of the laser beam reflected off a mirror strikes an object and is reflected off varying parts of the object. When these varying reflections of the laser beam react with the reference beam, they form a number of interference lines in the hologram. The hologram is only a middle step in holography. It holds an information pattern but does not bear a visual image of the object. When the hologram is lighted by another laser beam, the hologram is "translated" into a three-dimensional image of the object.

Optical Telescopes

Telescopes enlarge the image of far-off objects. Two telescopes in common use are *refracting* telescopes and *reflecting* telescopes. Refracting telescopes are often used as terrestrial (land-use) viewers. They consist of an objective lens, a long tube, and an eyepiece lens. Light rays from an object are refracted through a convex objective lens and form a real image in the tube of the telescope. However, the real image is *less* than one focal length of the convex eyepiece lens. As a result, the eye of the viewer sees the image of the object as a virtual image, inverted and enlarged. The magnification (m) of a refracting telescope is found by dividing the focal length of the objective lens (f_o) by the focal length of the eyepiece lens (f_e): $m = f_o/f_e$. The refractor described here is a Galilean type, like the telescope designed by the Italian scientist Galileo in 1602.

A reflecting telescope works in much the same way, but it uses mirrors instead of objective lenses to collect the light rays from an object. The incident light rays enter the telescope's tube and strike a concave mirror at the base of the tube. As the rays reflect off the base mirror, they strike a slanted mirror in the tube. The newly reflected light rays then converge at a focus in front of the eyepiece and the viewer sees an enlarged image.

The reflector shown here is modeled after one designed by the English scientist Isaac Newton in 1668. Reflecting telescopes can be more powerful than refractors because large mirrors can collect more light than can lenses.

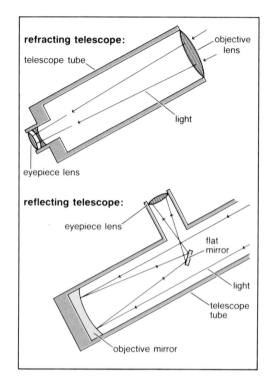

refracting telescope:
objective lens
telescope tube
light
eyepiece lens

reflecting telescope:
eyepiece lens
flat mirror
light
telescope tube
objective mirror

| How Light Waves Are Made | Scientists explain light production by first assuming certain events take place in an atom. The electrons of an atom spin around the nucleus in a variety of paths, or levels. Each level exists at a certain distance from the nucleus. Inner electrons are close to the nucleus, outer electrons are far. A fixed amount of energy is required for each electron to keep in its orbital level. Whenever an atom is jostled hard enough, one of its electrons may receive enough energy through heating to jump to a higher level; that is, spin farther from the nucleus. But it does not stay there long and will fall back to its original orbital level. As it falls back into position, it releases energy in the form of an electromagnetic radiation. The energy is released because the electron no longer needs it to stay in the original orbit. If the wavelength of the released radiation is in |

the visible range of the electromagnetic spectrum, light waves are produced.

Light seems to have a dual nature. It is believed to be a wave and a particle at the same time. It flows like a wave but comes in definite short bursts of energy, called *photons*. Photons of light are produced from an atom as long as its electrons continue to rise and to drop between energy levels.

Waves of radiation in the visible range have somewhat different wavelengths and frequencies. Because of this, white light contains a mixture of the colors of the visible spectrum. When white light is bent through a prism, seven distinct colors can be seen. Red has the longest wavelength and the lowest frequency in the visible light range; violet has the shortest wavelength and the highest frequency.

A source of white light radiates in all directions, scattering the light. As an object's distance from a source of white light increases, less and less light strikes the surface of the object because of scattering. However, this is not the case with a laser light beam. It is coherent. All its waves travel in step with each other. Because laser light only contains a single wavelength, it only has a single color (is *monochromatic*).

Laser Beams

A laser produces an intense beam of light. It produces its light energy by "pumping" atoms to high energy levels. As they are pumped, or stimulated, the atoms give off light waves. The name "laser" is an acronym of the technical description of its action—*L*ight *a*mplification from *s*timulated *e*mission of *r*adiation.

How Laser Light Is Made

A laser *amplifies* (builds up) light rays by shooting energy into atoms and causing their electrons to change energy levels. Light waves are emitted in the process. The light wave emitted by each excited atom stimulates another exited atom to produce a light wave that is in phase with the first one. That is, the crests and troughs of all the waves travel parallel to each other. This goes on and on until the emitted light waves are absorbed by enough unexcited atoms to stop the amplification.

A ruby laser produces a red laser beam. This type of laser consists of an artificial ruby rod containing chromium atoms. Chromium atoms can become excited by blue light. This wavelength of light is furnished by a flash tube surrounding the ruby rod. A mirror is at either end of the ruby rod to reflect and help amplify the stimulated emission of light. One mirror has a heavy coating of silver, which acts as a barrier to the light waves. The other mirror has a lighter coating of silver.

Blue light from the flash tube excites most of the chromium atoms in the ruby, causing their electrons to jump to a higher energy level. As they fall back to their original level (called the *ground state*), they release waves of red light. The energy of the light waves stimulates other excited chromium atoms to give off more light waves. During the process, the growing number of red light waves reflect back and forth in phase be-

Lasers are valuable tools in medicine, industry, communications, and other areas.

tween the mirrored ends of the ruby rod. When the waves acquire enough energy, they break through the partially silvered end as a beam of laser light.

Gas lasers produce beams of green light or other colors. These lasers maintain a steady lasing action by adding new atoms in the upper level continually as the old ones drop to a lower level after stimulation. As a result, the laser light does not become absorbed and the beam continues.

Laser Uses

Eye surgeons can use laser beams to "weld" detached retinas back onto the eyeball without cutting into the eye. The laser beam is directed onto the retina through the pupil of the eye. Scar tissue forms at the impact site of the laser beam and at that point fastens the retina to the inner surface of the eye.

Laser beams have been used for industrial purposes. The diamond dies through which extremely thin wire filaments are drawn can be drilled with a laser beam. The already narrow beam of light can be further reduced to a diameter of less than 0.001 inch. The energy concentrated in this tiny beam is known to be sufficient to cut through diamond.

Laser beams are sometimes used as reference points in building construction. They accurately mark straight lines along the course of large buildings. A laser beam is used by scientists to detect whether portions of a two-mile-long particle accelerator in Stanford, California, move out of alignment.

Three-dimensional images can be produced by laser beams. Holography, or laser photography, relies on the coherent beam of laser light to produce a *hologram,* a three-dimensional information record of an object on photographic film. A portion of a laser beam is reflected off the object and into the path of a reference beam of unreflected laser light. The interaction of the two beams produces a unique interference pattern in the film. When another laser beam is aimed through the hologram's interference "picture," a three-dimensional image of the original object is reconstructed. The image looks like a picture or a slide.

The distance between the earth and the moon has been measured accurately by means of a laser beam. Scientists recorded the time taken for a laser beam to bounce off a reflector placed by astronauts on the moon. Knowing the speed of light in a given period of time, scientists were able to compute the distance with accuracy.

Magnetic Fields and Magnets

Magnetism is a force. A *magnetic field* is a region in which a magnet will experience a magnetic force. Every magnet contains a north pole and a south pole. The rule is: opposite poles attract; like poles repel. For example, a magnet's north pole attracts a south pole but repels another north pole. The directions in the field along which the magnetic force acts are called "lines of force." A line of force can be followed in the region outside of a magnetic field from the north to the south pole. There are many such paths; they all come very close together near the poles but never cross each other. The greater the strength of the magnetic field, called the *flux density,* the closer are these imaginary lines of force. The flux density of a horseshoe magnet is greater than a bar magnet's, permitting the horseshoe magnet to attract more magnetic substances. The permanent magnetism of a bar magnet derives from spinning atomic electrons in the magnet. Any moving electric charge creates a magnetic field *(electromagnetism)*, and electrons are thought to spin so that they have a north pole-south pole axis. Two electrons with paired opposite spins would cancel each other's magnetic effects; unpaired electrons make "atomic electro-magnets" out of their atoms.

Magnets come in many different shapes and have their poles in different places. They have numerous, varied uses. *Bar magnets* can be placed inside cabinet doors to keep the doors closed. *Horseshoe magnets,* bar magnets bent into a horseshoe shape, are used in small motors, like those in slot cars. *Circular magnets* have applications in computers, where they store information. *Disk magnets,* which help create sounds from electrical impulses, are used in radio and television speakers. And *cylindrical magnets* have some special uses, such as holding magnetic substances in place on a machine.

An *electromagnet* is only magnetic while electricity flows through it; this type of magnet can be turned on and off. It makes a stronger magnetic field than a permanent magnet can. Electromagnets have many applications in the home, in industry, and in scientific research.

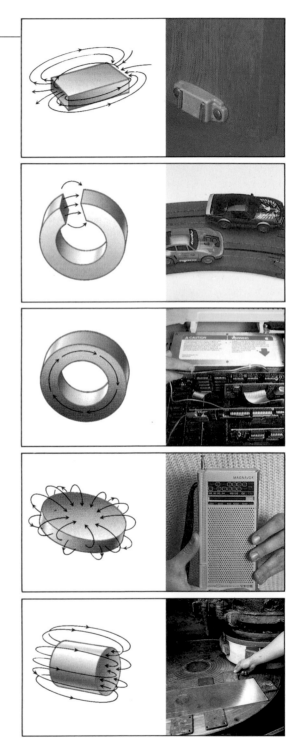

The Electromagnetic Spectrum

Different forms of energy spread across a range called the *electromagnetic spectrum*. Energy forms in this spectrum have both electrical and magnetic characteristics. They travel as electromagnetic waves. All waves have *wavelength* and *frequency*. A wave has an uppermost crest and a bottommost trough. Wavelength is the distance between the crest of one wave and the next (or between the trough of one wave and the next). Wavelength may be expressed in millimicrons. Frequency is the number of waves that pass a given point in a given time. Frequency is expressed in *hertz,* or cycles per second. An inverse relationship exists in the electromagnetic spectrum. As the wavelengths of energy forms grow longer, their frequencies diminish. Gamma rays have the shortest wavelengths and the highest frequencies; long radio waves have the longest wavelengths and the lowest frequencies. We can directly sense only a small portion of the electromagnetic spectrum. We can see visible light and feel the heat of infrared rays. Other forms require instruments that convert the energy into perceptible forms, such as gamma ray counters or radio receivers.

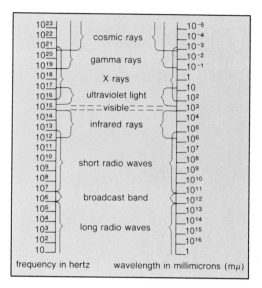

Electrical Circuits

An electric current is a flow of charged particles in the direction of the positive charges. Current flows whenever there is a potential difference in the amount of charged particles between one point of an electrolyte or conductor and another. Potential difference is measured in *volts*. The current's rate of flow is measured in *amperes* (amps). The resistance encountered in a metal conductor is measured in *ohms*. If any two of these three facts about a circuit are known, the other can be found by Ohm's law. It uses the formula: $R = \dfrac{V}{I}$, where R is the resistance, V is the voltage, and I is the amperage. An electric circuit can be structured in series or in parallel. A series circuit has a varying voltage, depending on the number of its power sources. Two 1½-volt batteries produce 3 volts when connected in series. A parallel circuit has a uniform voltage, no matter how many power sources. Two 1½-volt batteries connected in parallel produce 1½ volts.

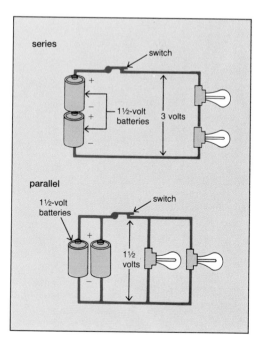

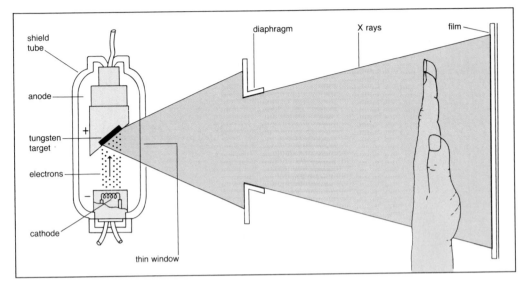

Generating X Rays

X rays are forms of radiation higher on the electromagnetic spectrum than closely related ultraviolet
waves. X rays have great penetrating power because their short wavelength and high frequency
lets them travel easily between the atoms of a substance. X rays are emitted from many sources in
the universe. They can also be generated for medical and industrial uses. When photographic film is
placed behind an object being X-rayed, the developed *roentgenogram* reveals a shadow picture of
the object. For instance, when a hand is X-rayed,
the roentgenogram shows the bones of the hand as
white shapes against a black background. This is
because X rays do not penetrate the dense, *radi-
opaque* bones as easily as the less dense flesh and
thus do not expose (darken) the areas of the film
covered by the bones. X rays can be produced by
high-vacuum X ray tubes. Such tubes consist of an
airtight glass container with two electrodes—one
positive and one negative—sealed inside. The cathode, or negative electrode, has a small coil of wire.
The anode, or positive electrode, consists of a
block of metal. In the diagram of an X-ray machine
above, an electric current flows through the cathode, causing it to become extremely hot. The heat
releases electrons from the cathode. At the same
time, a high voltage is applied across the cathode
and the anode. This voltage forces the electrons to
travel at high speeds toward the tungsten target.
When the electrons strike the target, X rays are
produced.

Releasing Nuclear Energy

The nucleus of an atom contains tremendous energy. This energy is needed to hold together, or bind, all the particles in the nucleus. Scientists estimate that the nuclear binding energy of one helium atom could light a 100-watt electric bulb for 220 years. Some atoms can release part of their nuclear energy during *radioactive decay*. In the process, radioactive elements transform into lighter elements, while emitting particles and radiation. Heavy radioactive elements, such as uranium-235 (a uranium isotope), can split when struck by high-speed neutrons. The *chain reaction* resulting from *fission,* or splitting, releases considerable energy. After a high-speed neutron splits an atom of uranium-235, two smaller atoms are produced and neutrons are released. The two smaller atoms, which may be barium, strontium, krypton, or xenon, among others, are also radioactive for a while, emitting gamma waves and beta particles until they acquire nonradioactive, stable forms. Meanwhile, the neutrons released by fission strike other atoms of uranium-235 and cause similar reactions. Each atom of uranium-235 releases some

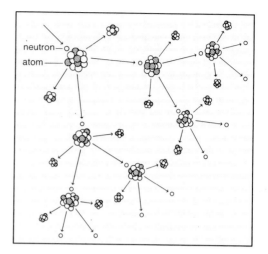

200-million-electron-volts of energy during fission. When fission takes place in a controlled setting, such as a *nuclear reactor,* the energy released can be used to generate electrical power. The heat produced by nuclear fission boils water, which in turn produces steam to drive the power turbines.

Color TV Picture Tube Operation

The picture tube transforms video signals into patterns of light. These patterns duplicate the scene in front of a television camera. One end of the picture tube is rectangular and almost flat; it forms the screen of the TV set. Inside the set, the tube tapers to a narrow neck. The neck of a color picture tube contains three electron guns—one each for the red, green, and blue signals.

Each electron gun in a color picture tube shoots a separate beam of electrons at the screen. Each of the three beams scans the screen.

The screen of most color tubes is coated with more than 300,000 tiny phosphor dots. The dots are grouped in arrangements of three dots each—one red dot, one green dot, and one blue dot. The dots glow red, green, or blue when an electron beam strikes them. When the TV set shows a color program, the three colored dots blend in the mind of the viewer to produce all the colors in the original scene.

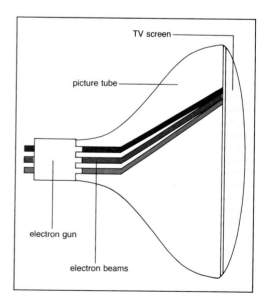

absolute zero Temperature at which an ideal gas has no volume—zero degrees Kelvin.

acid A chemical compound that forms a salt by exchanging its hydrogen with a metal or a positively electrovalent radical; usually tastes sour; can neutralize a base.

alpha particle A helium nucleus; a positively charged, low-speed particle with two protons and two neutrons, caused by some nuclear reactions.

angstrom Unit of electromagnetic wavelength measurement; one A = 0.00000001 centimeter.

angular acceleration Rate of increase of a body moving in a curve; directly porportional to the square of the linear velocity and inversely proportional to the curve's radius: $a = \frac{v^2}{r}$.

atom Smallest part of an element retaining the characteristics of the element.

atomic number Number of protons in an atom's nucleus; indicates place in the periodic table.

atomic weight Weight of an atom compared with the weight of a carbon-12 atom.

base A chemical compound that forms a salt when reacting with an acid.

Bernoulli's principle Pressure by a fluid on a surface decreases as the fluid's speed increases, and vice versa.

bond Chemical combining unit that equals the combining power of one hydrogen atom.

Boyle's law Gas volume varies inversely with pressure at a constant temperature.

burette A calibrated tube used in chemical analysis; its precise calibrations indicate how much of a reagent is dripped into a test solution.

British thermal unit (BTU) The amount of energy needed to increase the temperature of one pound of water one degree Fahrenheit.

calorie The amount of energy needed to increase the temperature of one gram of water one degree Celsius.

candela The amount of brightness of a 1/60-square-centimeter piece of platinum at its melting point.

catalyst Chemical substance that helps other chemicals react with each other without itself being affected by the reaction.

cathode The negative electrode of an electrolytic cell or an electronic tube.

cell A device that generates electricity.

Celsius Unit of temperature on the Celsius scale, which has 100 units between the freezing point of water (0°C) and its boiling point (100°C).

center of gravity Point where the weight of a body is concentrated.

Charles's law When pressure is constant, the volume of a gas is directly proportional to its absolute temperate, measured in degrees K.

chemical reaction Process in which chemical substances react with others, resulting in new chemical substances and the release of energy.

compound Two or more chemical elements combined to form a new substance having different properties than the precursor elements.

cosmic rays High-energy charged particles from interstellar space having great penetrating power.

covalent bond A strong bond created between chemical elements by sharing electron pairs.

cycle An entire oscillation, or vibration, of an alternating wave.

decibel Unit of sound intensity, or power per area unit, measured against a standard intensity of 10^{-16} watts per square centimeter.

density Mass of a unit volume of a substance; for example, aluminum's density is 2.7 grams per cubic centimeter.

dew point Temperature at which the atmosphere is filled with water vapor, causing condensation.

diffraction Scattering of waves in back of a solid object after they strike it; diffraction is greatest when the solid object is much smaller than the length of the diffracted waves.

direct current Single-direction movement of electrons through an electrical conductor.

dyne The metric unit of force needed to accelerate a mass of one gram at the rate of one centimeter per second each second the force is applied.

electrolysis Chemical breakdown of a substance in solution by an electric current.

electromagnetic spectrum Range of radiations having electrical and magnetic properties.

electromotive force The voltage, or potential difference, between poles of an electrical source.

electron A negatively charged atomic particle.

electron volt Energy acquired by an electron as it speeds through a potential difference of one volt.

energy The capacity to do work possessed by all matter; exists in many interchangeable forms, such as heat, light, electricity.

erg A metric unit of the work done when one dyne of force moves an object one centimeter.

Fahrenheit Unit of temperature on the Fahrenheit scale, which has 180 units between the freezing point of water (32°F) and its boiling point (212°F).

foot-candle The amount of illumination on a surface one foot away from a source emittng one candle of light.

foot-pound An English unit of work done when one pound of force moves an object one foot.

friction A force counteracting a body's movement on or through another substance.

fulcrum Point around which a lever turns.

fusion Release of energy from the combination of two light nuclei, such as hydrogen nuclei, into a heavier nucleus, such as a helium nucleus; source of solar energy.

gram A metric unit of mass equal to that of one cubic centimeter of water at 4°C.

gravitation The force of attraction exerted between all matter in the universe.

half-life Time required for half the atoms of a radioactive element to decay.

heat Energy released by molecular motion.

hertz Unit of wave frequency; one hertz equals one cycle per second.

hypothesis A scientific "guess" about why an observed event takes place.

inertia Resistance of matter to any change while it is either in motion or at rest.

ion An electrically charged particle made when an atom loses or gains electrons.

isotope An atom that differs from others of the same element by having fewer or more neutrons but the same number of protons.

Joule's law Heat developed in an electrical conductor is directly proportional to the square of the current, the conductor's resistance, and the rate of current flow; one joule equals 0.239 calorie.

Kelvin Unit of temperature on the absolute Kelvin scale; 0 K = −273.15°C (−459.67°F).

kinetic energy Energy of motion.

lambert One lumen of light reflected or given off from a one-square-centimeter surface.

law A scientific statement that a specific, observable event will take place every time it is tested.

lever A simple machine consisting of a bar that can rotate around a fulcrum.

light-year Distance that light traveling at 186,282 miles per second (299,792 kilometers per second) spans in one year.

line of force Imaginary line traceable to a north pole in a magnetic field or by a positive charge in an electric field.

lumen Amount of light on a one-square-foot area that is one foot from a light source of one candle.

magnetic field Space where a magnet experiences a force; present near a magnetic or an electric current.

magnetic force Attraction or repulsion experienced by magnets and electrical currents.

mass Amount of matter in a substance; permits substances to have inertia and react to gravitation.

matter Anything having weight and inertia.

mechanical equivalent of heat Work and mechanical energy expressed as heat; 1 calorie = 4.19 joules, 1 BTU = 778 foot-pounds.

meter Unit of length; expressed as equal to 1,650,763.73 times the orange-red color of krypton-86 in certain circumstances.

molecule Smallest amount of a substance that can exist freely and still keep all the chemical characteristics of the substance.

neutron Uncharged particle in an atom's nucleus; has a mass of 1.67×10^{-27} kilograms.

nucleus Central core of an atom; has a positive charge and contains most of the atom's mass.

Ohm's law The ratio between an electrical conductor's voltage and current flow through the conductor is constant at a given temperature.

orbit Path taken by a body moving around another, such as an electron around an atom's nucleus.

period Length of time for a complete vibration or revolution.

periodic table Orderly arrangement of chemical elements according to atomic number.

pH Number of free hydrogen ions in a solution; measures acidity.

pipette Thin, calibrated glass tube used for collecting, measuring, and transferring liquids.

proton Positively charged particle in an atom's nucleus with the same mass as a neutron.

quantum theory Idea that electromagnetic energy is given off in small parcels called *quanta,* also called photons.

radiant energy Energy that spreads in all directions from its source.

radioactivity Ability of the nucleus of a radioactive element's atoms to break down into lighter atoms, releasing small subatomic particles and energy in the process.

satellite A smaller body that circles around a larger one, such as the moon orbiting the earth.

shock wave Flow discontinuity when pressure and velocity change suddenly.

sound Energy level of vibrating matter sensed by the human ear.

superconductivity Zero resistance to electric current shown by metals at low temperature.

temperature Hotness or coldness of a substance in terms of its average molecular kinetic energy.

theory Explanation of observed events as supported by experimental evidence.

thermodynamics Study of low heat and other energy forms are related, and how conversions between the energy forms take place.

torque Force producing rotation; found by multiplying the force times the length of the arm it acts on.

velocity Speed and direction of a moving body.

volt Unit of potential difference between two sites in an electric field.

watt Unit of electric power from a one-amp current driven through a one-volt potential difference.

weightlessness Zero gravity; absence of gravity's pull.

work Force multiplied by the distance a body is moved by the force.

X ray Highly penetrating electromagnetic radiation having a wavelength shorter than an ultraviolet ray's.

Basic Information from the Earth Sciences

How much do you know about the planet on which you live? Could you tell someone what percentage of the earth is covered by land and what percentage is covered by water? What is the earth's atmosphere made of? Why does it rain? To understand the world around you, you must study the earth sciences.

This unit presents you with many interesting facts about the earth, its atmosphere, and its climates. The unit will help you to review some of the basic information you must know from the earth sciences.

Powerful forces within the earth cause
volcanoes such as Kilauea in Hawaii.

1

Land and Water
on the Earth

People have always been interested in finding out as much as they can about the place where they live, the planet earth. Their curiosity about what they see every day has created many sciences. Each of these separate sciences studies a different aspect of the earth.

Geology studies the solid parts of the earth, or the rocks, while *geochemistry* looks at the composition and chemical changes that occur on earth's crust. *Geophysics* studies the arrangements and interactions of the forces found there.

Other branches of the earth sciences study very specific things. *Seismology,* for example, studies earthquakes and attempts to predict them. *Mineralogy* studies the minerals found in the rocks. *Geodesy* measures shapes and sizes found on earth and the effects of gravity.

Still other sciences study other aspects of earth. Two sciences study earth's water. *Oceanography* explores the oceans, studying the water itself, the ocean floors, and the ocean's plant and animal life. *Hydrology* looks at the distribution of water on land, especially underground.

The air above the earth is studied by the *atmospheric sciences. Meteorology* examines the changes in temperature, moisture, and winds in the air to determine what the weather will be.

Climatology studies the patterns of these conditions over a period of time.

Each of these sciences has branches that look at parts of the total picture. Things learned in one area often affect studies in another. And you benefit by getting a constantly better idea of what your home is like.

Drifting Continents and Moving Plates

In 1912, German scientist Alfred Wegener suggested that the earth once consisted of only one supercontinent and that today's continents were the result of blocks of the great continent breaking off and drifting slowly away from each other. He gave these early land masses strange-sounding names like Pangaea, Laurasia, and Gondwanaland.

Scientists now think that Wegener was right when he observed that the continental coastlines seemed to fit together. Oceanographers have proved that the floor of the Atlantic Ocean is spreading at a rate of a few inches or centimeters each year, and that these continents are moving further and further apart.

A related theory, called the *plate tectonic theory,* involves the idea that the earth's crust is divided into about 20 rigid plates. Some plates follow continental boundaries, and others do not. Some plates include continental landforms and ocean basins, too.

Tectonic activity, thought to be powered by convection currents, takes place when the edges of the plates push against each other. Results of tectonic activity can include formation of mountains, occurrence of earthquakes, and creation of fault lines.

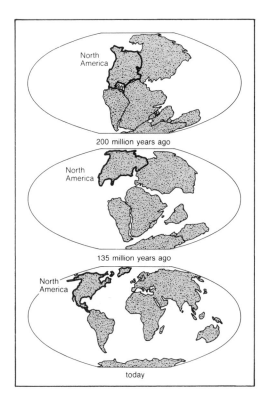

Earth's Surface

Less than 30 per cent of the earth's surface is actually land. Land is the rock of the earth's crust exposed to view in the form of continents and islands. This solid portion of the earth's crust is called the *lithosphere.*

More than 70 per cent of the earth's surface is covered by water. The oceans, rivers, lakes, and other bodies of water on earth are called the *hydrosphere.*

Of course, the land and the water are closely related. The rocky crust that lies under the surface of the land also extends under all of the ocean. The part of the earth's crust that lies under the ocean is called the *ocean basins.* The earth's crust varies in size or thickness, from about 5 miles (8 kilometers) under the oceans to about 25 miles (40 kilometers) under the continents.

The waters of the hydrosphere are important in many ways. Plants and animals need water to live. The waters of the oceans are important in their effect on weather and climate. Also, water wears away rock over long periods of time; some of this

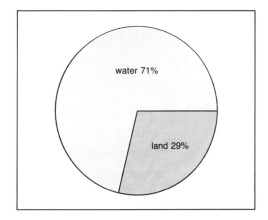

erosion may be harmful, but erosion is necessary in general to create new soil for the lithosphere.

A dramatic example of the power of water erosion can be seen in the Grand Canyon, in the Southwestern United States. The Colorado River created the canyon by cutting more than 1 mile (1.6 kilometers) into solid rock.

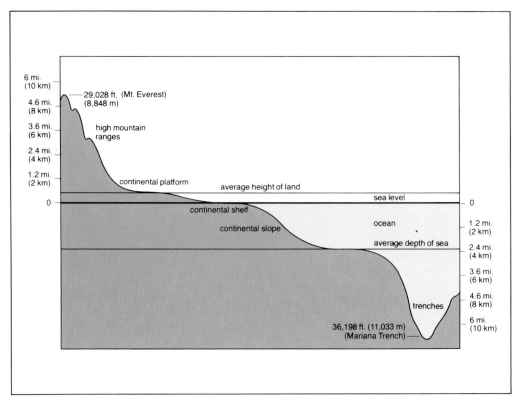

The Earth in Profile

It has been relatively easy for scientists to study the land portions of the earth. It has been known for a long time that land is usually the lowest along the coastlines of the oceans. As you move inland, the land slopes upward gradually toward various points where high mountains have been pushed up.

Only recently, during the 1900's, have scientists learned a very basic fact about the floors of the oceans: they are actually mirror images of the land forms that you can observe yourself. On page 141, you noted that the solid portion of the earth, also called the lithosphere, extends under the oceans, too. Modern exploring techniques have verified that the continental land mass—another name for a portion of the lithosphere—actually extends under the oceans, in the form of a continental shelf and a continental slope. The slope drops off to various depressions, or low points, called *trenches*.

All research to date indicates that the deepest trench, or the lowest point in the earth's crust, is

the Mariana Trench in the Pacific Ocean near the Philippine Islands. The Mariana Trench is 36,198 feet (11,033 meters) deep.

The highest mountain, or the most elevated point on the earth's crust, is Mount Everest, a mountain in the Himalaya range, on the borders of Nepal and Tibet. Mount Everest has been measured at 29,028 feet (8,848 meters) in height.

The diagram portrays a theoretical continental land mass and some of its features. The markings for the Mariana Trench and Mount Everest are included simply to give you an idea of the perspective involved, "the high" in contrast to "the low."

In any case, the high points and the low points in the earth's crust are unusual. The average height of land, including the land under the water on the continental shelf, is only about 2,700 feet (875 meters) above sea level. The average depth of the ocean floor is 12,400 feet (3,730 meters).

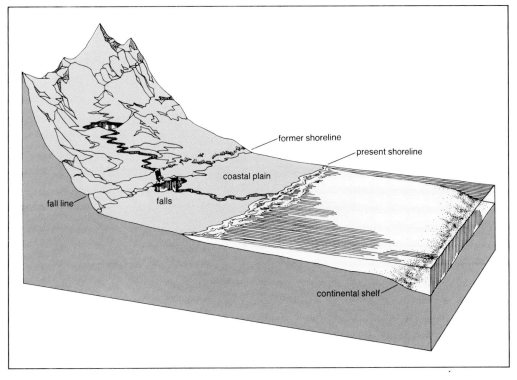

Earth's Lands: Shore Lands

Coastal plains are areas of low land located along the shore of the ocean. A coastal plain may be formed when rock from a mountain is slowly eroded away by running waters. The mountain need not be nearby, as long as there is a mountain steam running down to the shoreline to carry the rock. Naturally, it takes a very long time for a plain to be formed in this manner.

Sometimes the coastal plain merges with the part of the ocean basin known as the *continental shelf*. Or, the continental shelf may push up toward the shore to form a coastal plain. This, again, is a process that will take place over centuries. In such cases, scientists are usually able to detect where the former shoreline was, as shown on the diagram. Depending upon the size of the coastal plain, there can be a great distance between the former shoreline and the present shoreline.

On the land side, there is usually a distinct boundary marking the inland edge of a coastal plain. This boundary is called the *fall line* because the rivers that flow over it drop down this edge

from the harder, rocky land above to the softer ground below—that is, the "new" coastal plain.

A coastal plain often consists of rich, fertile land that attracts a considerable population. Such is the case with the Atlantic Coastal Plain. This plain is located along the eastern shore of North America, from New England to Florida. Many coastal plains have poor harbors or few harbors, but this does not happen to be the case with the Atlantic Coastal Plain.

A *flood plain* (not shown) is similar to a coastal plain, but it is formed near a river—rather than on the shoreline of an ocean. The mud and sand carried along by the river are deposited nearby, in small quantities normally and in great quantities during a flood (hence the name). Some rivers around the world with notable flood plains are the Mississippi in the United States, the Nile in Egypt, the Ganges in India, and the Po in Italy. The Nile flood plain contains some of the richest land in the world.

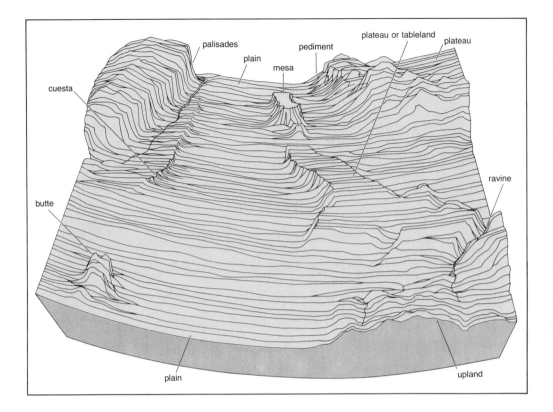

Earth's Lands: Flat Lands

Vast areas of lands along the seacoasts and far into the interior of the continents are flat lands, with only an occasional low raised area or shallow river valley. These vast areas are called the *plains*. By definition, plains are never very high above sea level, even when they are located great distances from the ocean. Large areas of level land found at high elevations are called *plateaus* or *tablelands*. Plateaus or tablelands often occur between mountain ranges.

Many features of plains and plateaus are the same, as you can see on this idealized composite of a plain and a plateau. Some very distinctive features may be more clearly defined, however, on a plateau. For example, rivers cut deep, narrow passages called *ravines* through the flat land of a plateau.

Ground raised above the surrounding region has the general name of *upland*. A high plateau or tableland with steep sides is designated a *mesa*. A small mesa is a *butte*. But in either case, with a mesa or a butte, the plateau rises sharply above the surrounding plain. A *pediment* is the sloping area at the base of a mountainous region in the desert or in a semiarid area. The pediment consists of bedrock covered by a thin layer of gravel eroded from the mountain.

A raised area that features a steep drop on one side but a long, gentle slope on the other side is called a *cuesta*. Very steep slopes that rise abruptly above the surrounding flat land are called *palisades*. Palisades reveal a cross-section of the rock of the region, often basalt rock.

Depending upon the amount of moisture in the atmosphere and the altitude of the plain or plateau, flat lands can be deserts, forests, or grasslands. Grasslands on the plains of North America are called *prairies*. In your own section of the country, or elsewhere when you are on vacation, you may be able to spot some of these land formations. For example, there are many beautiful and scenic palisades in California, and there are abundant grasslands in Nebraska and Kansas.

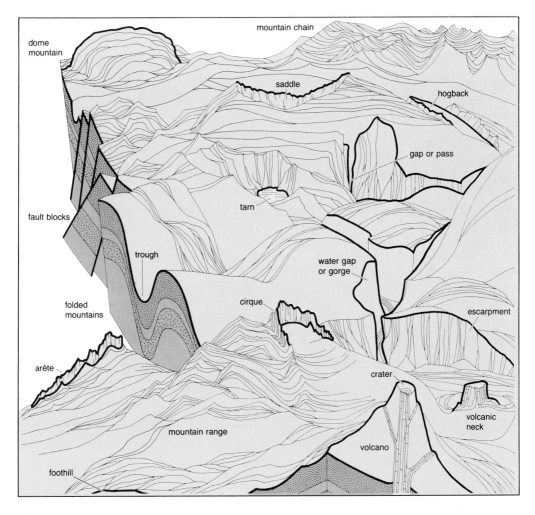

Earth's Land: High Lands

About one-fifth of the land portion of the earth is mountain land. Most frequently, mountains are formed by either folding or faulting. If the crust pushes up into rolling, wavelike shapes, *folded mountains* are formed as a result. The low part of each fold is called the trough; the highest part, the anticline. If the crust breaks so that some huge blocks move up while others move down, fault blocks, or block mountains, are formed.

A ridge formed by the tilted rock is called a *hogback,* and the steep side of a high ridge is known as an *escarpment.* Very often, folding and faulting occur together, with narrow openings called gorges, gaps, and passes between the steep heights.

Sometimes a single section of the earth's crust rises above the land around it to form a *dome mountain.* Or, magma (molten material from deep

inside the earth) may work its way up through the crust, causing an eruption of lava and ash that produces a *volcano.*

Whenever fault, folded, or volcanic mountains are connected to each other, they form a *mountain range.* A group of related mountain ranges form a *mountain chain,* or cordillera.

Other features of elevated areas are the result of various forces at work on the earth's crust. Glaciers have carved away vast areas of mountains, leaving behind high, irregularly-edged ridges called *arêtes* and broad, sloping areas called *cirques.* A *tarn* is a small lake formed in a cirque. *Foothills* are slightly elevated areas that essentially serve as borders between mountain zones and the surrounding lower plains.

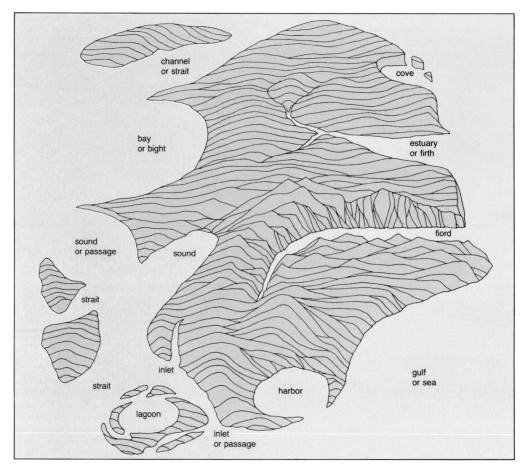

Earth's Water: Where Land Meets Water

As mentioned earlier in this section, seas, rivers, and lakes can have powerful effects on nearby landforms. The waters will erode away portions of land to make passages of various sizes and shapes, as shown on this idealized composite diagram. Note that the diagram portrays these passages in and around some small islands, but they also do appear on the great continents.

A *bay* is a portion of a sea or a lake that extends into the land. By common agreement, scientists define a *cove* as a smaller version of a bay and a *gulf* (not shown) as considerably larger than a bay.

A *harbor* is an area of fairly deep water protected from the currents and the winds. The definition of a harbor includes a practical element; it must be a place that has proven to be a shelter for ships that anchor there. Large population centers often spring up around a good harbor because of the shipping business that is generated.

Two larger bodies of water may be connected by a *strait* or *straits* through or between pieces of land. A *sound* is similar to a strait but is generally defined as a very long, narrow strip of water connecting two larger bodies of water. The Long Island Sound is a notable example of its type.

An *estuary* or *firth* is a small inlet of the sea into the land. A *lagoon* is a pond or small lake connected to some larger body of water. A lagoon at first glance may appear to be self-contained, but it will have one or more outlets.

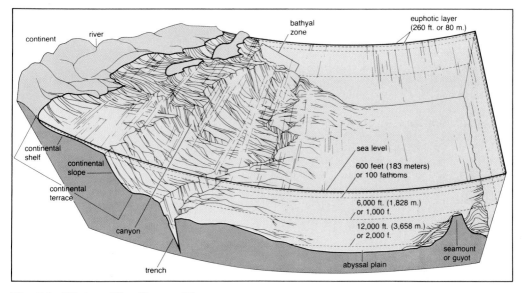

Earth's Water: The Ocean Floor

The edge of each continent extends under the ocean for a comparatively small distance; the area so encompassed is known as the *continental shelf*. The shelf slopes down gradually, as you can see in this idealized diagram, to a depth of about 600 feet (180 meters). Just before the shelf ends, it drops off to form an area known as the *continental slope*. Both of these features together may be referred to as the *continental terrace*.

A sharp cut or depression in the continental shelf is called a *canyon*, as on land. Sometimes the canyons are gigantic features that extend from the shelf, down to the slope, and down to the ocean basin itself. (The Hudson River Canyon off the Atlantic Coast of North America is a large canyon that has been studied in detail.)

The vast ocean basins begin where the continental slope leaves off. Taken together, the ocean basins cover almost three-fourths of the earth's surface. The most common feature of the ocean floor is a very broad, very flat area that resembles a plain on land and is, therefore, called an *abyssal plain*. The word *abyssal* is derived from the Greek words meaning "without bottom" and has been applied to the oceans since ancient times, when the seas were thought to be endless and literally bot-

tomless. This was long before scientific means of measuring the oceans were available.

Of course, the ocean floor is not totally flat or featureless. In some spots, hills or mountains rise up from the ocean basin. The generalized name for these features is *seamount*. A seamount with a flattened top is called a *guyot* and is thought to be volcanic in origin.

As mentioned above, a canyon may extend into the ocean basin from the continental shelf. In addition, the basin features large and deep cuts called *trenches*. The lowest recorded point in the earth's crust is a trench in the Pacific Ocean, the Mariana Trench (see also "The Earth in Profile," page 142). Not only is the Mariana located in the Pacific, but the greatest number of trenches in the ocean basin taken as a whole are located in that ocean. Trenches occur more frequently near edges of the ocean basin that are relatively near groups of islands or mountainous coastlines.

The *euphotic zone* or layer is that area of the water that receives sunlight. Thus, photosynthesis takes place in this zone, down to about 260 feet, or 80 meters, and new life is created there. The *bathyal zone* extends from about 600 feet (180 meters) to 6,000 feet (1,800 meters) below sea level.

2

Air around the Earth

Surrounding the land and water on the earth is another vital ingredient, the air. You cannot see, smell, or taste clean air, yet it is a very real and very vital substance. What is this vital substance made of? Air is a mixture of several gases (see the diagram on page 149, "Chemicals in the atmosphere").

Though air is a gas and not a solid, it still has weight. Also, air shows resistance to motion, so that you have to exert some force simply to walk along the ground. But the air itself, like any gas, flows easily and moves easily. Air expands under heat and compresses under pressure.

The "air ocean" surrounding the earth is referred to as the atmosphere. The atmosphere is much greater in size even than the vast oceans.

This section discusses the characteristics of the air or the atmosphere, including the layers of the atmosphere, chemical composition of the atmosphere, and atmospheric pressure.

Understanding the atmosphere is necessary to understanding all life on earth. Oxygen and nitrogen, two key elements in the air, must be present in order for plants and animals to live. Humans can survive for some time without food or water, but only for brief minutes without air. (See also Unit 4: "Basic Information from the Life Sciences," sections 2, 3, and 4.)

As you know, the "health" of the air has become a major concern in recent years. Air pollution has been on the increase, especially in large cities, as smoke and soot are poured into the air.

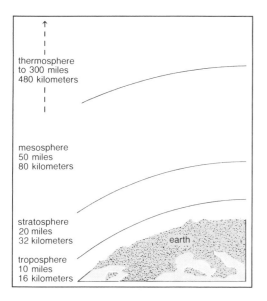

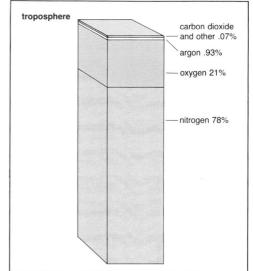

Layers of the Atmosphere

There are four layers in the atmosphere: the *troposphere*, the *stratosphere*, the *mesosphere*, and the *thermosphere*.

The *troposphere* is the layer in which humans live and in which weather occurs. When you think of "the air" or "the atmosphere," chances are that you are thinking of the troposphere—but this is only one layer. Note that the troposphere begins at the earth's surface and continues to about 10 miles (16 kilometers) up. At the earth's surface, the temperature averages 60°F. At the top of the troposphere, in the area called the tropopause, the temperature drops to −112°F. (−80°C). Changes in the weather are made possible by this occurrence of cold air on top of warm air in the troposphere.

The *stratosphere* extends from about 10 miles (16 kilometers) from the earth to about 20 miles (32 kilometers) out. At the base of the stratosphere, the temperature averages −67°F. (−55°C). But in this layer, the temperature rises—rather than falls—as you go up toward the top, reaching 28°F. (−2°C) in the upper area of this layer.

In the *mesosphere,* or the third layer from the earth's surface, scientists have regularly recorded the lowest temperatures in the earth's atmosphere. Near the top of that layer, the average temperature is −135°F. (−93°C). The mesosphere ranges from 20 miles (32 kilometers) to 50 miles (80 kilometers) above the earth's surface. At the top of the *thermosphere* (250 miles, or 400 kilometers, up) temperatures soar to 3600°F. (2000°C).

Chemicals in the Atmosphere

The diagram above shows the breakdown of chemical elements in the troposphere layer of the atmosphere. The gas of the atmosphere in this layer is broken down as follows: nitrogen, 78 per cent; oxygen, 21 per cent; argon, .93 per cent; and other (including carbon dioxide), .07 per cent.

Actually, these percentages are generally valid for the other areas of the lower atmosphere, up to 50 miles (80 kilometers) from the earth's surface. However, beginning in the stratosphere and continuing upward to the outer atmosphere, the percentage of ozone increases steadily. Ozone is vital to life on earth because it prevents harmful rays from the sun from reaching this planet. As you probably know, the percentage of oxygen in the atmosphere steadily decreases as you enter the outer atmosphere. This, and the thinness of the air, is why astronauts have to be equipped with special oxygen equipment for their space walks.

The lower atmosphere also contains, in addition to the chemicals mentioned above and depicted in the diagram, quantities of water vapor and solid particles called dust. The percentage of water vapor in the area varies from place to place on the earth's surface; there may be almost none or there may be as much as 4 per cent. Water vapor serves an important function; when the vapor condenses, precipitation forms and falls on the earth. The dust particles in the atmosphere are also thought to be crucial for weather patterns, as the concentration of atmospheric dust will determine cloud formation, including cloud type and cloud size.

Pressure in the Atmosphere

This graph illustrates how air pressure decreases, or goes down, as you go up in altitude. At sea level, the average air pressure is 14.7 pounds per square inch (101.3 kilopascals). By 10,000 feet from the earth's surface, air pressure has dropped to 10.2 pounds per square inch (70.1 kilopascals).

At 30,000 feet (9,000 meters) above sea level—or the height at which many jet planes are flown—air pressure has dropped to 4.5 pounds per square inch (30.8 kilopascals). By 50,000 feet (15,000 meters) above sea level, air pressure is a scant 1.8 pounds per square inch (12.1 kilopascals).

The figures on this graph cover only the troposphere, or the layer of the atmosphere closest to the earth's surface. But as you continue to go up in altitude, pressure continues to drop.

What exactly is air pressure? It is the weight of the air, or atmosphere, pressing from all sides on any object. Because the weight of the air is a key factor in air pressure, it is easy to see why air pressure falls as you go up in the atmosphere—there is less and less air to press down on that below.

A barometer is an instrument used to measure air pressure. On the weather report, you may hear the "barometric pressure" expressed as a single figure in millibars.

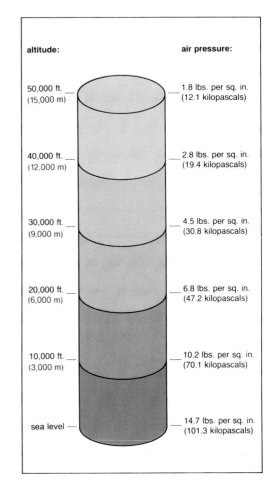

altitude:

50,000 ft. __
(15,000 m)

40,000 ft. __
(12,000 m)

30,000 ft. __
(9,000 m)

20,000 ft. __
(6,000 m)

10,000 ft. __
(3,000 m)

sea level —

air pressure:

__ 1.8 lbs. per sq. in.
(12.1 kilopascals)

__ 2.8 lbs. per sq. in.
(19.4 kilopascals)

__ 4.5 lbs. per sq. in.
(30.8 kilopascals)

__ 6.8 lbs. per sq. in.
(47.2 kilopascals)

__ 10.2 lbs. per sq. in.
(70.1 kilopascals)

__ 14.7 lbs. per sq. in.
(101.3 kilopascals)

Climate and Weather on the Earth

Weather consists of all the changes that occur each day in temperature, humidity, precipitation, and air pressure. Sometimes the words *weather* and *climate* are used interchangeably, but they actually have very different meanings. *Climate* is the correct term for a long-term pattern of weather changes in an area.

Facts about the earth's surface, the oceans, and the atmosphere are crucial to understanding weather and climate. The air uses moisture from the earth's waters to bring life-giving precipitation to the earth. The contours of the earth are an important factor in determining weather and climate. A mountainous region may have one type of weather pattern, and a valley nearby may have a very different weather pattern.

A cold front may bring strong winds and heavy rain or snow.

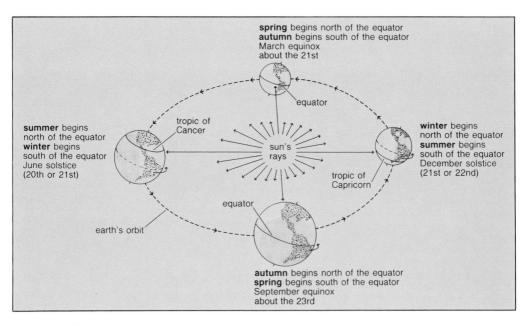

The Four Seasons

The four seasons—spring, summer, autumn (or fall), and winter—are crucial to both weather and climate. The sun supplies light and heat to all points on the earth. In this diagram, you can see how the seasons change as the earth travels in its elliptical orbit around the sun. (For more information on orbits, see "Features of Orbits" and "Planetary Orbits" on page 98.) As you will note, the seasons are reversed north and south of the equator. When it is winter in Montana and Wyoming, it is summer in Brazil and Kenya. The length of the day, and thus the amount of sunlight to be received in a given place at a given time, depends on two factors. One is the season of the year, and the other is the fact that the earth is tilted on its axis. These two factors are closely related in making the days short in the winter and long in the summer, in both hemispheres. Other factors enter into climate, however, and a "winter" day in a tropical country is quite warm when compared to one in the northern latitudes.

Recording Temperatures

In the 1700's, Gabriel Daniel Fahrenheit, a German instrument maker, perfected the thermometer by using mercury in a glass tube instead of alcohol. Fahrenheit designated 0° as the freezing point for a mixture of water, ice, and salt (written as 0° F.). The freezing point for water on his scale then became 32°; the boiling point for water, 212°.

Later in the 1700's, the Swedish astronomer Anders Celsius set up a different temperature scale, using an even 100 points between the freezing (0°C) and boiling points of water. The Celsius or centigrade scale is part of the international metric system. If you know a temperature in Fahrenheit, subtract 32 from that and multiply the number by

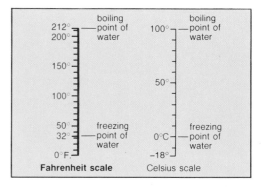

5/9 to get the Celsius reading. If you are starting with a Celsius reading, multiply by 9/5 and then add 32 to get the Fahrenheit equivalent.

Clouds and the Weather

A cloud is a mass of very small water drops or ice crystals. Clouds are the vehicle for bringing precipitation to the earth's surface. There are many varieties of clouds; some of the common types are shown in the diagram at right.

Different types of clouds are seen at various altitudes above the earth. *Stratus* and *stratocumulus* clouds are usually seen near the earth. The lower edges of most stratus and stratocumulus clouds are less than 6,000 feet (1,800 meters) above sea level. A stratus cloud looks like an even, smooth sheet. Light rain often falls from it. A stratocumulus cloud has light and dark areas on the bottom, and is less even in thickness than a stratus cloud.

Altostratus, altocumulus, and *nimbostratus* clouds usually appear from 6,000 to 20,000 feet (1,800 to 6,100 meters) above the earth. An altostratus cloud looks like a smooth white or gray sheet. An altocumulus cloud can appear in a number of shapes, such as unconnected piles of clouds or a layer of clouds piled together. A nimbostratus cloud, sometimes closer to the ground than 6,000 feet (1,800 meters), is a smooth gray layer. It is often obscured by falling rain or snow.

Cirrus, cirrostratus, and *cirrocumulus* clouds appear at elevations of 20,000 feet (6,100 meters) and higher. These types of clouds are formed entirely of ice crystals. A cirrus cloud looks like a delicate, wispy line. A cirrostratus cloud is a thin sheet of cloud that often makes a halo appear around the sun or moon. A cirrocumulus cloud, which rarely appears, may look like a small tuft of cotton.

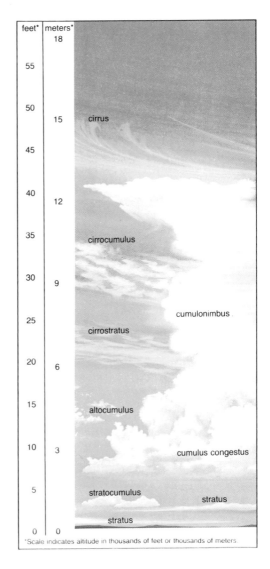

*Scale indicates altitude in thousands of feet or thousands of meters.

Fronts and the Weather

A *front* is the boundary of an air mass touching a second air mass that differs in temperature. When a front moves in, that means that the temperature is changing in the affected area. In the case of a *cold front* (top), cold air moves in, forcing the warm air that was there to move up and away. This makes sense when you recall from physics that heat tends to rise. If you happen to be outdoors when a cold front moves in, you can actually feel the temperature dropping rapidly. Cold fronts come very quickly, but this means that they may go quickly, too. Note the pointed symbol used to show the cold front on a weather map.

A *warm front* (center) precedes a mass of warm air moving into a particular area. A warm front moves more slowly than a cold front, and thus it may stay around longer, also. If you are outdoors when a warm front moves in, you might not notice it as the fronts are changing—because the warming trend is so slow and gradual. Note that as the warm front moves in, the warm air moves up (again, the principle of heat rising). The cold air is thus forced back in the direction it was coming from. The semicircular symbol is used to mark a warm front.

In the case of an *occluded front* (bottom), the cold front basically wins the "battle" between the two air masses, but the warm air is dispelled more gradually. Thus, the resulting temperature will be "cool" rather than "cold," because the warm air has some influence. Note that the symbol for an occluded front combines the cold front and the warm front symbols.

There are other types of fronts, but these are the three basic types to be familiar with. When any kind of front moves in, there are more changes than simply the change in temperature. Air pressure changes, too. A different type of cloud may appear in the sky, or the number of clouds in the sky may simply multiply. Precipitation generally results, either rain or snow, depending on the type of front and other factors. Note that precipitation is indicated with each of the fronts shown on the diagram.

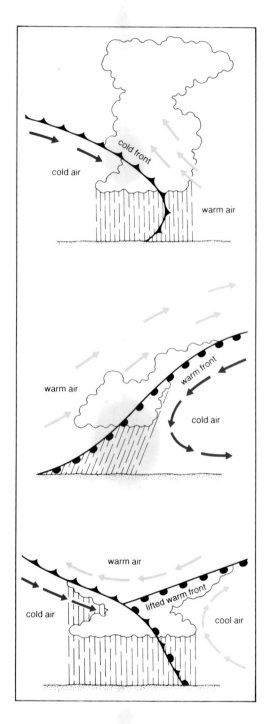

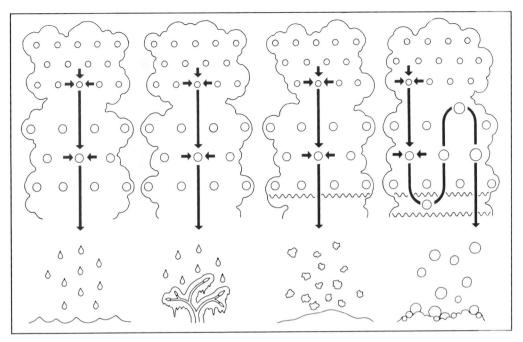

Precipitation

Water vapor is taken up into the atmosphere by means of evaporation. Water condenses to form clouds and eventually returns to earth as precipitation. To return to earth, water in the atmosphere must be made heavy enough to fall. It must be converted from a gas or a vapor into either a liquid or a solid. The only way to do this is to cool the air to below the point where it can hold water vapor. This temperature is called the *dew point*. It can vary, depending on the amount of cooling and the amount of water present.

Salt evaporated from sea spray, acids from pollution, and dust in the atmosphere all attract water vapor. They are the nuclei around which water vapor is converted into the four forms of precipitation.

Rain (far left) occurs when water-soaked nuclei attract other water drops until they become so large they can no longer be held up by air currents. Rain that is frozen by cold air near the ground turns to *sleet* (not shown).

Rain sometimes becomes very cold before it falls. Then it will fall as rain but freezes and becomes ice when it lands. This form of precipitation is called *glaze* (second from left).

Snow (second from right) is formed when water vapor is converted into its solid ice form directly, without first becoming a liquid. This process is called *sublimation*. Tiny six-pointed ice crystals form and collect into flakes.

Hail (right) is formed when raindrops become ice as they fall through freezing areas and then are carried up above the freezing point by strong air currents. (Note how the arrow in the diagram changes direction before the precipitation emerges.) Each time this frozen water tries to fall through the freezing point each particle picks up a new layer of ice until finally it is so heavy that the air currents can no longer hold it.

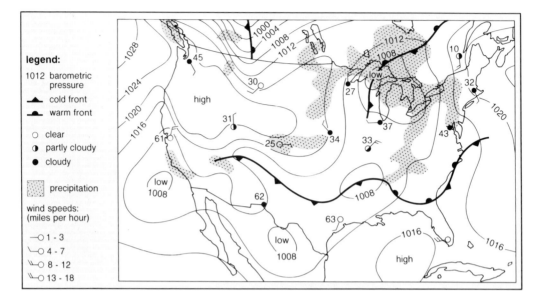

legend:

1012 barometric pressure

🔺 cold front

🔴 warm front

○ clear

◐ partly cloudy

● cloudy

▨ precipitation

wind speeds:
(miles per hour)

⟜○ 1 - 3

↘○ 4 - 7

↘↘○ 8 - 12

↘↘○ 13 - 18

Reading a Weather Map

Much of the science of weather forecasting, called *meteorology,* has been developed since 1900. Until about 1920, forecasts were based primarily upon reports of barometric pressure. Forecasters knew that areas of low pressure, called *cyclones* because the winds in them swirl around, bring wet weather and usually move to the north and east. High pressure areas, called *anticyclones,* with winds moving out from their centers, tend to move to the south and east and usually signal fair weather.

Today millibars of *barometric pressure* adjusted to sea level are noted on weather maps. Lines called isobars connect all the places with the same pressure reading.

After 1920, a group of Norwegian meteorologists began careful studies of weather patterns and found that the low pressure cyclones are formed by the meeting of cold and warm air masses. As a result, weather maps began to show the location of the cold, warm, occluded, and stationary fronts, and weather forecasting for longer time spans improved tremendously.

Meteorologists began establishing weather recording and reporting stations all over the world. This network was essentially complete by the late 1950's. It now consists of land observing stations, sounding stations that report events throughout the

troposphere, radar stations, and specially equipped ships, aircraft, and weather satellites.

Also in the 1950's, a series of standard procedures and codes was adopted on a worldwide basis. Numbers are used on maps to record instrument readings such as temperature and pressure, and symbols represent visual observations of precipitation and clouds.

On a weather map, a circle indicates a reporting station. The amount of the circle that is filled in corresponds to the amount of cloud cover. Numbers and symbols around the circle supply the details. The map above shows temperature in numbers and wind direction in the form of an arrow-like line. The line is placed to show the wind's direction, and the flags on it indicate the wind's speed in miles per hour.

To indicate larger weather features, shaded areas show precipitation and long heavy lines mark fronts. Cold fronts have triangular markings, and warm fronts, half circles (see also page 154). These symbols are placed on the side of the line in which the front is moving. An occluded front shows warm and cold symbols on the same side of the line, while a stationary front shows warm symbols on one side and cold ones on the other.

Climate Zones

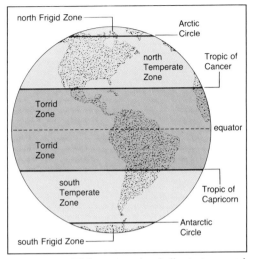

Weather, especially temperature, depends a great deal on the position of the sun overhead. Traditionally, the earth has been divided into five climate zones whose boundaries are the same latitudes that mark the changes of the seasons. The winterless Torrid Zone extends from the equator to the 23½° north and south latitudes, called the Tropic of Cancer and the Tropic of Capricorn respectively. Between 23½° and 66½° are the north and south Temperate Zones, which have warm summers and cold winters. Above the 66½° north and south latitudes, which mark the Arctic and Antarctic Circles, are the summerless Frigid Zones.

This classification accounts for the roles of the sun's light and heat on climate. But precipitation is another important factor in climate. Wet and dry variations occur at different times of the year throughout the Torrid and Temperate Zones. These variations have convinced scientists that it is necessary to establish many regional climate types and subtypes. There are a number of systems for classifying climates.

Types of Climates

These are the major climatic groups, according to the system devised by geographer Glenn T. Trewartha.

Tropical Climates. The tropical climates form a band around the equator. Temperatures are always warm, and heavy rainfall is common. There are two types of these climates. The *tropical wet climate,* where the tropical rain forests are found, has rain for at least 10 months a year. The *tropical wet-and-dry climate,* with its tall grasses or savanna, has less annual rainfall, a shorter wet season, and a longer dry season than the tropical wet climate.

Subtropical Climates. Here the seasons begin to become noticeable. There is some freezing, but at least eight months of the year have average temperatures of 50° F. (10° C) or more. There are two types of subtropical climates. The *subtropical dry-summer climate* has warm dry summers and mild rainy winters. The *subtropical humid climate* has more precipitation than the subtropical dry-summer climate, and summer is usually the wet season.

Temperate Climates. Called temperate because they occur between the zones of constant heat and constant cold, these climates have average temperatures of 50° F. (10° C) or more for at least four months, but not more than seven months, each year. There are two types of temperate climates. The *temperate oceanic climate* is warmed by mild oceanic currents. Precipitation is common all year around. The *temperate continental climate* has sharp weather contrasts, from cold winters to warm summers. Temperature ranges of over 50° F. or 30° C are common, and precipitation is generally lighter, with more than half the area experiencing subhumid conditions.

Boreal Climate. Winters are long and very cold and summers last no more than one to three months in these northern taiga regions dominated by coniferous forests. The impact of long days in summer and long nights in winter becomes significant on the *boreal climate*. Precipitation is limited, permafrost is common, and the growing season is short.

Polar Climates. Because low humidity accompanies low temperatures, precipitation is extremely low in the polar climates. For half the year, there is constant darkness; for the other half, constant light, with little warmth because of the steep angles of the sun's rays. There are two types of polar climates. The *polar tundra climate* has a few months with temperatures above freezing but none with temperatures above 50° F. (10° C). Permafrost prevents surface drainage, and swamps abound. In the *polar icecap climate*, long sunless periods and the ability of the snow surface to reflect back 80 per cent of the solar radiation it receives keep average temperatures below freezing.

Highland Climates. Altitude becomes an important factor in the *highland climates*. Above 6,000 feet (1,800 meters), the air grows thin, precipitation increases, and solar radiation becomes intense. There are large swings in temperature between day and night. The wet highlands are the sources of the major waterways.

Dry Climates. The rate of precipitation is always lower than the rate of evaporation in a dry climate. Arid deserts and semiarid steppes, transition belts around deserts, are found in the dry climate areas. Three main types are distinguished by their temperature conditions. Hot *tropical-subtropical dry climates* occur where dry, stable air masses form near the equator. *Cool coastal deserts* are refreshed by ocean currents. *Middle-latitude dry climates* occur deep inside continents when mountains block the arrival of water vapor from the oceans.

Cities and Their Climates

City or reporting station	Average temperature, °F. (°C)			Annual precipitation, in. (mm)
	Annual	Jan.	July	
Tropical wet climate:				
Belém, Brazil	78 (26)	77 (25)	78 (26)	108 (2743)
Kisangani, Zaire	76 (24)	77 (25)	74 (23)	69.4 (1763)
Singapore	80 (27)	79 (26)	81 (27)	95 (2413)
Tropical wet-and-dry climate:				
Calcutta, India	78 (26)	65 (18)	83 (28)	58.8 (1494)
Normanton, Australia	81 (27)	86 (30)	72 (22)	37.5 (952)
Subtropical dry-summer climate:				
Santa Monica, California	59 (15)	53 (12)	66 (19)	14.8 (376)
Perth, Australia	64 (18)	74 (23)	55 (13)	33.9 (861)
Naples, Italy	62 (17)	48 (9)	77 (25)	34.3 (811)
Subtropical humid climate:				
Charleston, South Carolina	66 (19)	50 (10)	82 (28)	47.3 (1202)
Sydney, Australia	63 (17)	72 (22)	52 (11)	47.7 (1212)
Buenos Aires, Argentina	61 (16)	74 (23)	51 (11)	39.1 (993)
Temperate oceanic climate:				
Paris, France	50 (10)	37 (3)	66 (19)	22.6 (574)
Hokitika, New Zealand	53 (12)	60 (16)	45 (7)	116.1 (2949)
Valentia, Ireland	50.8 (11)	44 (7)	59 (15)	55.6 (1413)
Temperate continental climate:				
New York City, New York	52 (11)	31 (−1)	74 (23)	42 (1067)
Montreal, Quebec, Canada	42 (6)	13 (−10)	69 (21)	40.7 (1017)
Moscow, U.S.S.R.	39 (4)	12 (−11)	66 (19)	21.1 (536)
Boreal climate:				
Yakutsk, Siberia, U.S.S.R.	12 (−11)	−46 (−43)	66 (19)	13.7 (348)
Fort Vermilion, Alberta, Canada	27 (−3)	−14 (−26)	60 (16)	12.3 (313)
Polar tundra climate:				
Sagastyr, Siberia, U.S.S.R.	1 (−17)	−34 (−37)	41 (5)	3.3 (84)
Upernivik, Western Greenland	16 (−9)	−7 (−22)	41 (5)	9.2 (234)
Polar icecap climate:				
South Pole, Antarctica	−57 (−49)	−20 (−29)	−74 (−59)	—
Eismitte, Greenland	−22 (−30)	−42 (−41)	12 (−11)	—
Highland climates:				
Quito, Ecuador	54.7 (13)	54.5 (13)	54.9 (13)	42.2 (1072)
Longs Peak, Colorado	37 (3)	23 (−5)	55 (13)	21.6 (548)
Tropical-subtropical dry climates:				
Phoenix, Arizona	70 (21)	51 (11)	91 (33)	7.2 (185)
Benghazi, Libya	69 (21)	55 (13)	78 (26)	11.9 (302)
Kayes, Mali	85 (29)	77 (25)	84 (29)	29.1 (739)
Cool coastal deserts climate:				
Lima, Peru	66 (19)	71 (22)	61 (16)	1.8 (45)
Middle-latitude dry climates:				
Santa Cruz, Argentina	47 (9)	59 (15)	35 (2)	6.1 (155)
Williston, North Dakota	39 (4)	6 (−14)	69 (21)	14.4 (366)
Ulan Bator, Mongolia	28 (−2)	−16 (−27)	63 (17)	7.6 (193)

Adapted from *An Introduction to Climate*, Fifth Edition, by Glenn T. Trewartha and Lyle H. Horn. Copyright © 1980, 1968 by McGraw-Hill, Inc. Used with the permission of McGraw-Hill Book Company.

absolute zero The temperature at which all molecular action stops; zero degrees on the Kelvin scale, or −273.15°C.

altitude Height above a base line. Altitude is usually measured from sea level.

anticline The high point of a fold in the earth's crust.

anticyclone An air mass that moves around a center of high pressure, also called a high pressure system, or high.

atmosphere The air around the earth.

bar A unit of measure of air pressure. Air pressure at sea level at 45° north latitude is 1.0132 bars.

cold front The forward edge of a cold air mass that is replacing a warm air mass.

continental drift The movement of the continents away from each other, caused by tectonic forces (see *plate tectonics*).

continental shelf The edge of each continent that extends under the ocean.

continental slope The area of steep dropping off of the continental shelf under the oceans.

cordillera A series of mountain ranges that forms a single system.

cyclone An air mass that moves around a center of low pressure, also called a low pressure system or low.

dew point The temperature at which air begins to condense as it cools.

diastrophism The process causing changes in the earth's crust that lead to movements on the surface, such as faulting and folding.

earthquake Movement of the earth's crust, usually caused by slippage along the sides of a fault or by volcanic activity.

epicenter The point on the earth's surface closest to the underground origin of an earthquake.

equinox A time occurring twice each year when the sun passes directly over the equator. Day and night are of about equal lengths all over the earth.

erosion The slow wearing away, or weathering, of soil and rocks by wind, rain, waves, and other weather forces.

faulting The breaking of the earth's crust into huge blocks, some of which move upward while others move downward, to form fault block or block mountains.

folding The upward and downward movement of the earth's crust into wavelike folds that form folded mountains. The high point of such folding is the anticline and the low point is the syncline.

gravity The attraction between the earth and other objects.

horizon The curved line where the earth and sky appear to meet.

hydrologic cycle The sequence in which the earth uses and reuses its water supply.

isobar A line on a weather map that connects areas having the same barometric pressure.

isotherm A line on a weather map that connects areas having the same temperature.

latitudes Distances north or south of the equator shown as parallel lines around the earth. The equator is 0° latitude.

lithosphere The solid portion of the earth's surface, often called the crust.

longitude Distance as measured east or west of a prime meridian, a line running north and south on the earth's surface. The meridian usually selected as 0° longitude runs through Greenwich, England.

mantle A thick layer of solid rock that begins below the earth's crust and extends 1,800 miles (2,900 kilometers) toward the earth's core.

mountain An area that lies at least 2,000 feet (610 meters) above the area around it. Most mountains are formed by the faulting or folding of the earth's crust.

occluded front The forward edge of a cold air mass that is overtaking a warm front and meeting the cool air ahead of it.

ocean The massive body of water that covers two-thirds of the earth's surface. There are five principal divisions of the ocean: The Atlantic, Pacific, Indian, Arctic, and Antarctic oceans.

ozone A form of oxygen that has three atoms of oxygen in each molecule (O_3). Ozone in the stratosphere absorbs the harmful ultraviolet rays of the sun.

permafrost Permanently frozen subsoil.

plate tectonics The theory that says that forces beginning below earth's crust cause the plates on which the continents are based to move about on earth's surface.

precipitation The removal of water vapor from the atmosphere and the form the water vapor takes as it falls to earth.

sial The rocky layer of the earth's crust that forms the continents.

sima The rocky layer of the earth's crust that lies under the continents and forms the ocean floor.

solstice A time occurring twice each year when the sun is farthest from the equator. The longest or shortest days of the year occur on the solstice.

stationary front The edge formed by a cold air mass and a warm air mass when neither is able to replace the other.

taiga The name in Russian for subarctic areas covered with coniferous forests. The name is also used for similar areas in North America.

talus The rocks and gravel piled up at the base of the cliff or slope from which they fell.

temperature inversion The condition that occurs when the air mass nearest the earth's surface is cooler than the mass above it. This is the opposite of the normal condition.

thrust The horizontal movement of the earth's surface in the process of diastrophism.

turbulence Irregular conditions in the atmosphere that cause violent winds.

uplift The upward movement of the earth's surface in the process of diastrophism.

volcano An opening in the earth's surface through which lava, hot gases, and rock fragments erupt. Volcanoes are also the mountains formed by the build-up of the material thrown out during eruptions.

warm front The forward edge of a warm air mass that is replacing a cold air mass.

water table The level in the ground below which the rock is saturated with water.

weather The effect of all conditions occurring in the atmosphere in one place during a short period of time.

weathering Changes in the earth's surface brought about by the forces of weather.

UNIT

4

Basic Information from the Life Sciences

Life, both plant and animal, is very complex. What are the basic parts of a cell? How do plants reproduce? How do animals breathe? Which bones make up the human skeleton?

This unit answers these and many other questions about living organisms. The unit is a handy, easy-to-use review of basic information from the life sciences.

Light from the sun makes life on earth possible
for people, animals, and plants.

1

A Look at the Cell

All living things consist of cells. The simplest forms of independent life are single cells. Each captures or makes its own food, uses the food for growth and cell repair, and divides into other cells like itself. Cells in more advanced living things are specialized into tissues and organs. Some types of special cells may form a food-manufacturing leaf in plants or a leg muscle in animals. The rule is: as the forms of life in the plant and animal kingdoms become more complex, their cells become more and more specialized into systems.

An ameba is an example of a one-celled animal. It has the attributes of a typical cell. And on a simpler level, it does many of the things done by many-celled creatures. The ameba's cell has *organization*. It is an orderly array of chemicals and cell parts organized in an efficient package to sustain life. The ameba's cell undergoes *metabolism* to get energy from food, grow, and repair worn out parts. The energy needed to power the cell comes from food, which is chemically broken down through *respiration* to extract its energy. The ameba *excretes,* or gets rid of, harmful waste products after the food is metabolized. It is capable of purposeful *movement,* one of life's attributes. It also shows *responsiveness;* that is, it can react to changes in its immediate surroundings. For example, an ameba will try to move away from a harsh chemical added to water around it. The ameba *reproduces* by cell division and splits into two daughter cells, each containing the ingredients and instructions needed for independent life. In more advanced organisms, reproduction is carried out by special sex cells.

The science of *biology* delves into the activities of all living things in their environment. *Botany* concentrates on plant activities, and *zoology* deals with the lives of animals. The general principles of life and the specialized adaptations made by plants and animals will be discussed in the first part of the following unit. Later in the unit, the human body and how it works will be explained.

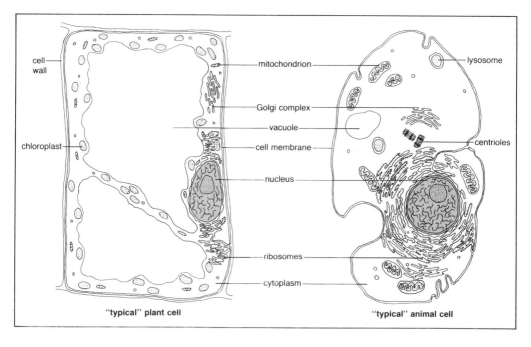

cell wall — mitochondrion — lysosome

Golgi complex

vacuole

chloroplast — cell membrane — centrioles

nucleus

ribosomes

cytoplasm

"typical" plant cell   **"typical" animal cell**

A Look at Typical Cells

A typical animal or plant cell contains three essential parts—the cell membrane, the cytoplasm, and the nucleus. The *cell membrane* separates the cell from its watery surroundings. It is a semipermeable membrane, allowing only select substances to pass through. Tiny molecules easily get through the membrane by simple diffusion. Larger molecules must be actively transported across the cell membrane, a process that requires cell energy. Still larger substances can be engulfed by portions of the membrane and brought into the cell, a process called pinocytosis. The *cytoplasm* is a watery-to-sirupy mix of nutrients and pigments in liquid suspension. Activities in the cytoplasm keep the cell alive. The *nucleus* is the control center of the cell. It contains coded information used by the cell for growth, repair, and reproduction.

The cytoplasm contains organelles, minute specialized parts, involved in producing energy for the cell. Other structures are concerned with making proteins to repair damaged cell parts. Food molecules are oxidized, or "burned" for energy, in each *mitochondrion*—one of the cell's many such "powerhouses." *Ribosomes*, located along membraned passageways in the cell called endoplasmic reticulum, manufacture the proteins needed for growth and repair. The *Golgi complex*, also called *Golgi*

apparatus, is a group of saclike storehouses where proteins made in the ribosomes are kept for future distribution.

A plant cell differs somewhat from an animal cell by having a rigid, cellulose *cell wall* around the cell membrane. The stiff cell walls give support to plant stalks and stems. The cellulose required for the cell wall is made in the cytoplasm of a plant cell. An organelle called a *chloroplast* is also found in a plant cell. Chloroplasts contain chlorophyll, the respiratory pigment used by green plants to manufacture food. *Vacuoles* are scattered through the cytoplasm of plant and animal cells, carrying dissolved food molecules for use by the mitochondria. Some cells have contractile vacuoles that help get rid of excess water by forcing it out of the cell. *Lysosomes* are similar to vacuoles but appear to digest food particles.

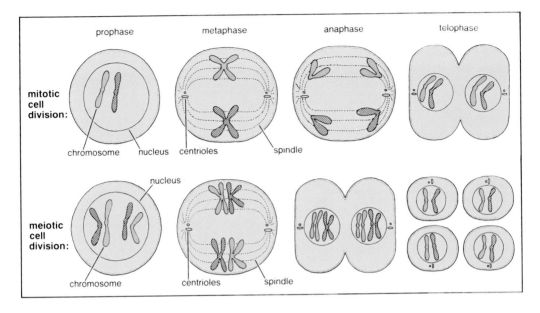

How Cells Divide

Body cells reproduce by *mitosis*. At the start of mitosis, strands of deoxyribonucleic acid (DNA)—the carrier of hereditary information—form into chromosomes. By *prophase,* the first stage of mitosis, each chromosome in the cell nucleus has duplicated. In the next stage, *metaphase,* the membrane around the nucleus disappears, *centrioles* are in place at opposite ends of the cell, *spindle* fibers appear between the centrioles, and homologous, or like, chromosomes line up at the cell midline. During *anaphase,* the third mitotic stage, one set of homologous chromosomes moves along the spindles toward each of the centrioles. In the final stage of mitosis, called the *telophase,* the centrioles and spindles disappear, a nuclear membrane forms around each set of chromosomes, and the cell membrane pinches in two. Two new body cells become formed, each with the same type and number of chromosomes as the parent cell (46 in a human body cell).

Sex cells, or gametes, reproduce by a two-step method called *meiosis.* During the first meiotic prophase, homologous chromosomes pair and duplicate into tetrads. The tetrads line up at the midline in the first meiotic metaphase, and separate and move toward a centriole during the first meiotic anaphase. By the end of the first meiotic telophase, two daughter cells form with the same number of chromosomes as the parent. However, meiosis keeps going on. During the second step, chromosomes *do not* duplicate. Four stages occur again, and four gametes are eventually produced from the original parent cell. But each new gamete contains only half the number of chromosomes in a body cell (23 in a human sex cell). Fertilization of a female gamete by a male gamete restores the original chromosome number.

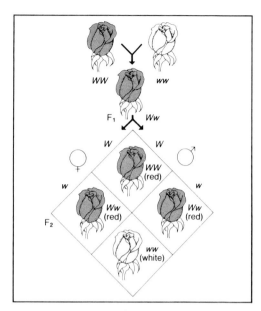

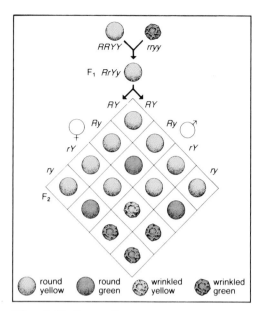

| round yellow | round green | wrinkled yellow | wrinkled green |

Mendel's Law of Segregation

Gregor Mendel, a 19th century Austrian monk, ex-
perimented with pea plants and discovered principles of inheritance that apply to all living things.
Physical traits, or *phenotypes*, are controlled by
gene pairs called *alleles* that reside on *homologous*, or like, chromosomes. Alleles for traits pass
from generation to generation in the gametes. Certain traits dominate others. For example, red flowers are dominant over white flowers. The *genotype*, or genetic makeup, of each allele remains in
independent, however, even when masked by a
dominant one. For example, the phenotype of red-
flowerness is caused by two *homozygous* alleles
with the genotype WW or by two *heterozygous* alleles with the genotype Ww. The phenotype of
white-flowerness results only from two homozygous alleles with the genotype ww. The alleles of
any given trait remain independent and will be segregated when new gametes form during meiosis.

Crossing a homozygous dominant rose plant with
red flowers (WW) with a homozygous recessive
rose plant with white flowers (ww) illustrates the
law. First generation offspring (F$_1$) are all heterozygous plants with red flowers (Ww) because all
received one of each allele from the parents' gametes. However, if two F$_1$ plants are crossed and
have four offspring (F$_2$), segregated alleles can
combine in a way that three offspring probably will
have red flowers and one will have white flowers,
in the 3:1 ratio shown above.

Mendel's Law of Independent Assortment

Mendel discovered another law of inheritance
while working with pea plants: different traits exist
independently of each other. If a trait is not expressed in one generation, it may be in another as
long as the allele for the trait exists.

Alleles for different traits are independently as-
sorted during meiosis and parceled out to the new
gametes. A gene for greenness of seed coat may or
may not be in a gamete with a gene for roundness
of a pea. However, a gene for greenness would
never be in a gamete with a gene for yellowness. A
Plunkett square, named after a British geneticist
who pioneered its use, shows the possible combinations that result from the independent assort-
ment of particular alleles. If a homozygous dominant plant having round, yellow peas (RRYY) is
crossed with a homozygous recessive plant having
wrinkled, green peas (rryy), the first generation
(F$_1$) offspring all will be heterozygotes and will
show the dominant phenotypes because of their
RrYy genotypes. But combinations of the different
traits will appear in the F$_2$ generation. Of 16 possible offspring from crossing two F$_1$ heterozygotes, 9
could have round, yellow peas (1 RYRY, 2 RYrY,
2 RYRy, 2 RyrY, 2 RYry); 3 could have round,
green peas (1 RyRy, 2 Ryry), 3 could have wrinkled, yellow peas (1 rYrY, 2 rYry); and 1 would
have wrinkled, green peas (rryy). The 9:3:3:1 ratio of predicted phenotypes is shown in the illustration above.

DNA—The "Ladder" of Heredity

The genes in chromosomes are strands of DNA. The genetic code that carries traits lies in the sequence of chemical groups in the DNA gene. The DNA molecule looks like a twisted ladder or a spiral staircase, which scientists call a *double helix*.

Each side of the molecule consists of an alternating chain of *deoxyribose* sugar and *phosphate* groups; that is, these chemical groups repeat themselves along the DNA molecule. Attached to each deoxyribose sugar molecule is a nitrogenous base molecule.

DNA contains four nitrogenous bases—*thymine* (T), *adenine* (A), *guanine* (G), and *cytosine* (C). The two chains of a DNA molecule are linked by complementary base pairs, the "steps" of the ladder. Complementary objects are connected together like a key in a lock. Adenine and guanine are chemically called purines; thymine and cytosine are pyrimidines. Purines complement pyrimidines. This means that adenine always pairs with thymine and guanine always pairs with cytosine in a DNA molecule. The A-T and G-C linkages are hydrogen bonds, fairly weak but still strong enough to hold together both chains of the DNA molecule. However, the ends can become "unzipped" and nearby bases can pair with complementary partners on the separated strand of DNA.

adenine

thymine

guanine

cytosine

phosphate

deoxyribose

How DNA Duplicates Itself

The DNA molecule is able to *replicate*, or make an exact copy of itself, because of its unique pairing of complementary bases. This important attribute enables it to pass on its genetic information to other DNA molecules.

Each new DNA contains the same sequence of deoxyribose sugar-phosphate group-nitrogenous base units, or *nucleotides*, as the parent molecule. As an example, assume that a DNA molecule has the following sequence of nine nucleotide pairs:

A-T T-A C-G G-C C-G T-A A-T C-G C-G. The nucleotide sequence on one side of the molecule would be: TAGCGATGG. The sequence on the other side would be: ATCGCTACC. Each nitrogenous base is linked with its complementary partner by hydrogen bonds. When those bonds break, the molecule becomes separated and "unzips." However, the bonding sites on the separated bases are now free to accept other complementary nucleotides to restore the molecule to its unbroken

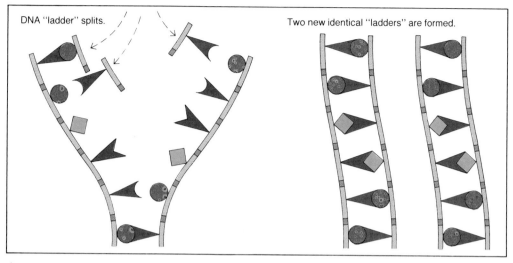

DNA "ladder" splits.

Two new identical "ladders" are formed.

form. Thus, both sides can form new molecules. As the TAGCGATGG side of the old molecule is free, nearby nucleotides attach to their complementary partners until the entire molecule is re-formed: A-T T-A C-G G-C C-G T-A A-T C-G C-G. This also happens with the other side of the old molecule, where ATCGCTACC becomes A-T T-A C-G G-C C-G T-A A-T C-G C-G also.

An original DNA molecule can be replicated with the same sequence of nucleotides for generation after generation, unless a *mutation* occurs to break the sequence of nucleotides. Groups of three nucleotides are called *codons*. The codon sequence in the DNA molecules of any particular living thing makes up its *genetic code*. From our prior example, the codons of the DNA molecule are: ATC GCT ACC. These codons are a *template*, or pattern, on which a nucleic acid called *ribonucleic acid* (RNA) is formed.

RNA transcribes the genetic code and carries it to special sites in the cell—ribosomes—where proteins are manufactured. Protein synthesis, or manufacture, is an extremely important cell activity. Proteins give form to many living things and are used in cell, tissue, and organ repair. Proteins are also important in the energy transactions of a cell. The catalysts that help chemical reactions in a cell are proteins. All proteins are made from basic building blocks called *amino acids*. The amino acids must be in a certain sequence for the making of any given protein. The amino-acid sequence is in an "order form" determined by the sequence of codons in the genetic code of an organism. A codon usually contains the instructions for the assembly of a specific amino acid in a protein molecule. However, some codons can call a halt to the assembly process.

How RNA Carries the Genetic Message

Ribonucleic acid (RNA) is similar to DNA. The RNA "backbone" has alternating sugar and phosphate groups like DNA. However, the RNA sugar is *ribose* instead of deoxyribose. Also, RNA contains a pyrimidine called *uracil* (U), in addition to adenine, guanine, and cytosine. Uracil is closely related to DNA's thymine, and the adenine nucleotide of DNA can combine with uracil as well as with thymine. This important ability allows RNA to be the "translator" of genetic information in the DNA molecule. RNA is usually a single-stranded

molecule, but it can pair complementary bases like DNA and thus assume a double-helix shape.

A typical cell contains two kinds of RNA—*messenger* RNA (mRNA) and *transfer* RNA (tRNA). The mRNA is made from a template, or pattern, of separated DNA strands. Free RNA nucleotides in the cell nucleus combine with complementary nucleotides on the "unzipped" DNA molecule and form strands of mRNA. These new molecules contain an altered transcription of the genetic code that will revert back into the original genetic mes-

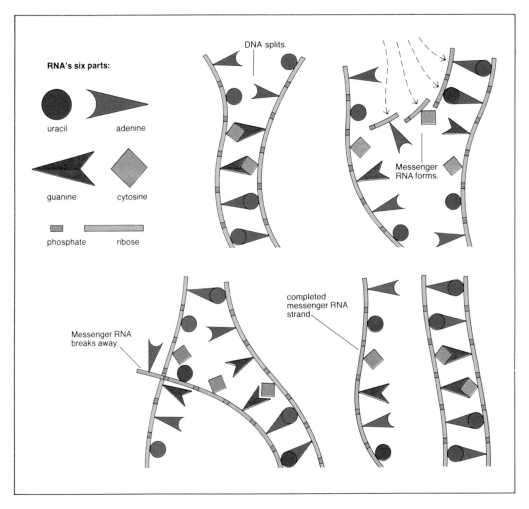

RNA's six parts:

uracil   adenine

guanine   cytosine

phosphate   ribose

DNA splits.

Messenger RNA forms.

completed messenger RNA strand

Messenger RNA breaks away.

sage during protein manufacture. For example, if the nucleotide sequence of a separated DNA strand is TAGCGATGG, the nucleotide sequence of the mRNA strand will be AUCGCUACC (the adenine of DNA links with uracil of RNA).

After completion of the code transcription, the mRNA strand breaks free from the DNA template, leaves the cell nucleus, and travels to *binding sites* on ribosomes in the cytoplasm. There, the mRNA strand acts as a template for the assembly of amino acids into "beginner" proteins called *peptides*. The tRNA molecules are extremely small. They consist of triplet nucleotides, like the codons of DNA.

Each tRNA triplet has an amino acid attached to it. As tRNA and its amino acid arrives at the ribosome's binding site, it temporarily links with its nucleotide complement on the mRNA strand lo-

cated there. If the nucleotide sequence of the mRNA molecule contains the message AUCGCUACC, then three tRNAs with the nucleotides TAG, CGA, and TGG would link one after the other with the mRNA and drop off their amino acids for assembly into a peptide. Thus, the original DNA message TAGCGATGG is restored and the peptide ordered by the DNA is made.

One of the nucleotide sequences of the mRNA strand calls a stop to the synthesis, and the newly made peptide or polypeptide (if long enough) breaks free and travels to wherever it is needed. The rule is as follows: one gene (DNA codon) orders the synthesis of only one kind of peptide. However, a given mRNA strand may contain many thousands of A, U, C, or G nucleotides, resulting in the synthesis of heavy, long-chained polypeptide molecules (proteins).

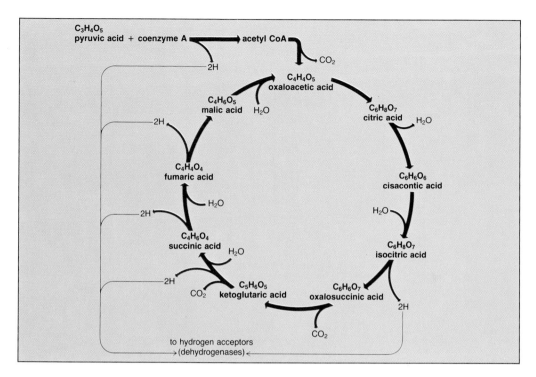

The Krebs Cycle—A Cell Energy Provider

The *Krebs cycle*, also called the *citric acid cycle*, is a series of chemical reactions that occur in all cells that require oxygen to live. It is an important part of *metabolism*, the process by which living things turn food into energy and living tissue.

The Krebs cycle begins with pyruvic acid and coenzyme A reacting to produce acetyl coA. In turn, acetyl coA acts on oxaloacetic acid to form citric acid. The cycle continues until its completion, when oxaloacetic acid is formed again and acetyl coA restarts the cycle. In short, what happens is that pyruvic acid is broken down into carbon dioxide molecules. Also, pairs of hydrogen atoms are transferred to a group of hydrogen-accepting coenzymes that are part of the *respiratory cycle*. ATP and water molecules are produced during the respiratory cycle. The coenzymes NAD (nicotinamide adenine dinucleotide) and FAD (flavin adenine dinucleotide) are oxidized in the process. Involved also are dehydrogenase and a chemical group called the cytochromes.

The oxidation-reduction reactions that result in ATP formation take place in the cell's "powerhouses"—the mitochondria. The process is called *oxidative phosphorylation*. Oxidative phosphorylation is responsible for energizing a host of cell activities, including the active transport of large molecules across the cell membrane. It also provides the energy needed for carbohydrate, fat, and protein synthesis.

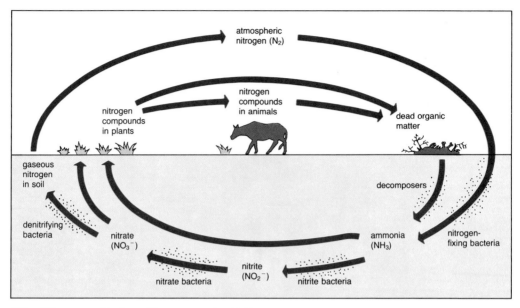

The Nitrogen Cycle—Necessary for Life

Nitrogen is one of the most important chemicals of life. All living things need nitrogen for protein construction. Nearly 80 per cent of the atmosphere is made of free nitrogen in gas form. But most living things cannot use nitrogen gas for protein synthesis. It must be combined with oxygen and other chemicals into nitrate compounds. Animals cannot use nitrogen compounds directly to manufacture proteins and must eat plants or other animals to get the necessary nitrogen.

In nature, free nitrogen is converted into usable nitrogen compounds by a cycle containing two processes—one requiring lightning energy and the other using a chemical conversion by certain bacteria. Lightning flashes combine nitrogen and oxygen gases into nitrogen dioxide, which then joins with the water in rainfall to form nitric acid. Soil chemicals react with the nitric acid to form nitrate compounds, which green plants take up through their roots and use for making proteins. Later, some animals eat the plants and use the plant protein for making animal protein. But the lightning method of making nitrates does not provide enough usable nitrogen to fulfill the needs of all living things. The conversion action of *nitrogen-fixing* bacteria provides the rest.

Some bacteria are able to *fix* nitrogen, or transform nitrogen gas in the air directly into the nitrates needed by the bacterial cells for their own protein manufacture. These bacteria live on the roots of legume plants, such as peas, clover, and alfalfa. The extra amounts of nitrates made by the nitrogen-fixing bacteria go into the soil, where they can be taken up by plant roots. When plants and animals die, decay bacteria break down body proteins and release ammonia, a gas that contains nitrogen and hydrogen. The ammonia that remains in the soil is changed into nitrite by *nitrifying* bacteria. Oxygen is then added to the nitrites by bacteria to form usable nitrates again. However, some of the body proteins during plant and animal decay are converted to nitrogen gas by *denitrifying* bacteria and released into the air for another turn of the nitrogen cycle.

2

Facts about Botany

Botany is a study of plant life. The plant kingdom is a very large part of the living world. More than 350,000 different kinds of plants exist. They range from tiny, one-celled plants, such as bacteria, to giant redwood trees. At the lowest level of the plant world, plants and animals are sometimes indistinguishable because some "plants" behave more like "animals." However, at more advanced levels, plants are clearly distinguished from animals.

A key characteristic of plants is the way that most plants get food. They make it directly from carbon dioxide and water by *photosynthesis*. The action of sun energy on plant chlorophyll makes possible the conversion of carbon dioxide and water into glucose, a food sugar. One of the by-products of plant photosynthesis is free oxygen, which helps maintain oxygen levels in the air. This is important for animals, too, because they also need oxygen for their life processes. However, not all plants are able to photosynthesize their food. Some are parasites, drawing their food directly from other organisms. Fungi are examples of parasites. They sometimes can be seen growing on decaying tree trunks. These fungi perform a valuable service by preventing the accumulation of dead matter. Bacteria are other examples of plant parasites. However, they can cause harmful diseases in animals and humans.

The plant kingdom is broken down into two major categories—*nonvascular* plants and *vascular* plants. Nonvascular plants lack the roots, stems, and leaves that characterize the vascular plants. Examples of nonvascular plants are algae, fungi, and mosses. Blue-green algae are the simplest plants and have been on earth the longest. Their fossils were found on 2-billion-year-old rocks. They can live in many places and even have been found in hot springs where temperatures reach 80°C (176°F.). The simplest nonvascular plants reproduce by simple cell division. The more complex ones have a two-stage life cycle. A gametophyte, or egg, stage is produced first, followed by a sporophyte stage, in which a stalk grows from the fertilized egg. Eventually, spores develop from the stalk tip and become the first steps in the next gametophyte stages. In the vascular plants, which are more advanced, the sporophyte stage is the main plant you commonly see—the leaves, stem, and roots. A vascular network of nutrient-carrying tubes allows food and liquids to spread throughout the plant. The roots can penetrate deep in soil to find moisture and soil chemicals needed for the plant's life processes. The stem can support many leaves, the "food factories" in which photosynthesis takes place, and thus helps increase the plant's likelihood for survival. Though important, the reproductive (gametophyte) parts of vascular plants are smaller than the main plant (sporophyte).

Vascular plants are divided into two major divisions— spore-bearers and seed plants. Ferns and other related plants reproduce by spores, which have life cycles that result in new plants. Seed plants have male (pollen) and female (egg) sex cells that produce fertilized seeds, which will grow into new plants. Seed plants are further divided into *gymnosperms* and *angiosperms*. Pines, spruces, and many other evergreen trees produce their pollen and seeds in cones. They rely on the wind to spread fertilized seeds through their range. Maples, elms, and other angiosperms produce their pollen and seeds in flowers. Although some angiosperms can fertilize themselves to produce seeds, those with flowers rely on insects to cross-pollinate flowers and produce seeds.

Seeds—Future Plants

Botanists classify angiosperms according to whether the plants produce *monocot* seeds or *dicot* seeds. All angiosperms produce seeds in the ovaries of their flowers. After the fertilization of an ovule, each seed develops a tiny embryo that will grow into a new plant. The seed leaves of plant embryos are called *cotyledons* (*cots*, for short). Some angiosperms produce seeds with a single cot (monocots) and others produce seeds with two cots (dicots). The corn kernel is an example of a monocot seed. The corn embryo is protected by a *seed coat,* or testa, that completely surrounds the seed contents. A *silk scar* on the coat marks the point where the pollen tube of the corn plant, or *silk,* penetrated the ovule to fertilize it with pollen.

The cotyledon will furnish the growing corn embryo with food from the starchy *endosperm* until it develops leaves and can produce its own food. The cotyledon also protects the *plumule,* the baby plant's first bud. The plumule will develop into the stem of the new plant. The *hypocotyl* is the future root of the new plant. Its tip, the radicle, is the first part of the baby plant to break out of the seed coat. The bean is an example of a dicot seed. It has two cotyledons, but is very similar to a monocot seed. The *hilum,* also part of the monocot seed, is a scar at the point where the ovule was attached to the parent plant's ovary. The *micropyle* is a tiny hole where the pollen tube entered the ovule and fertilized it. However, unlike the grassy monocots, the bean embryo will use up all its endosperm by the time the seed germinates.

Both monocot and dicot seedlings are further classified according to the positions of their cotyledons after germination. Those seedlings that show *epigeal* germination keep their cotyledons above the ground while developing. They are usually green and can perform photosynthesis right away. Those seedlings with *hypogeal* germination, such as corn, keep their cotyledons in the soil.

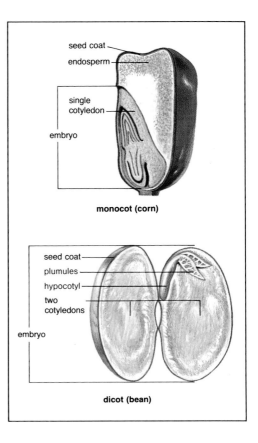

monocot (corn)

dicot (bean)

Flowers Form Seeds

The flower's male reproductive part is the *stamen*. It consists of an *anther* and a stalklike *filament*. Pollen grains are made and held in the *anther*. A number of stamens usually circle the flower's female reproductive part, the *pistil*. The pistil consists of a topmost *stigma* connected by the *style* to the vase-shaped *ovary*. When pollen grains are ripe, they are released from the anthers and caught by the sticky stigma.

Insects attracted to the flower help move pollen to the stigma. Each pollen grain then sends a pollen tube through the style and into an ovule in the ovary. Plant sperm cells in the pollen tubes fertilize the ovules, and seeds begin to develop.

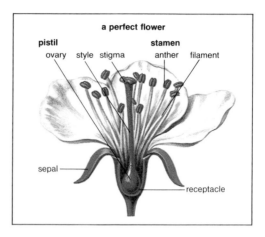

a perfect flower

pistil — ovary   style   stigma

stamen — anther   filament

sepal

receptacle

Kinds of Roots

The root is one of the first parts of a plant to start to grow. A *primary root* develops from a plant's seed. It quickly produces branches, or *secondary roots*. The *root cap* at the tip of each root protects the delicate tip of the root as it pushes through the soil. Roots draw in water and dissolved minerals from the soil. These materials are transported to the leaves by the stem's vascular system to provide the raw materials of plant growth. The root contains many *root hairs* in back of the *root tip*. Water absorbed by the root hairs is conducted upward by osmosis. Osmotic pressure pushes the water molecules in the soil upward through the plant, in order to replace the water vapor lost from the leaves by transpiration.

Two kinds of roots are illustrated— *fibrous* and *taproot*. Fibrous roots are stringy and pierce the upper soil in many directions to extract a maximum amount of water. Taproots store food in addition to providing anchorage.

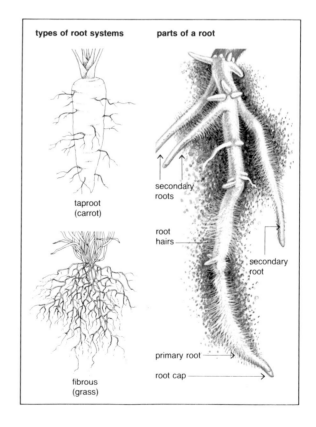

types of root systems

parts of a root

taproot (carrot)

fibrous (grass)

secondary roots

root hairs

secondary root

primary root

root cap

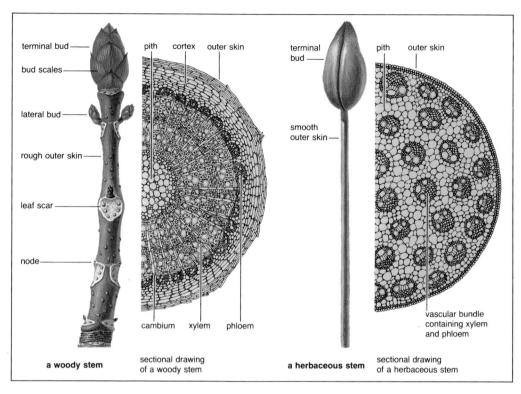

terminal bud — / bud scales — / lateral bud — / rough outer skin — / leaf scar — / node — / pith / cortex / outer skin / cambium / xylem / phloem / terminal bud — / smooth outer skin — / pith / outer skin / vascular bundle containing xylem and phloem

a woody stem — sectional drawing of a woody stem — **a herbaceous stem** — sectional drawing of a herbaceous stem

Stems Support Plants

The stems of plants support the flowers and leaves. Stems hold these parts up to the air and sunlight for photosynthesis. Stems also conduct water and minerals from the roots to the leaves, where they are used for food manufacture. After food is made, the stem carries the sugary *sap* throughout the plant. Cells that carry water upward make up the stem's *xylem* tissue. Cells that carry sap make up the *phloem* tissue.

Depending on the species of plant, a stem may be large or small. The stem of an oak tree, for example, consists of the trunk, branches, and twigs. By contrast, the stems of a cabbage or lettuce plant are so short that the plants seem stemless. The stems of still other plants, such as the potato, are not apparent because they grow underground. Stems that grow underground are called *subterranean stems;* those that grow above ground are *aerial stems.* Aerial stems are either *woody* or *herbaceous.*

Dicots produce woody stems, and monocots produce herbaceous stems. Woody stems have a rough, brown skin. A *terminal bud* is at the topmost portion. When this bud grows, the plant grows taller. Leaflike *bud scales* protect the terminal bud and the *lateral buds* that grow from *nodes* on the stem. Lateral buds will grow either into branches or into flowers or leaves. The *leaf scar* is where a leaf petiole has separated from the stem.

A microscopic view of a cross section of a woody stem would reveal many vascular bundles of cells contained in the *cortex* under the outer skin. The cortex is comprised of woody xylem and phloem. The *cambium* is the narrow layer where xylem and phloem cells are made. New cells grow from the cambium each year. These annual rings can be seen in crosscut stems. Pith cells store food. They are in the center of woody stems. A herbaceous stem has a different arrangement. It has a smooth, green skin and has very little xylem. A crosscut view reveals many vascular bundles occurring randomly through the stem. The bundles consist of xylem and phloem. They are separated by pith.

Makeup of a Flowering Plant

Flowering plants are the most common members of the plant world. Each flowering plant contains four main parts—the roots, stems, leaves, and flowers. Roots, stems, and leaves are called the *vegetative* parts of the plant. Flowers and their fruits and seeds are the *reproductive* parts.

The flowers develop the seeds that will allow the plant to reproduce and continue its line in the plant kingdom. The seeds are enclosed in *fruits* that develop after the female parts of the flower have been fertilized by pollen, the male sex cells of plants. Each part of a flowering plant is the result of adaptation over millions of years. the first plants were tiny, one-celled organisms capable of making their own food by photosynthesis. Eventually, communities of cells arose that were better able to cope with changing conditions of the environment by banding together into many-celled organisms. The functions of these cells in the organism became increasingly specialized—some cells becoming solely involved in reproduction activities, others developing into tissues concerned with transporting food raw materials and with food storage, and still others concentrating on the important job of food making.

Plant propagation is the responsibility of the plant's reproductive parts. When pollen is wind-blown or carried by insects from the flower's anthers to its stigma, the sticky, sugary surface of the stigma causes the pollen to germinate. A pollen tube develops and grows through the stigma and style to the ovary. In the ovary, the pollen tube penetrates an ovule, and one of the sperm cells in the tube fertilizes the egg in the ovule's *embryonic sac*. This fertilized cell will eventually develop into a new plant through a series of mitotic cell divisions that will result in different plant tissues. Another sperm cell in the pollen tube fuses with *polar nuclei* given off during meiotic cell division in the ovary and produces endosperm tissue. The endosperm will nourish the embryonic plant until it can produce food on its own.

After the ovules of a flowering plant are fertilized, they develop into seeds and the ovary becomes a fruit that encloses the seeds. Having fruit is a way the plant can scatter its seeds over a wide area. When an animal eats the fruit, the seeds are deposited in the animal's solid wastes wherever the animal flies or roams. Some seeds rely so heavily on animals that the seeds cannot germinate unless softened during animal digestion.

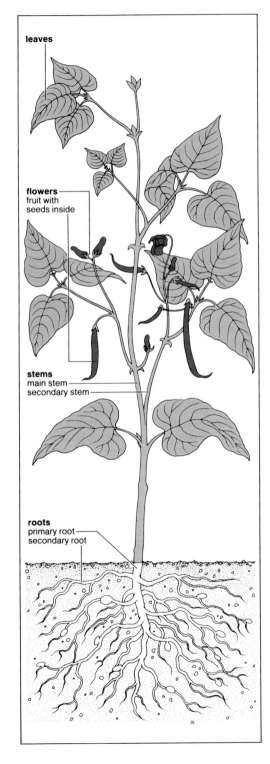

leaves

flowers
fruit with
seeds inside

stems
main stem
secondary stem

roots
primary root
secondary root

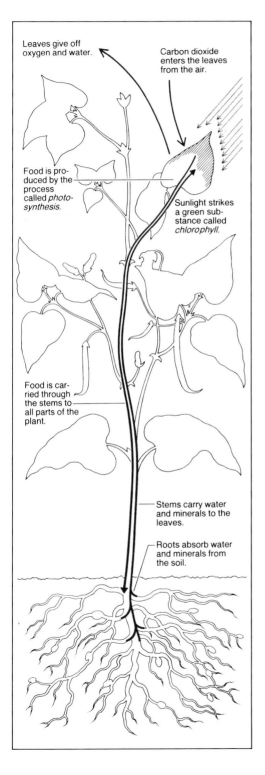

Leaves give off oxygen and water.

Carbon dioxide enters the leaves from the air.

Food is produced by the process called *photosynthesis.*

Sunlight strikes a green substance called *chlorophyll.*

Food is carried through the stems to all parts of the plant.

Stems carry water and minerals to the leaves.

Roots absorb water and minerals from the soil.

Photosynthesis—How a Green Plant Makes Food

Photosynthesis is the process by which green plants make food. The term *photosynthesis* comes from Greek words meaning "light" *(photo)* and "put together" *(synthesis).* Light energy puts together carbon dioxide and water into glucose—a sugar used by the plant for food. Carbon dioxide in the air enters the leaves through the stomata on their undersides. Water is absorbed by the plant roots from the soil and conducted to the leaves through the stem's vascular system. After glucose is made, it is transported to all the plant cells, where it is *oxidized,* or burned, for the energy needed for their life processes.

The oxidative process, called *respiration,* requires oxygen. So, a plant both gives off and takes in oxygen. The atmospheric amount of carbon dioxide and oxygen is kept in balance because more carbon dioxide is used by plants during the day when they photosynthesize food, and more oxygen is used during the night for the ongoing task of cell respiration.

Photosynthesis always requires a chlorophyll pigment, chlorophyll *a* or chlorophyll *b* being the most common. Chlorophyll *a* has a blue-green color; chlorophyll *b* is yellow-green. The chlorophyll molecule absorbs wavelengths of light and transfers the light energy into chemical energy. The chlorophyll molecules are contained in chloroplasts in the leaf or stem. A large number of chloroplasts are located near the upper surface of the leaf, where their chlorophyll molecules can be stimulated by sunlight. For example, a 1-millimeter-square section of leaf contains some 400,000 chloroplasts. Chlorophyll and sunlight will break down six molecules of carbon dioxide (CO_2) and six molecules of water (H_2O) into one molecule of glucose $(C_6H_{12}O_6)$ and six molecules of oxygen gas (O_2). This is chemically written as: $6\ CO_2 + 6\ H_2O \xrightarrow{\text{sunlight}} C_6H_{12}O_6 + 6\ O_2 \uparrow$. Respiration in the plant cells is the reverse of photosynthesis. Glucose combines with oxygen to form carbon dioxide and water. The chemical equation for respiration is: $C_6H_{12}O_6 + 6\ O_2 \rightarrow 6\ H_2O \uparrow + 6\ CO_2 \uparrow$.

Although a green plant constantly undergoes photosynthesis during the day, not all the glucose is used for instant food. Some is changed into other sugars, or converted into starch and fats for storage, or changed into cellulose—the stiffening material for plant cell walls.

Where Photosynthesis Takes Place

Under a microscope, a section of a leaf reveals the structures involved in photosynthesis and food transportation. Two kinds of cells contain chlorophyll—the green pigment of photosynthesis. They are column-shaped *palisade cells* located under the upper epidermis and the irregular *spongy cells* between the palisade cells and the lower epidermis. Water and minerals are carried to the food-making cells by the xylem tissue of the leaf veins.

The palisade and spongy cells contain chloroplasts, structures bearing the light-energy-absorbing chlorophyll. The glucose made in the chloroplasts is carried away to other parts of the plant through the phloem tissue.

Stomata are scattered throughout the lower epidermis. Each stoma contains *guard cells* that circle the stoma pore. They regulate the amount of carbon dioxide taken in and the amount of oxygen and water vapor released through the pores. The guard cells regulate the amount of gases and moisture passing through the pores.

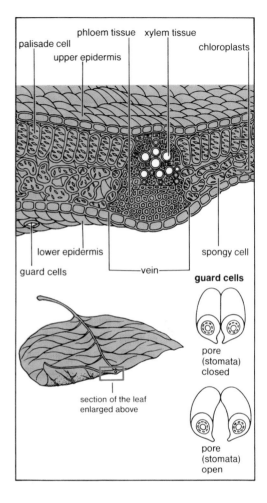

section of the leaf
enlarged above

Leaf—A Plant Food Factory

Leaves have the important job of making plant food. Each leaf is divided into two main parts—the *petiole* and the *blade*. The base of the petiole is wider than the rest of the leaf stem and holds the leaf firmly to the plant stem. Some petioles have *stipules,* tiny leaflike structures that help provide food for the plant. The blade consists of an *epidermis,* or outer cover, that encloses a network of veins and a spongy inner area that contains chlorophyll cells. Water needed for photosynthesis is carried through the plant and into a leaf through the petiole. The water then moves through the veins to the "factory" areas of chlorophyll cells.

When light strikes a leaf, it filters through the upper epidermis and floods the cells below. A number of pores, called *stomata,* pierce the epidermis of the leaf's underside. Stomata are valves. They let in air containing the carbon dioxide needed for photosynthesis, and they let out oxygen waste and water vapor. Stomata usually open during the day and close at night, when the plant rests and requires less carbon dioxide.

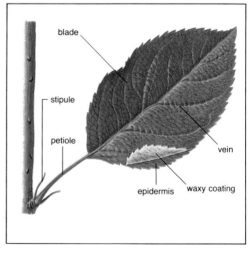

From Seed to Grown Plant

The seed of a green plant *germinates,* or sprouts into a new plant, when it gets the proper amount of moisture, oxygen, and warmth. Moisture softens the seed coat and allows the embryonic plant parts to break through. Oxygen is needed for cell respiration and growth during germination. In most places, seeds lay dormant over the winter and sprout in spring. Scientists have determined that the best temperature range for germination is between 18°C (65°F.) and 29°C (85°F.).

Prior to germination, all the embryonic plant parts are held in by the seed coat. As the seed coat softens and splits, the *hypocotyl* emerges and forms the primary root. The *epicotyl* grows upward and begins to form the plant stem. After the stem breaks through the soil, the *cotyledons* open and free the *plumule.*

Cotyledons provide food for the seedling until it can make its own. As the stem grows upward toward the sunlight, the plumule develops into the first leaves, which begin to make plant food by photosynthesis.

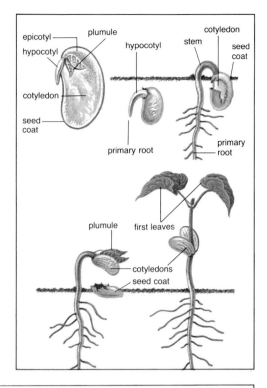

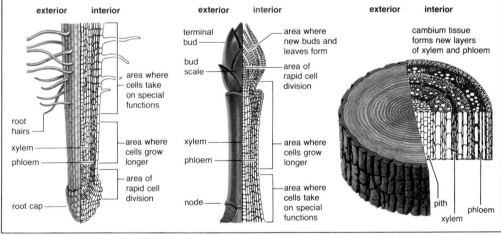

How a Plant Grows Larger

Plants grow rapidly at the tips of their roots and stems. There, the cells undergo rapid mitotic divisions and push deeper into the soil or higher into the air. Cells behind the rapidly dividing ones grow longer because of auxin growth hormones.

Farther back within the plant, cells develop into specialized tissues and structures. Trees and many other plants grow wider because of a ringlike area of cell division below the bark called cambium. Each year, cambium cells lay down new xylem and phloem tissues in the roots and stems.

The root tip is protected by a tough root cap. When encountering a hard object, the root cap "tells" cells behind it to move in another direction.

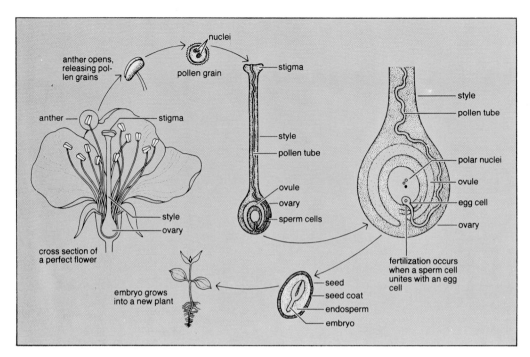

How Flowering Plants Reproduce

The flower is the reproductive structure of angio-
sperm plants. A flower is a short branch of a stem
containing specialized sex parts. The anthers of the
flower break open and release pollen, the male sex
cells. Pollen grains contain high-energy fats and are
surrounded by a tough covering, permitting pollen
to survive even after being blown many miles from
a plant. When pollen falls on the sticky stigma of a
flower, it sends a pollen tube through the style.
The tube carries sperm cells, one of which will fertilize an egg in the ovary and produce a seed. The
other sperm cell will fertilize the polar nuclei, and
the result will be nutrient endosperm for the seed.
This double fertilization is unique to angiosperms.
After germination, the seed will develop into a new
plant.

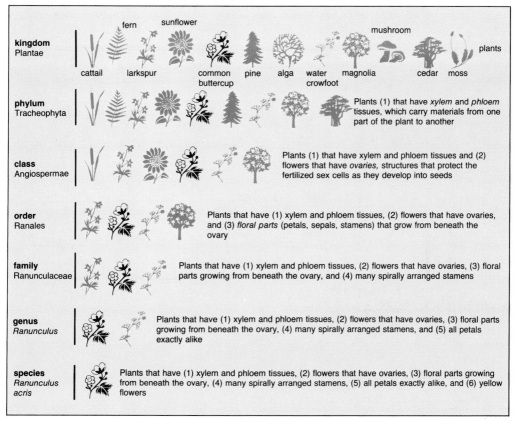

The Plant Kingdom

Most plants and animals have common names in all languages of the world. But if scientists did not have a working knowledge of all these languages, they would have a difficult time discussing or writing about living things by common names. As a result, an international committee of scientists has formulated a Latin scientific name for every living thing. For example, the scientific name of a tea rose is *Rosa odorata*. *Rosa* is the name of the *genus*, or group, to which the plant belongs; *odorata* is the *species*, or individual name.

The generic and specific names are always given together. This is called the binomial (two-name) nomenclature system of classifying living things. It was devised by Carolus Linnaeus, an 18th century Swedish botanist.

All living things are ordinarily classified in seven major groups. Each descending rank narrows the classification of the plant of animal. The groups are: (1) kingdom, (2) phylum (plural: phyla), (3) class, (4) order, (5) family, (6) genus, and (7) species.

The plant kingdom *Plantae* is divided into 10 phyla. All plants with vascular tissues belong to the phylum *Tracheophyta*. All tracheophytes with flowers are in the class *Angiospermae*. Angiosperms with floral parts beneath the plant ovary belong to the order *Ranales*. If the stamens of these plants occur in spirals, they belong to the family *Ranunculaceae*. If members of this family have petals that are exactly alike, they belong to the genus *Ranunculus*. Any member of this genus having yellow flower petals is *Ranunculus acris*, a flower that you commonly call a "buttercup."

3

Facts about Zoology

Zoology is the study of animals. There is an enormous number of animals on earth, about a million species. Unlike most plants, animals are *heterotrophs;* they must get food energy from plants or from other animals that they eat. Animals live nearly everywhere on earth—in the oceans, on land, in trees. Some attach themselves to underwater rocks and never budge from the site; others run or fly great distances. Animals have a wide variety of body forms and structures. A paramecium consists only of a single, specialized cell. A whale, the largest kind of animal, contains millions of cells.

Basically, animals are divided into *invertebrates,* or animals without backbones, and *vertebrates,* or animals with backbones. Ninety-five per cent of all animals are invertebrates. Some of them are simple animals, such as sponges. Jellyfish and sea anemones are more advanced than sponges because they contain two kinds of basic tissue, an inner *endoderm* that lines the digestive cavity and an outer *ectoderm* that covers the body. Planarians are still more advanced, having a third, bulky tissue called *mesoderm.*

The largest phylum of animals consists of the arthropods, a group that includes insects, shellfish, and spiders. Three out of four animal species are arthropods. Vertebrate animals have protected spinal cords. The great classes of vertebrates are fish, amphibians, reptiles, birds, and mammals. The first three are cold-blooded; birds and mammals are warm-blooded and have heat regulators to help them survive drastic temperature changes.

How Invertebrates and Vertebrates Differ

The nerve network in the bodies of many kinds of animals helps them respond to changes in the *environment*, or surroundings. Nerves with incoming messages about conditions in the environment are called *sensory* nerves. Nerves with outgoing messages telling the body how to react to environmental changes are called *motor* nerves. Sensory and motor nerves in some kinds of animals are contained in a main nerve called the *spinal cord*.

Invertebrate animals, such as the centipede, lack a protective backbone around the main nerve. The invertebrate's main nerve usually lies unprotected near the *ventral*, or belly, part of the body, as shown in the diagram (the simplest invertebrates do not have a main nerve). Invertebrates include amebas, sponges, starfish, mollusks, and insects. Invertebrates are commonly known as *lower animals*.

Vertebrates, animals with backbones, are *higher animals*. The main nerve of a vertebrate is located near the *dorsal*, or back, part of the body. The main nerve of vertebrates is protected by a bony enclosure, as illustrated. Vertebrates include fishes, amphibians, reptiles, birds, and mammals. A small marine animal called amphioxus has a *notochord*, a rod of cartilage that serves as a backbone and partly protects the main nerve. The amphioxus is regarded as the link between the lower and higher animals. A notochord is present in the embryos of all vertebrates. However, as the embryos of the higher vertebrates develop, the notochord cartilage is replaced by bone, and *vertebra*, or bony segments, develop around the spinal cord.

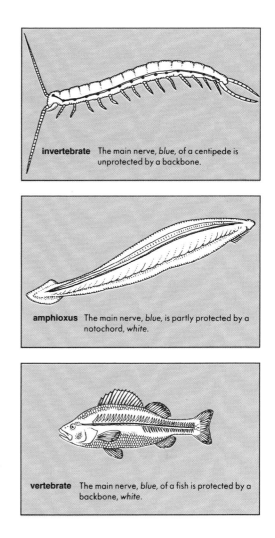

invertebrate   The main nerve, *blue*, of a centipede is unprotected by a backbone.

amphioxus   The main nerve, *blue*, is partly protected by a notochord, *white*.

vertebrate   The main nerve, *blue*, of a fish is protected by a backbone, *white*.

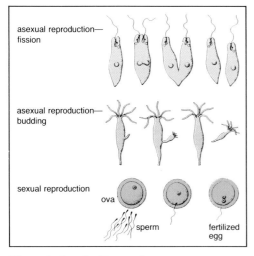

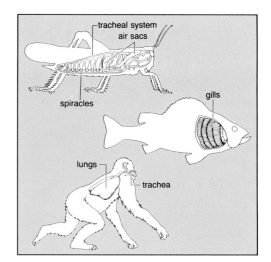

How Animals Reproduce

All species of animals *reproduce,* or make more of their kind. Offspring are formed by one of two ways—asexual reproduction or sexual reproduction. *Asexual reproduction* requires only one parent to produce offspring. *Sexual reproduction* requires a male and a female parent. Many of the simplest animals usually reproduce asexually. These include protozoans, sponges, jellyfish, and sea squirts. But they sometimes reproduce sexually. Most other animals reproduce only sexually.

One kind of asexual reproduction involves division of the parent into two new organisms. Planarians reproduce in this way. Some sponges and hydra reproduce asexually by budding. Small projections, or buds, grow from the side of the parent's body. Some of the buds develop their own feeding organs, and then break off from the parent as individuals.

Animals that reproduce only sexually have special sex cells to produce their young. Female sex cells are called *eggs,* or *ova*. Male sex cells are called *sperm*. In the process of fertilization, a sperm unites with an egg, and the resulting *zygote* develops into a new individual. Some animals that reproduce sexually never meet their mates. For example, sea urchins release millions of eggs or sperm in the ocean for random fertilization. Some sperm cells eventually drift to the egg cells and fertilize them.

Most kinds of animals that reproduce sexually require mating. By a variety of attracting methods, including sounds and scents, male and female animals come together in order to allow the sperm cells to fertilize the egg cells.

How Different Animals Breathe

Oxygen is essential for animal life. Land animals take in oxygen from the air. Water animals get their oxygen from dissolved gases in the water. Each type of animal has special respiratory organs used for oxygen intake. A few animal species live where oxygen is not freely available. These animals, which include tapeworms and other parasites, live in intestinal organs and take in oxygen from the host's food.

Insects, the most common invertebrates, take in oxygen through air tubes called *tracheae*. *Spiracles,* or pores, on the outside of the insect body are connected to a tracheal air system. Body muscles pump in oxygen through the pores. The tracheal system distributes oxygen throughout the insect body. Carbon dioxide, the waste product of respiration, is pumped out through the spiracles.

Vertebrate animals ordinarily breathe with gills if they live in water or with lungs if they live on land. A fish gulps water and passes it over the thin tissues of its gills. The oxygen dissolved in water becomes absorbed by gill tissue (the oxygen concentration in water is *higher* than in the gills), and carbon dioxide in the gills passes into the water (the carbon dioxide concentration in water is *lower* than in the gills). The gulped water is forced out through the gill openings.

The bodies of land vertebrates develop pressure changes to bring oxygen into the lungs. Warm-blooded animals—birds and mammals—need much oxygen because their bodies use considerable energy to control temperature. Air with oxygen is inhaled into the lungs through the *trachea* and then exhaled.

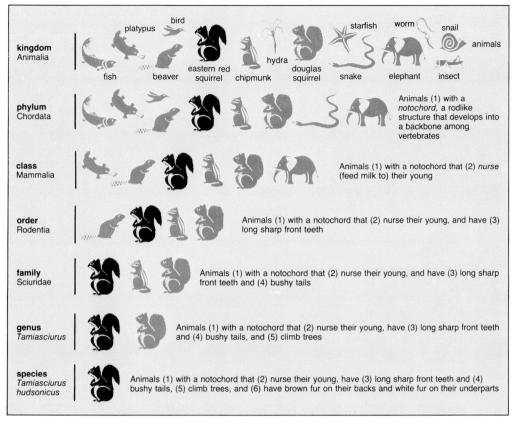

| kingdom Animalia | | |
| class Mammalia | | |

The Animal Kingdom

Most plants and animals have common names in all languages of the world. But if scientists did not have a working knowledge of all these languages, they would have a difficult time discussing or writing about living things by common names. As a result, an international committee of scientists has formulated a Latin scientific name for every living thing. For example, the scientific name of a bottle-nosed dolphin is *Tursiops truncatus. Tursiops* is the name of the *genus,* or group, to which the animal belongs; *truncatus* is the *species,* or individual name.

The generic and specific names are always given together. This is called the binomial (two-name) nomenclature system of classifying living things. It was devised by Carolus Linnaeus, an 18th century Swedish botanist.

All living things are ordinarily classified in seven major groups. Each descending rank narrows the classification of the plant or animal. The groups are: (1) kingdom, (2) phylum (plural: phyla), (3) class, (4) order, (5) family, (6) genus, and (7) species.

The animal kingdom *Animalia* is divided into 26 phyla. All animals with a notochord belong to the phylum *Chordata.* All chordates that nurse their young are in the class *Mammalia.* Mammals that have long, sharp front teeth belong to the order *Rodentia.* If these rodents have bushy tails, they belong to the family *Sciuridae.* If members of this family climb trees, they belong to the genus *Tamiasciurus.* Any member of this genus having brown fur on its back and white fur on its underparts is of the species *Tamiasciurus hudsonicus,* commonly called an Eastern red squirrel.

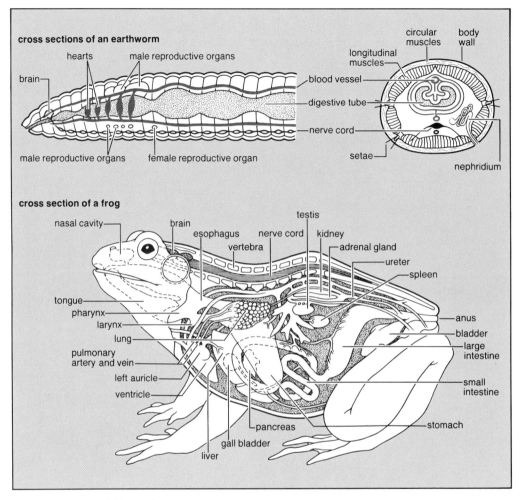

cross sections of an earthworm

hearts   male reproductive organs

brain

circular muscles   body wall

longitudinal muscles

blood vessel

digestive tube

nerve cord

male reproductive organs   female reproductive organ

setae

nephridium

cross section of a frog

nasal cavity   brain   testis

esophagus   nerve cord   kidney

vertebra   adrenal gland

ureter

spleen

tongue

pharynx   anus

larynx   bladder

lung   large intestine

pulmonary artery and vein

left auricle   small intestine

ventricle

pancreas   stomach

gall bladder

liver

Earthworm and Frog Anatomy

The earthworm, an annelid worm, and the frog, an amphibian, are commonly dissected in classrooms to study their internal anatomy.

The earthworm body is divided into a number of segments. A lengthwise cut of the body wall reveals the internal organs in the segments. In the forward part of the body are the earthworm's five hearts, which pump blood between the dorsal (top) and ventral (bottom) blood vessels. The digestive tube spans the entire body. The nerve cord, an extension of the brain, runs along the ventral part of the body cavity. A cross-cut of a segment reveals the longitudinal and circular muscles used by the worm to crawl. In addition to digestive tube, blood vessels, and nerve cord, *setae* and *nephridia* are exposed. Setae are bristles that prevent the worm

from slipping. A nephridium removes waste products from the bloodstream and excretes them through one of many excretory tubules.

The internal anatomy of the more complex frog is best studied system by system. The *circulatory system* includes the heart, arteries, and veins. The *respiratory system* includes the skin, nose, pharynx, and lungs. The *digestive system* includes the mouth, stomach, intestines, and liver. The *excretory system* includes the skin, kidneys, and bladder. The *nervous system* includes the brain, spinal cord, nerves, and sense organs. The *endocrine system* includes the pituitary, thyroid and adrenal glands, and the pancreas and sex organs. The *reproductive system* includes the sex organs and their ducts, or outlet tubes.

4

Facts about the
Human Body

Human physiology deals with the manner in which the various systems of the human body work to maintain life. Some body activities go on unnoticed by us because they are not controlled on a conscious, or aware, level. Food digestion is an example. But we are quite aware of other body events, such as a toothache or the hunger pains resulting from an empty stomach.

All the body structures play some role in either getting energy from food, using that energy for cell respiration, nerve impulse energy, or muscle contraction energy, or for the generation of offspring. The skeletal and muscle systems support the body and make it move. The respiratory system maintains normal breathing so that vital oxygen is continually inhaled and carbon dioxide is exhaled. The digestive system breaks down food into its basic chemical parts, which then can be carried by the circulatory system to all body cells for energy uses. An endocrine system of hormones—chemical messengers—starts and stops many body activities at the correct time. The urinary system removes poisonous wastes from the bloodstream and excretes them from the body. The reproductive system, which is closely related to the urinary system in the body, and which is primarily under the control of hormones, prepares the stage for producing human offspring. All of these systems are under the control of the nervous system and its chief organ—the brain.

When the body systems are not operating in tune, illness results. Malfunction of the body can result from bacterial or viral invasion, lack of proper food or other nutrients, or inherited body errors. However, medical and nutritional steps can correct most of these situations. Preventive medicine is a field that attempts to maintain healthy bodies by teaching persons about how the body operates and what it needs for health.

Table of Facts about the Body

Your body is an amazing complex of parts coordinated in a way that allows it to function as a healthy unit. The facts in this table are only a few of the facets of the human body. All weights and volumes are average figures for adults. Some figures are slightly lower for females because the data is based on body weight and females ordinarily weigh less than males.

Total number of bones—206.

Number of vertebrae—26 in all (7 cervical, 12 thoracic, 5 lumbar, 1 sacral [made of 5 fused bones], and 1 coccygeal [made of 4 fused bones]).

Total volume of blood—about 5 qts. (about 5 l) in a 155-lb. (70-kg) person.

Number of cells in one cubic millimeter of blood:
Red blood cells (erythrocytes)—4.5 million–5.5 million.
White blood cells (leucocytes)—6,000–10,000.
Platelets (thrombocytes)—200,000–800,000.

Total volume of body water—65% of male body weight; 55% of female body weight.

Normal body temperature—98.6° F. (37° C).

Weight of the human heart—about 11 oz. (310 g) in males; about 9 oz. (255 g) in females.

Average number of heartbeats per minute—72 (the heart will beat about 3 billion times in a 70-year period).

Weight of the human brain—about 50 oz. (1,400 g) in males; about 45 oz. (1,260 g) in females.

Length of the small and large intestines—28 ft. (8.5 m)

Daily weight of sweat secreted from the skin—24.5-31.5 oz. (700-900 g).

The Heart Pumps Blood

The heart has four chambers—*right atrium, left atrium, right ventricle,* and *left ventricle.* The ventricles are separated by a thick *septum.* The atria are separated from the ventricles by valves. Once blood moves from the atria to the ventricles, the valves prevent it from backing into the atria. This is also true of the valves in the pulmonary artery and the aorta.

Each heartbeat has two stages—a relaxation stage (diastole) and a contraction (systole). During the first part of the relaxation stage, deoxygenated blood from the body enters the right atrium from the inferior and superior venae cavae. At the same time, oxygenated blood from the lungs enters the left atrium from the pulmonary veins. As the atria fill, the *tricuspid* and *mitral valves* open, allowing blood into both ventricles. An electrical wave from the heart's pacemaker in the right atrium causes the ventricles to contract. Blood in the right ventricle pushes open the *pulmonary semilunar valve* and moves through the pulmonary artery to the lungs for oxygenation. At the same time, blood in the left ventricle pushes open the *aortic semilunar valve* and moves into the aorta for distribution throughout the body.

Like other muscles, the heart needs blood with food and oxygen, and it requires removal of waste products. The *coronary* arteries and veins provide for this crucial blood circulation to the heart.

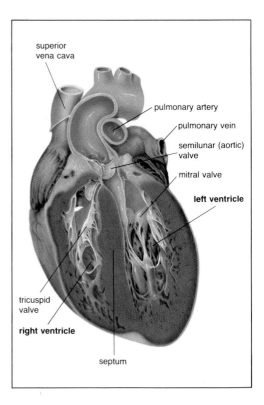

superior vena cava

pulmonary artery

pulmonary vein

semilunar (aortic) valve

mitral valve

left ventricle

tricuspid valve

right ventricle

septum

The Male Reproductive System

The male reproductive system shares many of its parts with the urinary system that removes liquid wastes from the body. The primary male reproductive organ is the *testicle*, or testis. Each of the two testes contains many tiny tubes in which sperm cells develop.

The testicles are suspended from the body in a saclike *scrotum*. Suspension in the scrotum keeps the sperm in the testicles away from the destructive heat of the abdominal cavity. Accessory reproductive structures transport the sperm cells out of storage sites on top of the testicles during the process of *ejaculation*.

The *penis* consists of spongy tissue around the urethra, a tube between the *urinary bladder* and the end of the penis. When the bladder becomes filled, voluntary muscles in the penis can relax and permit a flow of urine. Each *vas deferens*, one of a pair of tubes from the testicles, connects with the urethra. An involved process of stimulation allows blood to engorge the spongy tissue of the penis, causing it to become erect. Before ejaculation, sperm cells are mixed with lubricating secretions of the *seminal vesicles, prostate*, and other glands, resulting in a fluid called *semen*. During ejaculation, the semen is discharged from the penis.

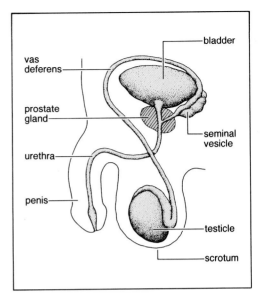

The Female Reproductive System

Inside the female body, *ovaries*—the primary female reproductive organs—produce *ova*, or eggs. Accessory reproductive organs in a female help move an egg to a place where it can be fertilized by a male sperm or harbor the developing human embryo when fertilization occurs and pregnancy begins.

The monthly cycle of egg release, pregnancy preparation, and uterine tissue breakdown if pregnancy does not occur is called the *menstrual cycle*. It usually lasts 28 days. Hormones from the brain start the menstrual cycle by triggering development of a *follicle* in an ovary. The ripening follicle releases its own hormones, called *estrogens*, which thicken the lining of the uterus and develop a rich blood supply in readiness for harboring a fertilized egg. At about the 14th day of the menstrual cycle, *ovulation* occurs. An egg is released from an ovary, captured by the fingery end of a *Fallopian tube*, and transported through the tube to the uterus. If sperm are in the tube, one of them will probably fertilize the egg. But if the egg is not fertilized, it dies within 12 hours and passes out of

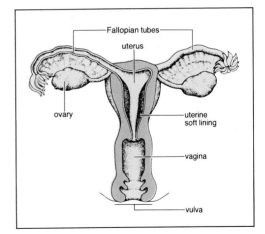

the body. The uterine lining will then be sloughed off at the end of the cycle, and discharged from the body through the *vagina* and past the *vulva*. However, if fertilization takes place, the developing embryo will implant or attach itself to the uterine lining, and a baby will grow in the uterus until it is born nine months later.

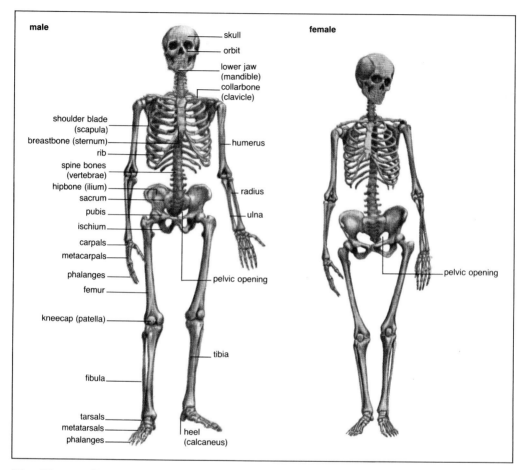

The Human Skeleton Gives Support

The skeleton is the framework of the human body. Its hard, strong, calcium-containing bones are connected by tough cords called *ligaments*. The bony framework is divided into two components—the *axial* skeleton and the *appendicular* skeleton. The *axial skeleton* includes the skull, rib cage, and the vertebral column. The *appendicular skeleton* comprises the body limbs.

Enclosing the brain, the skull consists of close-fitting bones. It has two main parts—the *cranium* and the *face*. The cranium has eight bones—*frontal*, two *temporals*, two *parietals*, *occipital*, *sphenoid*, and *ethmoid*. The 14 bones of the face include the two *maxillae* (upper jaw) and the hinged *mandible* (lower jaw), the largest bones of the face. The other facial bones include the *palatine* (forming the back of the mouth roof), the *nasal* (nose bone), and the *zygomatics* (cheekbones).

The *vertebral column,* or backbone, contains 26 bones (33 in the embryo but 9 bones fuse into 2 bones in development). The seven *cervical* vertebrae form the neck. The first cervical vertebra is the *atlas;* it supports the skull and pivots with the second cervical vertebra, the *axis.* The 12 *thoracic* vertebrae have ribs attached to them. The first seven pairs of ribs connect directly to the *sternum,* or breastbone. The next three pairs are joined to the ribs directly above them by cartilage. The last two pairs of ribs, called *floating ribs,* are unattached to any other. Five *lumbar* vertebrae connect the upper body with the lower body. Linking the two bony portions of the hips is the *sacrum,* made of 5 fused bones. The *coccyx,* or tailbone, is made of 4 fused bones.

The upper appendicular skeleton consists of the *pectoral girdle,* or shoulder, and the arm and hand bones suspended from it. The pectoral girdle consists of two *scapulae,* or shoulder blades, and two *clavicles,* or collarbones. The head of the *humerus,* or upper arm bone, fits into a socket under the *coracoid process* of the scapula. This ball-and-socket hinge allows the arm to have a wide range of motion. The *radius* and *ulna* are the two forearm bones. Their overlapping ends give the forearm its distinctive rotation. The eight carpal bones constitute the wrist. The five *metacarpals* form the hand and lower thumb. Fourteen *phalanges* make up the fingers and the thumb.

The lower appendicular skeleton consists of the *pelvic girdle* and the lower limb bones attached to it. The pelvic girdle consists of two hipbones formed from three fused bones (in adults)—the *ilium, ischium,* and *pubis.* The head of the *femur,* or thighbone, fits into a socket in the hipbone. The *tibia* and *fibula* are two bones that make up the lower leg. The tibia, or shinbone, is linked with the femur by a swinging joint, capped by a kneebone called the *patella.* Seven *tarsal* bones make up the ankle. The *calcaneus,* largest of the tarsals, forms the heel of the foot. Five *metatarsal* bones make up the foot itself, and 14 *phalanges* form the toes.

Models of the human skeleton can be useful teaching aids.

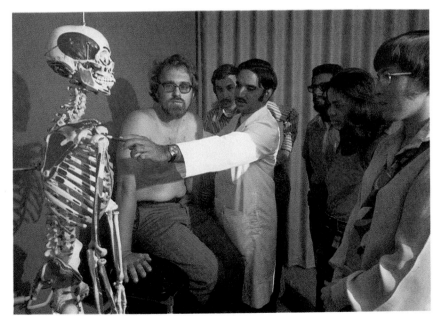

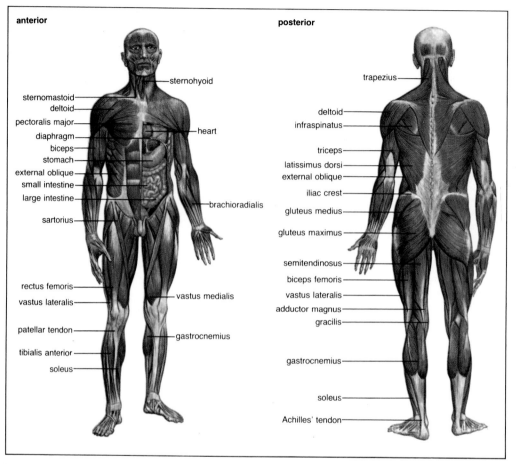

anterior

sternohyoid
sternomastoid
deltoid
pectoralis major
diaphragm
heart
biceps
stomach
external oblique
small intestine
large intestine
brachioradialis
sartorius
rectus femoris
vastus lateralis
vastus medialis
patellar tendon
gastrocnemius
tibialis anterior
soleus

posterior

trapezius
deltoid
infraspinatus
triceps
latissimus dorsi
external oblique
iliac crest
gluteus medius
gluteus maximus
semitendinosus
biceps femoris
vastus lateralis
adductor magnus
gracilis
gastrocnemius
soleus
Achilles' tendon

Muscles Make the Body Move

The human body contains more than 600 muscles. They make up some 45 per cent of the total body weight. Each muscle is made of long cells called muscle fibers. These, in turn, consist of many, very thin fibers that can slide on each other. When the nerves attached to muscles trigger muscle contraction, the muscle fibers shorten as their component fibers slide over each other. During contraction, the muscle fibers shorten to about half their normal length. When a muscle is not in a state of contraction, it relaxes. The body contains three kinds of muscles—*voluntary, involuntary,* and *cardiac*.

Voluntary muscles are so called because we can control their contractions. Many of them are attached to the body's bony framework and are thus called *skeletal* muscles. They are responsible for body movement and posture. Involuntary, or smooth, muscles are part of the various digestive and endocrine organs, and also line the blood vessels. Their contractions are controlled by portions of the brain that operate at below-conscious levels, making us unaware, for instance, of every contraction of blood-vessel muscles. Cardiac, or heart, muscle fibers are interconnected in a way that allows a uniform spread of the electrical signals that trigger a heartbeat.

A skeletal muscle consists of three sections—*origin, body,* and *insertion*. The origin is one end of the muscle ordinarily fixed to an anchoring bone. The body is the bulk of the muscle. The insertion is the other end, fixed to the bone it will move. Some skeletal muscles are grouped in *antagonistic* pairs. When one contracts, the other relaxes.

Some of the major skeletal muscles are illustrated at left. However, it is important to remember that individual body movements are usually the result of many muscles acting together as mechanical units. The facial muscles, such as the *frontalis,* the *orbicularis oculi,* and the *orbicularis oris,* give rise to the facial expressions so characteristic of humans and other primates. The *buccinator,* another facial muscle, controls cheek movements. The *masseter* is the powerful muscle that closes the jaw. The *sternomastoid* is a neck muscle that draws the head downward toward the shoulder. The *deltoid* is a large, triangular shoulder muscle that *abducts* the arm—pulls it away from the side of the body. The *biceps* flexes the arm and forearm. Its antagonist, the *triceps,* pulls the arm downward and parallel to the body. The *pectoralis major* muscle *adducts* the arm—pulls it in toward the side of the body. The *gluteus* muscles in the lower back move and rotate the thigh. The *gracilis,* a thin muscle on the inner edge of the thigh, pulls the thigh in toward the center of the body and flexes the leg. The *sartorius,* which is the longest muscle in the body, flexes the thigh and leg, and also rotates the thigh. The *biceps* of the leg flexes and rotates that limb. The *gastrocnemius* makes up most of the leg calf. It and the *soleus* flex the foot.

People of all ages take classes or exercise at home to keep their muscles strong and limber.

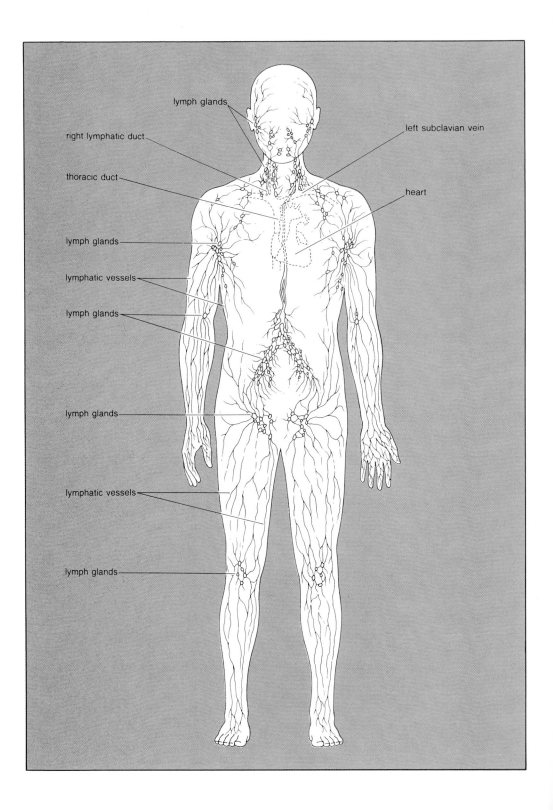

The Lymphatic System—Drainage and Defense

The lymphatic system has two functions—it helps the veins drain body tissues, and it plays a major part in body defense against infection. Like the circulatory system, the lymphatic system is a network of tubular vessels. They carry tissue fluid called *lymph* and range from capillary size to large-diameter vessels. However, the lymphatic system is not a closed system and eventually drains into the large veins below the neck. The *thoracic duct,* the main collector of lymph fluid, empties into the left subclavian vein. The lymphatic vessels also serve to drain fat particles from the body's tissues after fatty foods are absorbed by the intestine.

The work of body defense goes on in *lymph glands,* filters scattered throughout the lymph pathways. Bacteria and other harmful substances easily get into the lymphatic system through the many lymph capillaries in the skin and elsewhere. Once in the lymph flow, bacteria can infect the entire body. However, as lymph fluid filters through the lymph glands, special cells in them attack and destroy the bacteria.

The *spleen,* a lymphoid organ near the left kidney, also fights infection. Both the spleen and the lymph glands manufacture *lymphocytes,* which are special cells that can destroy foreign substances in the body.

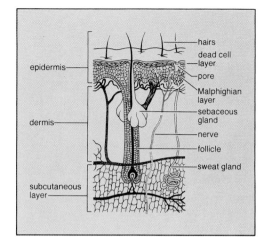

Nerve Endings in the Skin

Sensation receptors are located in the skin and other body sites. The receptors range from bare nerve endings to highly specialized organs involved in sight and hearing. Some receptors respond to touch, some to chemicals, and some to light.

The skin has many nerve endings. Four sensations can be detected by skin receptors: cold, warmth, touch, and pain. Cold and warmth are detected by nerve endings deep in the skin. Tactile sensation, or light touch, is sensed by cup-shaped nerve endings just below the *epidermis,* the top layer of the skin. Pressure, or very heavy touch, is detected by bulb-shaped nerve endings deep in the *dermis* of the skin and in tendons and other deep body tissues. Pain is detected by bare nerve endings in the upper portions of the dermis, as well as within the linings of certain body cavities.

Nerve fiber stimulation is basically an electrical event. The exchange of sodium and potassium ions in the nerve fiber changes the polarity of the fiber and starts a wave of depolarization—an *action potential,* or nerve impulse—along the fiber. The nerve impulses move at an incredible speed from fiber to fiber across links called *synapses.*

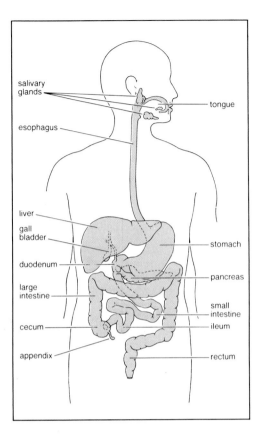

salivary glands
tongue
esophagus
liver
gall bladder
duodenum
large intestine
cecum
appendix
stomach
pancreas
small intestine
ileum
rectum

The Digestive System

The digestion of food begins in the mouth. Enzymes from the *salivary glands* begin to reduce starches into sugars, and the *tongue* starts the swallowing process. Chewed food is swallowed down the 10-inch-long (25 centimeters) *esophagus* into the *stomach*. Stomach enzymes and acids continue to reduce starches to sugars and break down proteins to peptides and amino acids. The stomach churns and stores the digested food, now called *chyme*, and releases small amounts of it into the 12-inch-long (30 centimeters) *duodenum*, the first part of the small intestine.

Blood vessels in the many wall projections of the small intestine absorb the digested food molecules for distribution throughout the body. Muscles in the walls of the 22-foot-long (7 meters) small intestine contract in a rhythmic wave called peristalsis that moves the chyme to the *ileum* of the small intestine and into the *cecum*, the start of the *large intestine*. The cecum has a functionless *appendix*, which sometimes becomes seriously inflamed. When chyme gets to the 5-foot-long (1.5 meters) large intestine, most of the food has been absorbed into the bloodstream. Water is removed from the liquidlike remains in the large intestine until a hard feces is formed and eliminated.

Some accessory organs aid food digestion and distribution. The *liver*, the largest internal organ, receives food from the digestive system and determines if it will be used or stored. The liver also removes poisons from the blood and reduces them to bile. The *gall bladder* stores and concentrates bile, and empties it into the digestive tract. The *pancreas* produces insulin, an important hormone in carbohydrate metabolism, and the pancreas also makes digestive enzymes.

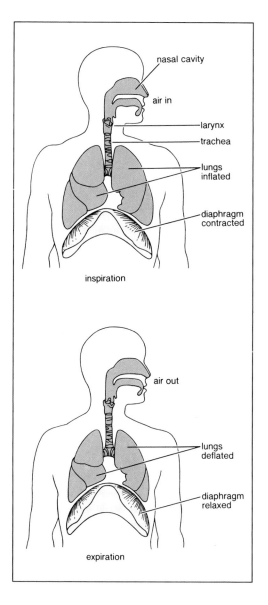

nasal cavity

air in

larynx

trachea

lungs inflated

diaphragm contracted

inspiration

air out

lungs deflated

diaphragm relaxed

expiration

How You Breathe

Breathing is a rhythmic activity that brings oxygen-rich air into the lungs and removes carbon-dioxide-filled air from them. The *diaphragm,* a large, dome-shaped muscle that separates the chest cavity from the abdominal cavity, plays a key part in breathing. Rib and belly muscles also help. When the diaphragm contracts, the chest cavity becomes larger and gains volume. Because of this, a suction develops as pressure in the chest drops. Outside air rushes in through the nasal cavity and/or the mouth and then down the *trachea,* or windpipe, to inflate the lungs. This process is called *inspiration.* During *expiration,* the diaphragm relaxes and reduces the chest volume. As a result, pressure builds in the chest cavity, deflating the lungs or forcing air out of them.

At the ends of the long air passages are spongy air sacs called *alveoli,* surrounded by many capillaries. Oxygen enters the bloodstream and carbon dioxide leaves it at the alveoli, which eventually link with the trachea.

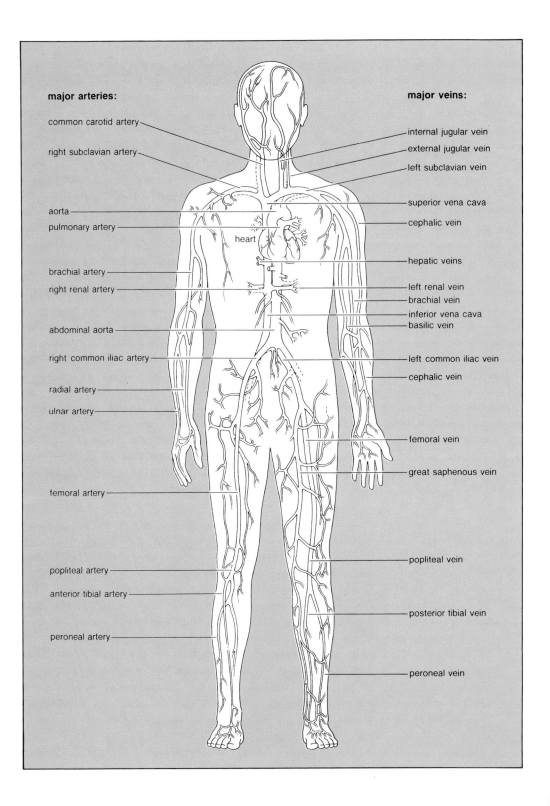

major arteries:

common carotid artery

right subclavian artery

aorta

pulmonary artery

heart

brachial artery

right renal artery

abdominal aorta

right common iliac artery

radial artery

ulnar artery

femoral artery

popliteal artery

anterior tibial artery

peroneal artery

major veins:

internal jugular vein

external jugular vein

left subclavian vein

superior vena cava

cephalic vein

hepatic veins

left renal vein

brachial vein

inferior vena cava

basilic vein

left common iliac vein

cephalic vein

femoral vein

great saphenous vein

popliteal vein

posterior tibial vein

peroneal vein

Blood Circulates through the Body

Blood is the life stream of the human body. This red fluid performs many tasks, and no part of the body can live without it. Blood carries vital food and oxygen to all cells and removes the waste products of metabolism. With cells able to destroy harmful bacteria and viruses, blood is important in the body's fight against disease. Blood consists of a solid part and a liquid, or *plasma,* part of carbohydrates, fats, and proteins in a watery solution.

Blood has three kinds of cells—*red blood cells* (erythrocytes), *white blood cells* (leukocytes), and *platelets* (thrombocytes). Red blood cells are disks with flattened centers where nuclei once existed. They contain a red protein called *hemoglobin.* Oxygen combines with hemoglobin and is carried by the erythrocytes to other cells for respiration. Every minute, the body needs 250 cubic cm of oxygen. Red blood cells wear out quickly and are replaced constantly. The body makes about 21 billion erythrocytes each day. White blood cells mobilize and attack foreign substances that invade the bloodstream. These defense cells have chemical sensors that detect bacteria, viruses, or other harmful intruders. Some white blood cells are *phagocytes;* they eat the intruders. Others coat the intruders in a way that makes them "tasty" to phagocytes. Still others maintain a memory system to help the body defend against similar intruders in the future. The platelets plug small leaks in the blood vessels. They work in combination with fibery proteins in plasma to seal small holes and cuts with *blood clots.*

The circulatory system is a closed network of *arteries, veins,* and *capillaries.* Arteries carry oxygenated blood from the lungs to the rest of the body. Arteries are linked with veins, which bring blood back to the lungs for more oxygen. Tiny, thin-walled capillaries are the links. All body tissues have capillaries. Oxygen and food molecules pass from the capillaries into surrounding tissue cells. In turn, carbon dioxide and nitrogenous wastes pass into the capillaries for removal. Carbon dioxide is transported to the lungs for exhalation; nitrogenous wastes are carried to the kidneys for excretion.

Arteries and veins have slightly different structures. The walls of arteries are circled by involuntary (smooth) muscles and elastic tissue. The elastic nature of the arterial wall maintains the wave, or *pulse,* of high-pressure blood flow when blood is pumped from the *heart.* The walls of veins have less elastic tissue and have longer openings than arteries to accommodate the low-pressure blood flow back to the heart. Most arteries have namesake veins; and most blood vessels occur in pairs, one for each side of the body.

The *aorta* is the major artery. Oxygenated blood returned from the lungs through the *pulmonary* veins (the only case of a vein carrying oxygenated blood) is pumped to the body through the aorta. The *common carotid* and *subclavian* arteries are offshoots of the aorta. Blood is pumped to the head through the common carotid and to the upper limbs through the right and left subclavians. The *brachial* artery feeds the upper arm; the *radial* and *ulnar* arteries, the forearm and hand. The *internal* and *external jugular* veins drain the head. The *pulmonary artery* carries deoxygenated blood to the lungs for oxygenation (the only case of an artery carrying deoxygenated blood). The *abdominal aorta* brings arterial blood to the trunk and lower limbs. Offshoots of the abdominal aorta transport blood to the digestive glands and organs. The *renal* arteries feed the kidneys and carry waste products there for excretion. The abdominal aorta splits into the *common iliac* arteries, which continue into the legs as the *femoral* arteries. The *popliteal* artery threads in back of the knee joint, the *anterior tibial* artery runs the course of the shinbone, and the *peroneal* artery ends near the heel. Deoxygenated blood from the lower limbs first flows through the *great saphenous* veins, into the *common iliac* veins, and then into the *inferior vena cava,* which drains the lower limbs and trunk. The *hepatic* vein stems from the liver to the inferior vena cava. The *basilic, brachial,* and *cephalic* veins drain the arm. The *subclavian* veins connect with the *superior vena cava.* Through the two venae cavae, all venous blood flows back into the heart, where the blood will again be pumped to the lungs for more oxygen and again throughout the body.

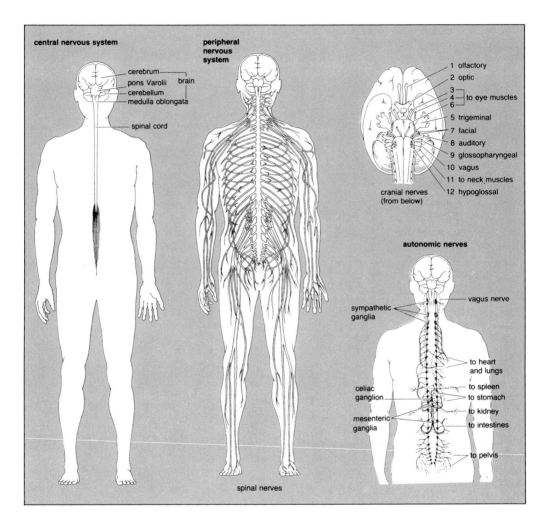

central nervous system

cerebrum
pons Varolii — brain
cerebellum
medulla oblongata

spinal cord

peripheral nervous system

1 olfactory
2 optic
3
4 ┐ to eye muscles
6 ┘
5 trigeminal
7 facial
8 auditory
9 glossopharyngeal
10 vagus
11 to neck muscles
12 hypoglossal

cranial nerves
(from below)

autonomic nerves

sympathetic ganglia

vagus nerve

celiac ganglion

mesenteric ganglia

to heart and lungs
to spleen
to stomach
to kidney
to intestines

to pelvis

spinal nerves

The Nervous System—A Communications Network

The *central, peripheral,* and *autonomic* nervous systems make up the body's communications network. The central nervous system consists of the *brain* and *spinal cord.* The peripheral nervous system contains *cranial* and *spinal* nerves. The autonomic nervous system has cranial nerves and nerves from bundles called *ganglia* near the spinal cord. Most nerve information is sent to the brain for interpretation and then to the muscles for action. Nerve impulses can only travel in one direction. Incoming signals are passed along *sensory* nerves, while outgoing signals are passed along *motor* nerves.

The brain is the key part of the nervous system. The *cerebrum* controls memory, awareness, moti-

vation, and other "higher" mental activities. The *pons, cerebellum,* and *medulla* control "lower" activities, such as balancing or breathing.

The 12 cranial nerves have sensory, motor, or combined fibers. Some of the major sensory nerves are: the *olfactory* (smell), *optic* (sight), and *auditory* (hearing). The *vagus* has motor fibers that control many internal activities, including heartbeat.

In the autonomic system (over which you have no conscious control), the *sympathetic* ganglia serve autonomic nerves in the upper body; the *celiac* and *mesenteric* ganglia send off fibers to the stomach, intestines, and other abdominal organs.

The Eye—Your Window to the World

Incoming light rays enter the eye through the clear *cornea*. Then they pass through the *pupil*, an adjustable hole controlled by the *iris* muscles. The light rays are focused by the *lens*—made thicker or thinner by the *ciliary muscle* to accommodate near and far objects—as a reduced and inverted image on the *retina*.

The watery *aqueous humor* behind the lens maintains the eyeball shape. The *sclera* is the tough, white outer coat of the eyeball.

The *choroid* layer contains blood vessels. The retina has rods, cones, and nerve cells that transmit information about the inverted retinal image along the optic nerve to a visual center in the brain. There, the image is reverted to its right-side-up position. The *fovea centralis* is the center point of the retina. The *blind spot* is a small area where the retinal blood vessels emerge; it is insensitive to light.

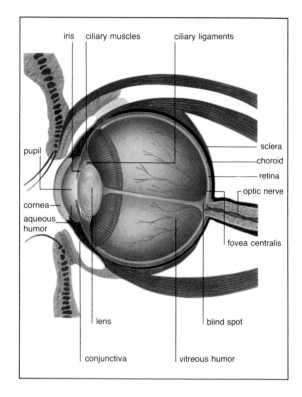

Taste Buds in the Tongue

Taste, like smell, is a chemical sense. *Taste buds* capable of sensing chemicals in the mouth are located on the top and side surface of the tongue.

The surface covering of the tongue senses the texture and the temperature of food. The taste buds are housed in bumpy projections called *papillae*. The *vallate* papillae, which range in number between 8 and 12, are in a V-shaped row on the rear surface of the tongue. The mushroom-shaped *fungiform* papillae, more numerous than the vallate, are scattered over the sides and the tip of the tongue. The taste buds attach to sensory nerves that carry taste messages to the brain.

In varying degrees, the taste buds can distinguish four tastes; sweetness, bitterness (alkalinity), sourness, and saltiness. The sweet taste is usually detected by taste buds in the forward edges of the tongue. Bitterness is registered mainly at the back surface. Sourness can be discerned at the middle edges. And saltiness can be distinguished over a wide area of the tongue. However, few tastes can be clearly distinguished at the center surface of the tongue.

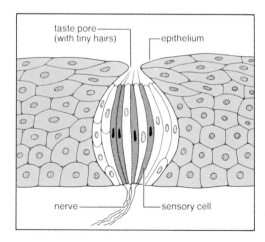

The Ear Enables You to Hear

The ear is a complex hearing and balance organ. In the outer ear, sound waves are received by the *pinna* and channeled through the *auditory canal* to the *tympanum,* or eardrum.

As sound vibrates the eardrum, the vibrations are transmitted through three delicate bones of the middle ear—*the malleus, incus,* and *stapes*—to the *oval window*. There, the vibrations are passed to fluid in the *cochlea* of the middle ear. Hair cells in the cochlea pick up the vibrations and send them along the *cochlear nerve* to the brain for translation as sounds.

Three *semicircular canals* in the inner ear contain fluid and tiny "pebbles" that shift position whenever the body tilts out of line. This information is sent to the brain very rapidly over the *vestibular nerve* for corrective muscle action to restore body equilibrium.

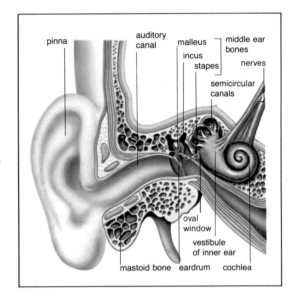

The Nose—Organ of Smell

The sense of smell is a chemical sense closely linked with the process of breathing. Currents of air brought in each *nostril* during an inspiration, or breath intake, swirl up to the top of the nasal cavity. Air circulates over outcropping called *conchae* in the nasal sinuses, or passages, to be warmed or cooled to body temperature before going to the lungs. At the top of the nasal cavity are free nerve endings of the *olfactory nerves*. They project through openings in cranial bone from the *olfactory bulb,* the terminal of the first cranial nerve. The olfactory nerve cells are very sensitive to odors. Odors result from the volatile, or vaporous, components of various substances breathed in. Much of the "taste" of food is the result of odors intercepted by the olfactory nerves and transmitted to the brain. For example, you have probably observed that when you have a head cold and your nasal passages become filled with fluid, almost everything you eat tastes the same.

The nasal cavity is the beginning of the pharynx, the part of the body where the breathing and eating processes cross each other. The *epiglottis* is a "valve" that keeps food out of the windpipe. When food is swallowed, it forces the epiglottis over the windpipe as it passes into the *esophagus*. The Eus-

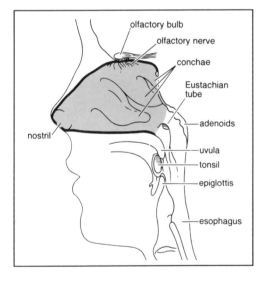

tachian tube, a "pressure valve," connects the pharynx with the middle ear.

The pharynx also has lymphoid tissues, such as the *adenoids* and the *tonsils*. The tonsils are located in the throat near the point where the *uvula* hangs from the roof of the mouth.

Teeth and the Dental System

Teeth are the hardest tissues of the human body. A tooth consists of a *crown,* an underlying *dentin,* and a soft *pulp.* The crown is the hard, white part of the tooth that appears above the gum line. The *neck* of the tooth is at the gum line, and the *root* is anchored in the bony jaws. These parts of the tooth are shown and labeled in the diagram at the right.

The crown is made of carbonate apatite crystals filled in with calcium phosphate. It is nonliving material; holes or cracks in the enamel cannot be repaired by the body. Most of the tooth consists of living dentin. Similar to bone in its composition, dentin is about 50 percent calcium phosphate. Blood vessels and nerves from the pulp infiltrate the dentin and make it alive. If the enamel becomes decayed or cracked, the exposed dentin can convey the sensations of warmth, cold, and pain. The tooth root is covered by bonelike *cementum.* Tiny fibers extend from the cementum and anchor the root into the bony tooth socket.

The adult mouth contains 32 teeth. The maxilla, or upper jaw, contains four *incisors,* two *canines,* four *bicuspids,* and six *molars.* The mandible, or lower jaw, contains the same kind and number of teeth. The incisors and canines bite and tear food. The premolars crush and the molars grind food.

Humans develop two sets of teeth—primary, or deciduous, teeth and permanent teeth. The central incisors are the first primary teeth to erupt through the gums. They appear when a baby is about 6 months old. The lateral incisors appear next, at about 8 months old, followed by the bicuspids, at about 14 months of age. The first and second molars erupt between 14 and 36 months after a baby is born.

The permanent teeth start to replace the baby teeth at 6 years of age and end the process about 6 years later. However, the third molars, or "wisdom" teeth, do not usually erupt until a person is between 18 and 22 years old—or, in some cases, even older.

Preventive care is considered especially important by dentists and dental hygienists. Most dentists advise that young people have their teeth checked by a dentist every six months. And many school systems require a dental checkup at least once a year—that is, before the student starts school in the late summer or early fall.

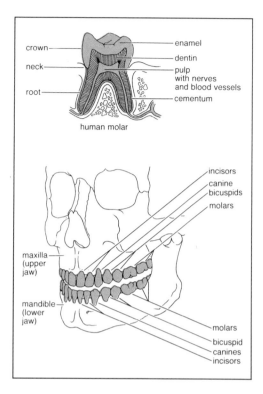

human molar

Table of Conditions for Life

Certain conditions are necessary for life. All the requirements are found in a thin region called the *biosphere* near the surface of the earth.

Temperature range	Most living things exist within a narrow temperature range between 0°C (32°F.) and 80°C (176°F.). As a rule, life processes stop near 0°C— the freezing point of water— and at about 80°C. Very few plants or animals can live at temperatures that exceed 80°C.	Water	Living things need water, which is a main component of protoplasm—the living substance of a cell.
		Carbon dioxide	Green plants need carbon dioxide from the air plus water for photosynthesis.
Altitude range	Some birds live as high as 27,000 ft. (8,230 m) above sea level. No animals are known to live at a depth greater than 35,800 ft. (10,910 m) below sea level.	Oxygen	Most plant and animal cells require oxygen from the air or dissolved in water for cell energy processes.
		Food	Green plants make their own food; animals acquire energy by eating green plants or other animals.
Sunlight	Most plants require sunlight for the energy to make their own food by photosynthesis.	Carbon	Needed for carbohydrate fuel.
		Nitrogen	Needed for making proteins for body growth.

UNIT 4   Glossary

adrenal (uh DREE nuhl) gland The endocrine gland on each kidney. These glands secrete hormones that include epinephrine (adrenaline), a substance that causes a rise in heartbeat, increased blood sugar, and other body responses to emergencies.

alveoli (al VEE uh ly) Spongy air sacs in the lungs, where oxygen and carbon dioxide exchange occurs.

amino (uh MEE noh) acids Nitrogen-containing compounds that form proteins when strung together.

anaerobic (AN air OH bihk) respiration The process of breaking down carbohydrates in the absence of free oxygen.

angiosperms (AN jee uh spurmz) The flowering plants. They form the largest subphylum of the plant kingdom.

artery A vessel that carries blood away from the heart.

axon A nerve cell part that conducts impulses away from the cell body toward another nerve cell.

bacteria (bak TIHR ee uh) Microscopically small organisms divided into three groups: bacilli (rod-shaped), cocci (round-shaped), and spirilli (spiral-shaped).

biology The study of all living things.

blood The vital fluid in higher animals that carries food, gases, and disease-fighting substances.

bone marrow A substance inside the body's long bones where blood cells are made and fat is stored.

botany The study of plants.

bronchi (BRAHNG ky) Branching tubes connecting the lung's alveoli with the trachea.

cell The basic unit of life. The cell consists of a nucleus, cytoplasm, and enclosing membrane.

chromosomes (KROH muh sohmz) Combinations of nucleic acid and proteins in body and sex cells engaged in transmitting hereditary information.

dendrite (DEHN dryt) A nerve cell part that conducts an impulse toward the cell body from another nerve cell.

DNA Deoxyribonucleic acid; a chemical in the cell nucleus that stores genetic information.

drug A nonfood substance that changes body makeup or activity. Drugs are used to control or cure disease; addiction can occur when the body tolerates increasing dosages of certain drugs.

ecology (ee KAHL uh jee) The study of how living things interact with their surroundings.

endocrine (EHN doh krihn) system A body system of ductless glands that secrete chemical hormones into the blood. Target organs are influenced by the hormones.

enzyme A protein serving as a catalyst to speed up or slow down chemical processes in the body.

fetus (FEE tuhs) In higher animals, a developing embryo. The human embryo is referred to as a fetus between three months of age and birth.

flagella (fluh JEHL luh) Threadlike projections in some microorganisms, used for locomotion.

gametes (GAM eets) Sex cells produced during meiosis.

gene (JEEN) The unit of biological inheritance; a specific sequence of nucleotides in a DNA molecule in a chromosome.

gymnosperms (JIHM nuh spurmz) Evergreen plants, or conifers. These plants bear naked seeds in cones.

heterozygous (HEHT uhr uh ZY guhs) Type of gene pairing where each of the two genes is different.

homozygous (HOH muh ZY guhs) A type of gene pairing where the two genes are similar.

kidney A structure in animals that filters liquid waste products from the blood but retains the water.

meiosis (my OH sihs) A type of cell division that produces gametes, which contain a haploid number of chromosomes.

metabolism The chemical processes that occur in living things; a combination of the *anabolic* buildup of cell materials and the *catabolic* breakdown of them.

mitochondrion (MIHT uh KAHN dree uhn) A cell organelle where energy transformations occur; a cell "powerhouse."

mitosis (mih TOH sihs) A type of cell division that produces body cells containing the diploid number of chromosomes.

neuron (NUR ahn) A nerve cell. The cell conducts nerve impulses from other neurons through its dendrites and transmits them to still other neurons through its axons.

nucleolus (noo KLEE oh luhs) A round mass in a cell nucleus where RNA is located. This mass disappears during mitosis.

nucleotide (NOO klee uh tyd) A chemical combination of a sugar, phosphate group, and nitrogenous base that forms the basis of the nucleic acids.

nucleus The "master control" of the cell. The nucleus controls life processes in all living cells except bacteria.

organelle A cell structure having a special task.

osmosis (ahz MOH suhs) Diffusion of small molecules through a *semipermeable*, or selective, membrane.

ovulation (OH vyuh LAY shuhn) The release of an egg cell during the midpoint of the menstrual cycle.

parasite An organism that lives in or on a host organism and gets its food from the host. The parasite is often harmful to the host.

peristalsis (peh ruh STAL sihs) Waves of muscular contractions and relaxations of the gastrointestinal tube that move food through the human digestive system.

phenotype (FEE nuh typ) How genetic makeup appears as body traits; examples are tallness, shortness, skin coloration.

pituitary (pih TOO uh tehr ee) gland The endocrine gland beneath the brain; the source of important hormones that trigger hormone secretions from other endocrine glands.

radial symmetry A wheel-like body structure. Two equal parts result, with similar structures in each part, no matter how the body is divided.

regeneration The ability of some organisms to grow new body parts when injured or severed.

respiration (REHS puh RAY shuhn) An energy process requiring oxygen and giving off carbon dioxide.

ribosomes (RY buh sohmz) Cell structures where proteins are made.

RNA Ribonucleic acid; carries genetic information from DNA in the cell nucleus to the ribosomes.

saprophyte (SAP ruh FYT) An organism that lives off dead organic substances.

synapse (sih NAPS) The junction between axons of one neuron and dendrites of another.

thorax A body part between the head and abdomen. This part is enclosed by ribs in humans.

tissue A group of cells in the body having the same makeup and function.

trachea (TRAY kee uh) An air tube.

vein (VAYN) A vessel that carries blood back to the heart.

X chromosome The chromosome determining "femaleness."

Y chromosome The chromosome determining "maleness."

yolk The food stored to feed a growing embryo.

zygote (ZY goht) A fertilized egg resulting from the union of male and female sex cells.

Index

Acknowledgments

The publishers acknowledge the following illustrations. Credits read from top to bottom, left to right, on their respective pages. Charts and diagrams prepared by the *World Book* staff unless otherwise noted.

Cover Illustrations: Yoshi Miyake. Alex Ebel; Robert Demarest; Trevor Boyer, Linden Artists Ltd. Photos: Fermilab; World Book photo; Richard J. Feldman, National Institutes of Health; Les Blacklock, Tom Stack & Associates; © California Institute of Technology; Teisaku Kobayashi.
1 World Book photo. 27 Bettmann Archive.
94 Genentech, Inc. 97 Lick Observatory.
128 Chuck O'Rear, Woodfin Camp, Inc.
139 Robert Goodman, Black Star. 151 © Anthony Edgeworth, The Stock Market. 163 Edmund Nagele, FPG. 193 Rush Medical College, World Book photo. 195 © Annie Griffiths, West Light.